LIVING AT THE EDGE

Explorers, Exploiters and Settlers of the Grand Canyon Region

BY MICHAEL F. ANDERSON

GRAND CANYON ASSOCIATION
GRAND CANYON, ARIZONA, USA
1998

Development begins at the
southcentral rim

The Grand Canyon
Railway arrives

Theodore Roosevelt
proclaims Grand Canyon a
National Monument

Tourism arrives at
the North Rim

Congress creates
Grand Canyon
National Park

1896

1901

1908

1917

1919

COVER PHOTOS

The Santa Fe Railroad initially allied with Martin Buggeln to control tourism at the southcentral rim. Here, the Grand Canyon Railway delivers visitors around 1910-15, by which time the Santa Fe and Fred Harvey Company controlled all accommodations at Grand Canyon Village. GRCA 7448

Buckey O'Neill (second from right), Yavapai County sheriff, 1880s.
Sharlot Hall Museum, PO1116P

Miners in front of the cook shack on Horseshoe Mesa, ca. 1903. GRCA 8810

Editors
Sandra Scott
L. Greer Price

Publications Manager
Pamela G. Frazier

Project Manager/Art Director
Kimberly Buchheit

Book Designer
Rebecca Markstein

Additional Editorial Assistance
Faith Marcovecchio

**Grand Canyon Association, Post Office Box 399
Grand Canyon, Arizona 86023
Tel.: 520.638.2481 Web: www.thecanyon.com/gca**

*Grand Canyon Association is a not-for-profit organization.
Net proceeds from the sale of this book will be used to support
the educational goals of Grand Canyon National Park.*

ISBN: 0-938216-55-4   LCN: 97-78140

*Printed in the United States of America
on recycled paper using vegetable-based inks.*

ACKNOWLEDGMENTS

A first book is like any major project, it seems. It takes twice the time and three times the effort as first expected, and works best when good people participate. My fortune is to have had many such folks help get this history to print.

Since I was born a little late to have personal knowledge of Grand Canyon's settlement period, I must thank early artisans, photographers, cartographers, and authors of books, articles, and myriad primary documents with whom this story originates. They are identified, each and every one, within the endnotes.

I also thank the institutions, archivists, and librarians who safeguard these materials and often pointed me in the right direction. With a wealth of well-organized records at Grand Canyon National Park, I spent much time with Sara Stebbins in the research library; Carolyn Richard, Colleen Hyde, and Mike Quinn in the study collection; and Doug Brown in professional services, all of whom have helped me write Grand Canyon histories since 1990. Further gratitude is owed archivists at Northern Arizona University, Arizona State University, and the University of Arizona; public libraries in Flagstaff, Fredonia, and Kanab; the Mohave County Historical Museum in Kingman; the National Park Service's Denver Service Center; and the National Archives.

Many people participated in this project simply because I or the publisher asked for their help. My thanks to Andy Wallace, Ben Huseman, and David Miller, who let me go along as they retraced the Ives' Expedition of 1857-58 and helped in other ways as well. Appreciation goes to Debra Sutphen, a colleague at the canyon for several years, and Teri Cleeland, archaeologist and historian for the United States Forest Service in Williams, for their unpublished studies of canyon history which helped my research. Bill Suran, George Billingsley, Greer Price, Jim Babbitt, George Lubick, Charles Meister, Doug Brown, Pam Frazier, Richard Quartaroli, Cecil Cram, Karoline Tisdale, Linda Anderson, Andy Wallace, and Valeen Avery all studied the initial manuscript and improved its content. I especially thank Val for her confidence in my abilities since my return to school in 1988. With her help, and the rest of my doctoral committee at Northern Arizona University (Andy Wallace, George Lubick, and Karen Powers), I may yet graduate in this millennium.

Grand Canyon historians benefit from many regional residents who remember the settlement era, contributed to canyon history in some way, or recall efforts of their parents and grandparents. It was a genuine pleasure to interview Fred and Jeanne Schick, Jim Shirley, Harvey Butchart, Jim Babbitt, Steve Verkamp, Gale Burak, Bill Suran, Steve Church, Ben Hamblin, Loren and Sarah Hamblin Broadbent, Dart Judd, Keith and Carol Judd, Ron Mace, Billy Swapp, Paul McCormick, Stanley White, Quentin Rust, Anna Brown, and Walapai Johnny Nelson. Special gratitude goes to those who endured multiple interviews: Cecil Cram, who rode with me (not always on roads) to explore the Arizona Strip and point out dozens of historic sites; and Mardean Frost Church, who told the tale of North Rim hunting camps then introduced me to many other helpful residents. I deeply regret that Mardean did not live to read the work she helped create.

My thanks to Tom Carmony who drove with me to discover Bill Bass's roads and the Caves, and to Harvey Howell at Redlands Ranch for pointing us to this all but invisible pioneer campsite when we failed to find it on our own.

I cannot thank enough Pam Frazier and the Grand Canyon Association for trusting an unpublished writer and helping him turn out a readable history, and Kim Buchheit and Rebecca Markstein, two imaginative designers, for making the story better than its words. I also am indebted to Sandra Scott for her fine editorial skills and her attention to every detail.

Last on the gratitude list but most important to me are brother David, who consistently accompanies me into wilderness and points out natural values a historian might miss; sisters Diane and Mary, and their children, Bob, Tammy, Tina, Mike, Dan, and Jason, the latter three hiking into the canyon with me at a young age and who, I hope, still remember the experience; my mother, Dorothy, who died in 1991 but still influences my life; father, Francis (Toby), who has always been there for me; and the in-laws, Jenny, Pete, Don, Missy, Tim, Ed, and Amy for their fortitude in taking care of the Anderson clan. And especially to my wife of thirty years, Linda, who has given me reasons to live since we were sixteen years old and to whom this book is dedicated.

After studying the human history of Grand Canyon for the past six years, I am moved to also acknowledge the men and women of the United States Forest Service and National Park Service for their administration of the most beautiful place on Earth. They have difficulty succeeding in their dual mission of preservation and public access and have failed at times, but the historical record reveals dedicated people undertaking the often thankless task of protecting landscape both for and from its legal owners, the American public, as well as speaking for its native plants and wildlife. ■

ABOUT THE AUTHOR

Michael F. Anderson is a public historian and doctoral student at Northern Arizona University. Since 1990 he has been researching and writing histories of Grand Canyon's trails, roads, and pioneers, and is currently writing an administrative history of the national park for Grand Canyon Association.

Mike lives with his wife, Linda, and his two dogs, Cerca and Doc, in Strawberry, Arizona.

TABLE OF CONTENTS

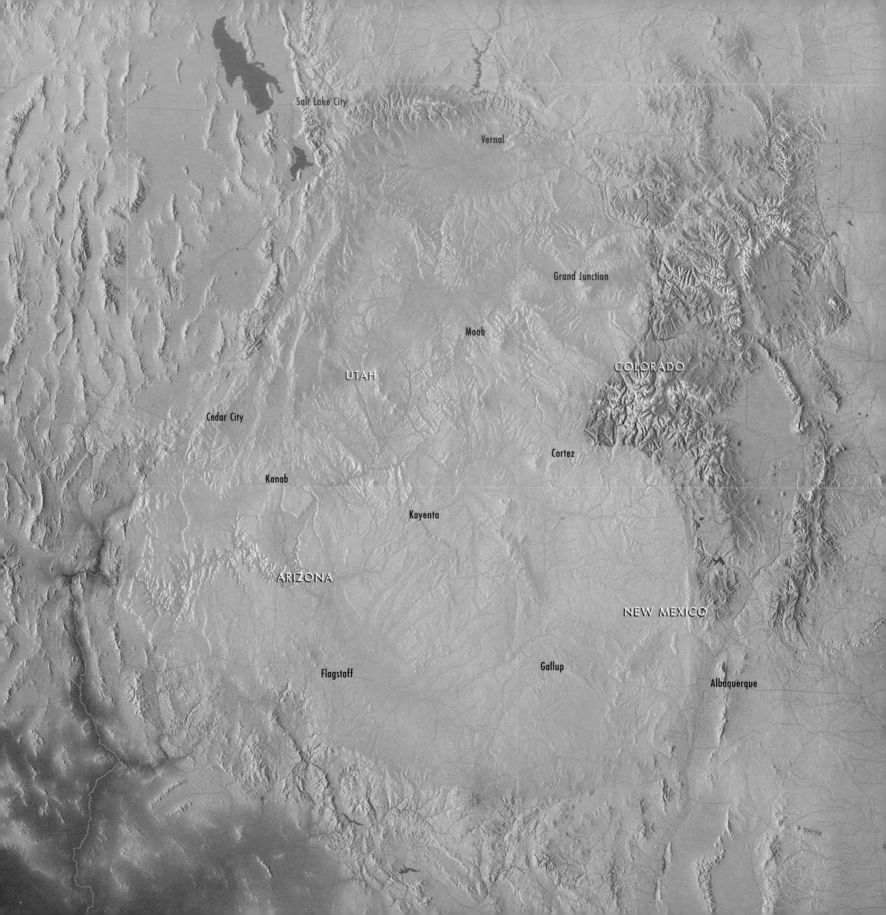

LIVING AT THE EDGE

*American Indian
cultures arrive in the
Grand Canyon region*

*European-American
trappers rediscover
the region*

*U.S. Army explorers lead
the way to settlement*

*Latter-Day Saints arrive
on the Arizona Strip*

CA.
8000 B.C.

1821

1851

1858

J.W. Powell runs
the river through
Grand Canyon

Prospectors begin to comb
the inner canyon

European-Americans begin
to settle the southeast rim

Primitive hotels and camps
appear at the southeast rim

1869

1873

1883

1885

INTRODUCTION
The Grand Canyon Region

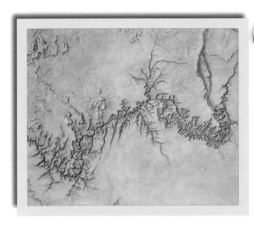

The Grand Canyon from Earth orbit reveals the Colorado River canyon cutting through the inhospitable Colorado Plateau from Lake Powell (upper right) to Lake Mead (left center). Regional explorers and immigrants found little to cheer about.

The broadly delineated Colorado Plateau (opposite) with the Sonoran Desert to the south and southwest and Great Basin to the west.

Courtesy of Chalk Butte Inc. © 1995

THE GRAND CANYON OF THE COLORADO RIVER SLICES DEEPLY ACROSS NORTHWESTERN ARIZONA. River, wind, rain, ice, thaw, and gravity have been at work here for several million years, chiseling with nature's indifference an enormous gash measuring 277 miles in length, averaging ten miles in width, and in places a full mile in depth.

Nowhere else on earth have the elements sculpted such a landscape, a natural classroom for scientific investigation. Paleontologists have long marveled at the fossil record within near-vertical rock strata which contrast a seemingly dead world in the gnarled 1.75-billion-year-old Vishnu Schist at the bottom of the chasm to a planet teeming with life in the 250-million-year-old Kaibab Limestone on canyon rims. Biologists revel in the presence of nearly all earth's habitable zones with their attendant diversity of plants and animals. Geologists grin ever more broadly as they descend from rim to river through half our world's stony past, laid bare in crisply delineated layers of color and form.

Others of a less scientific bent who try to understand then describe the natural scene have a more difficult, if equally rewarding, time. Artists and photographers have labored for more than a century to picture the essence of this place. Their works grace walls from Verkamps Curios at the canyon's South Rim to the Capitol in Washington. Writers, too, have struggled to wrap imaginations around the scenic splendor. Their books, essays, and poems number in the thousands. Wonderful as many of these works are, no single image despite its breadth, or words despite their insight can adequately express the sensory experience gained from a few moments spent along canyon rims.

Since this book is most concerned with the history of exploration and settlement in the Grand Canyon region, I am spared the hopeless task of translating the natural scene for the reader's soul. I admit to walking the canyon's brow and most major trails to the Colorado River, gaining along the way some appreciation of what others have tried to say. I have gazed, questioned, reflected, and looked again into the depths from above and to the rims from below, no doubt experiencing something others have

felt, but cannot say for sure what it is. My advice to those of a romantic bent is to circumvent the middle men: saunter up to the edge, linger long, and feel Grand Canyon first hand. Then take the time to stroll down one of the trails, if only for a few hundred yards, to gain an entirely different perspective.

While taking in what Grand Canyon has to offer today, imagine for a moment what this place meant to explorers and settlers who approached, not in automobiles on asphalt highways, but on foot or horseback upon dusty trails at best. Arriving from centers of civilization, they asked profoundly different questions than we ask today. At first, *Where are we going, how will we get there, what and who will we find?* Later, *Where do we put the road, build the town, raise our families?* Ultimately, *How do we make a buck from this magnificent hole in the ground?* Our appreciation of Grand Canyon

derives from values fully realized only in this century which prompt us to cherish nature for its own sake. Early visitors had other thoughts entirely.

Apply pioneer concerns to the regional landscape. Grand Canyon occupies the south-western corner of the Colorado Plateau, a land mass of 130,000 square miles that has been rising for tens of millions of years at a rate of several inches per century. This ponderous uplift combined with persistent erosion and volcanic eruption accounts for elevations ranging from 1,200 feet above sea level at the base of the Grand Wash Cliffs to 12,600 feet on the San Francisco Peaks. In between lies very little one might call flat and little more that early European Americans considered habitable.

The canyon begins at a spot long used by regional travelers to cross the Colorado River and ends where chasm and Colorado Plateau abruptly relent to desert lowlands. Its eastern portal is Lees Ferry, a tiny pocket of nearly level alluvial soil beneath the junction of the Echo and Vermilion Cliffs at the Paria River's mouth. Here, explorers, prospectors, cattlemen, settlers, and desperados from 1871 through 1928 ferried wagons, livestock, and families aboard flat-bottomed vessels to continue journeys between southern Utah and northern Arizona.

A float down the Colorado River reveals why Lees Ferry served so long as an important regional intersection despite its hazardous crossing. After a brief moment in full sun at the ferry site, the river regains anonymity within Marble Canyon, a sixty-mile prelude to Grand Canyon proper. Marble Canyon's seemingly sheer cliffs form a half-tunnel, breached solely by a few rugged tributary drainages and visited even into historic times only by a few American Indians, river runners, and backpackers. As the river bends in a more southerly direction, broader views are obtained of buttes and pinnacles, terraces and talus slopes, receding to distant rims often unseen from river level. Although one is nearly a mile below the rim at the Little Colorado River confluence, a practiced eye can pick out occasional routes to the top. Anything wider than a horse trail, however, even to a modern engineer, is difficult to imagine.

The Colorado sweeps westerly from the Little Colorado confluence, entering Grand Canyon proper while continuing to scour deeper into ancient stone. Here and there, as at Unkar Delta downstream of the Tanner Trail, the river's Inner Gorge grudgingly gives way to a few sandy acres and terraced slopes where subsistence agriculture, building sites, and transcanyon routes are possible. Farther along, fewer opportunities to till, build, or walk erect present themselves as the river enters an underworld named Granite Gorge. At long last the Colorado emerges into sunshine and open vistas at Grand Canyon's western portal, the Grand Wash Cliffs. Here also, nearly three hundred river miles from Lees Ferry, early travelers took advantage of comparatively level terrain to move north and south across the region.

A few early Grand Canyon explorers obtained this daunting visage from river level, and what they reported to the outside world did little to encourage settlement. The canyon's true dimensions and impediment to travel or livelihood, however, are fully realized only from points along inner-canyon trails. Today's hiker along the Tonto Trail from Red Canyon to Bass Canyon notes that, although he is fifteen hundred feet above the river, lofty rims seem no nearer. The favorable vantage upon the

Tonto Platform also reveals as no river view can that Grand Canyon is filled with immense and complex side canyons, soaring buttes, continuous sheer cliffs of Redwall Limestone and Coconino Sandstone, and intervening talus slopes receding far back toward the North Rim. A transcanyon road through this? A likely spot to support a family? The more common concern in earlier times was *How do we get out of here?*

The monumental crevasse even today stymies north and south movement of wheeled conveyances; and, before the dawn of tourism, thwarted attempts to earn a living. Early explorers and settlers would have been content with a level east-west passage or settlement sites near its northern and southern edges. Irregular topography combined with unfavorable climate hampered these efforts as well.

The Grand Canyon itself offered few opportunities to pursue traditional nineteenth-century occupations like ranching or farming. Even mining was hampered by local topography. GRCA 3866

3

HOME IS A HAZARDOUS PLACE

While Grand Canyon pioneers worked hard to secure a marginally adequate water supply, Havasupai Indians for centuries have had more than they can handle. Perennial Havasu Creek is historically one of the most voluminous and dependable water supplies in the region, more than sufficient to irrigate fields and orchards through the hottest summers and greatest droughts. The down side: runoff from summer thunderstorms and snowmelt from the Coconino Plateau drains through Cataract, Hualapai, and Lee Canyons where they converge below Havasu Springs and often submerges the small village of Supai before continuing to the Colorado River.

Havasupais built simple wickiup homes, hand-constructed irrigation works, and cliffside storage bins as traditional adaptations to their flood environment. When summer floods came, always with little warning, residents sprinted for cliffs, munched on their cached supplies, watched the flood rise and ebb, then returned to rebuild quickly or moved up to the plateau a little earlier than usual. But as the historic record shows, transition to European-American economies over the last hundred years has created an escalating natural hazard, more costly as each decade passes.

Flora Gregg, teacher at the Supai reservation school, witnessed a severe flood in summer 1901 that announced its approach with a ten-foot wall of water through the narrows above the village. The deluge destroyed fields, orchards, and homes, yet Gregg wrote that all "set up temporary housekeeping" in cliff shelters, then returned to repair homes, collect and dry out their furnishings, and replant in a leisurely, even cheerful manner. This was a purely traditional response to their fickle environs.

On 2 January 1910, five days of winter thaw followed by heavy rains produced a ten- to fifteen-foot wall of water through the narrows. Havasu Creek surged twenty feet above flood stage, engulfing the entire canyon from wall to wall. Stone agency buildings that had survived the 1901 flood melted as "so many lumps of sugar," leaving the terrified agent and his wife up a nearby cottonwood in their undergarments. Flagstaff's *Coconino Sun* reported the devastation under the headline "Village Destroyed by Flood Will Undoubtedly be Thing of the Past," but fortunately nearly all tribal members were on the plateau and unaware of anything amiss. When they returned, however, the transitional—not traditional—response was to build more elaborate, equally flood-prone irrigation works and go to work as part-time wage laborers.

By the end of the pioneer period at Grand Canyon's South Rim, the formerly self-sufficient Havasupais had nearly completed their transition to a cash economy. A major summer flood in 1928 left 25 percent of Supai's residents destitute and all in need of emergency provisions and transportation from the government. Low-wage labor to repair flood damage had become a major source of income. That condition only worsened by the 1940s as residents diversified into tourism, yet expensive camp and trail improvements disappeared with each new flood. A summer inundation in 1990 produced several million dollars in damages, and floods since that year have hardly given the people time to catch their breaths.

The 1975 Grand Canyon National Park Enlargement Act returned more than two hundred thousand acres to the Havasupai, and the tribe's own plans have called for a partial return to traditional plateau occupation. But even then, home in Havasu Canyon will remain a hazardous place.

Recommended Reading:
Stephen Hirst, *Life in a Narrow Place: The Havasupai of Grand Canyon* (New York: David McKay Company, 1976)

Above: Supai Charlie in front of a traditional Havasupai home at Supai. Grand Canyon photographer H.G. Peabody preserved this image in 1899 when the tribe still lived in traditional abodes. The wickiup and other simply built structures like earthen irrigation ditches were deliberate adaptations to the people's flood-prone canyon home. GRCA 8991

The region immediately north of Grand Canyon between St. George, Utah, and Lees Ferry, Arizona, has long been called the Arizona Strip for its isolation from the remainder of the state. Elevations range from 4,500 to 9,000 feet, amenable terrain only in comparison to the nearby yawning abyss. Nearly at its center, what practical Mormon pioneers called the Buckskin Mountain and reflective Southern Paiutes termed the "mountain lying down," the Kaibab Plateau rises like a thick violet cloud to separate semiarid eastern and western sectors of the strip. The plateau at 7,500 to 9,000 feet in elevation supports a healthy ponderosa pine forest and abundant mule deer. Add twenty-seven inches of annual precipitation nurturing rich grasses within aspen-lined meadows, and it held promise for early settlers. Troublesome tributary canyons, sometimes three hundred inches of snowfall in a single winter, and shallow limestone soils limited its use, however, and suggested easier transportation routes.

Eastern and western sectors of the Arizona Strip lie between 4,500 and 6,000 foot elevations. Numerous washes lead generally south from the strip's northern border at the Vermilion Cliffs, and their canyons gouge ever deeper as they approach Grand Canyon. The most significant of these is formed by Kanab Creek, the only easily accessible stream located between the widely separated Paria and Virgin Rivers. Along its upper, level banks lie two towns that figure prominently in North Rim history: the sister communities of Fredonia, Arizona, and Kanab, Utah. During the pioneer period, east-west travellers hugged the colorful cliffs to access a few perennial springs and passed near these town sites as they rounded the Kaibab Plateau. Mormon pioneers who built the towns realized

through trial and error that marginal rainfall discouraged dry farming and fickle Kanab Creek limited irrigation. They had to think twice before locating homes in this arid place and ever after to sustain marginal livelihoods.

Topography immediately south of Grand Canyon is no more amenable to east-west travel, while precipitation and groundwater flow are even less favorable for settlement. The broad Coconino Plateau begins at the South Rim roughly a thousand feet lower in elevation than the Kaibab Plateau and descends gently to the south, with somewhat more precipitous drops to the east beyond Desert View and west in the vicinity of Ash Fork. Annual precipitation varies from fifteen inches at points along the canyon lip to seven inches and less within the eastern Painted Desert and western lowlands approaching the lower Colorado River. There are no perennial streams atop the Coconino Plateau, although Cataract Creek emerges near Williams and with its tributaries flows intermittently, dissecting two thousand square miles of semiarid terrain before converging at the Havasupai village of Supai within Havasu Canyon. The combination of Cataract's canyons, the imposing San Francisco Peaks, and aridity convinced 1850s road surveyors to follow springs straddling the thirty-fifth parallel of latitude, well south of the canyon's edge.

When European Americans finally settled at Grand Canyon in the 1880s, they learned that precipitation, whether it falls in violent summer

Early depictions of Grand Canyon often expressed mood, not reality, as this drawing, published in John Wesley Powell's 1895 book, Canyons of the Colorado, *indicates. NAU.PH.268-16*

thunderstorms, gentle winter rains, or snow, does not remain long in one place. The surface of the Colorado Plateau is alternately water-resistant sandstone which sends torrents immediately rushing to the region's lowest points (ultimately, to the Colorado River) and highly fractured limestone that draws rain and snowmelt deep beneath the surface then releases it sparingly at difficult locations. At Grand Canyon, permeable limestone of the Kaibab Formation supports no natural lakes, other than small sinkholes on the North Rim, or appreciable aquifers within easy range of the well driller's rig. Rather, the best regional water sources are found several thousand feet below the canyon's rims at Indian Garden, Havasu Springs, Thunder River, and Roaring Springs, none of which were tapped for rimside settlements until the pioneer period had lapsed.

. . .

This 300-mile-wide, 150-mile-long slice of northwestern Arizona is certainly a place of matchless beauty to twentieth century visitors, but as the foregoing physical description implies, it proved a difficult region for early European Americans to transit then settle. When they did arrive in the middle years of the nineteenth century, they brought along certain ideas that had accompanied all westward immigrants since long before the American Revolution. Uppermost was their perception of the West as "wilderness," free for the taking despite American Indian occupants. Pioneers did

not have to think of Indians as savages to justify taking whatever land they wished, though many felt exactly that way. Others simply believed that Indian occupants did not use the land to best advantage, had too much of it, and would not miss a section here and there put to better use.

Pioneer concepts concerning free wilderness land to the west lay firmly ensconced within land policies of our United States government, which had pieced together its public domain through war for independence, purchase, boundary negotiations, and war for acquisition. Policies concerning land distribution had evolved since the nation's founding, beginning with sales of large tracts designed to fill the national treasury then shifting toward free distribution of small parcels to encourage continental occupation by United States citizens. The 1862 Homestead Act with subsequent amendments represented the culmination of the later democratic ideal. Armed with a long heritage of take and subdue, those who arrived at the canyon's edge in the 1880s and 1890s found themselves within a piece of the public domain that essentially had no protective status. Take and subdue they did, holding onto the land through squatter's rights until federal surveys allowed sections to be homesteaded, or until enterprising settlers found other ways to legally claim their chosen parcels.

The most often used "other way" to turn federal land into private property, especially in the Grand Canyon region, involved mining claims. The 1866, 1870, and 1872 Federal Mining Acts encouraged

prospectors to file claims almost anywhere within the public domain and, later, national forests. Miners, like homesteaders, could gain ownership through patent if they actually developed minerals of value, but could also control mineral-barren land without patent if they simply made modest annual improvements. Federal laws allowed local mining districts to set their own rules and the size of individual claims, typically measuring from one to twenty acres. The truly liberal aspects of federal law, however, which would ultimately ignite conflicts at Grand Canyon's South Rim, were those that allowed one person to hold any number of claims and permitted any type of development on them: mine, mill, farm, ranch, nightclub, jewelry stand—anything.

Pioneers who wished to develop Grand Canyon resources, whatever they might be, also benefitted from acts of the Arizona territorial legislature in the 1870s and 1880s that allowed anyone to build roads and trails across state lands or the public domain and to charge tolls for as long as fifteen years to recoup construction costs. Prior to 1920, individuals and companies built dozens of roads leading to and along canyon rims and dozens more inner-canyon trails. Only one trail developer chose to impose tolls, but others officially recorded their modest pathways as toll roads, and each felt a strong proprietary interest in those segments of the pioneer transport grid he had created.

These liberal homestead, mining, and transportation laws coupled with the democratic ideal of unregulated development of the early public domain are crucial to understanding the pioneer period at Grand Canyon. They sowed seeds of conflict which would sprout at the turn of the century among individuals, corporate powers, and conservation-minded federal agencies. The earliest settlers, who worked unbelievably hard to develop the remote region, would learn that, just as Grand Canyon began to attract large numbers of paying tourists, the federal government—the same government that had encouraged them to settle—wanted to impose regulations to protect natural and built environments. Conflict between public and private interests would churn beneath the routine of everyday life for nearly thirty years. Ultimate control taken by the United States Forest Service and National Park Service would bring an end to the pioneer period and begin what we experience today as Grand Canyon National Park.

Private acquisition and private use versus public preservation are underlying themes of this book. The reader is alerted to these themes and asked to consider them in each chapter. They illuminate and often explain each pioneer family's approach, tenure, and departure from Grand Canyon. They also involve something larger, having to do with successive land managers wresting control from prior occupants, a process that never ends, and the notion that large tracts of land can be set aside and preserved in a more or less natural state despite developmental pressures.

Since Grand Canyon is a rather large place, it is no surprise to learn that people did not arrive all at once or in any particular order to every point along its edge, nor did they come from the same direction and stay equal lengths of time. Chronology alone cannot portray

settlement complexity so the story is told in temporal order, more or less, within geographical segments. American Indian occupation and early explorers encompassing the entire region are presented first, followed by settlement near the southwestern, southeastern, and southcentral rims. The canyon's north side is considered last, not because its pioneer settlement is less important, but because it developed later and to a lesser extent, ended later in some respects, and unfolded in ways entirely different from its southern counterpart only ten air-miles distant.

Dropping well below the canyon's rim, one encounters Shinumo Creek.
Courtesy of Mike Buchheit

Folsom point preform found in the Nankoweap area in 1993. *GRCA 14051*

7

CHAPTER ONE
Earliest Residents

T HE PRESENCE OF PALEO-INDIANS IN THE AMERICAN SOUTHWEST PROBABLY DATES TO THE LAST ICE AGE, ten thousand years ago, and although little is known of them, scholars suggest they led nomadic lives following the tracks of mammoths and other large animals in hopes of securing a meal. A single projectile point recently discovered in a remote corner of the canyon confirms that these early people passed this way in their incessant search for food.[1]

Archaic peoples replaced or descended from Paleo-Indians and exploited the Southwest with a greater awareness of natural resources. They hunted both large and small animals, collected a wide variety of plants and seeds, and shaped these products to enrich their lives. Fragments of Archaic baskets, sandals, and fiber nets as well as stone tools and projectile points have been found in and around Grand Canyon. The most intriguing artifacts unearthed within inner-canyon limestone caves are beautifully crafted, four-thousand-year-old split-twig figures of deer and mountain sheep, some found skewered with diminutive spears, suggesting prayers or celebration for successful hunts.[2]

Life among Archaic peoples eased considerably about 200 B.C. with the introduction of corn cultivation from Mexico. This early agricultural revolution prompted nomads to adopt a more sedentary culture that enveloped much of the Colorado Plateau and all of Grand Canyon. These early residents, called Prehistoric Pueblo (formerly termed Anasazi) by archaeologists, at first used the canyon sparingly during periods of above average precipitation, but by A.D. 900 inhabited eastern portions of the inner canyon as well as its northern and southern edges[3]. By A.D. 1075, they had replaced early wood and thatch pithouses with stacked-stone dwellings, were raising a variety of crops on arable inner-canyon terraces, crafting fine ceramic pottery, and occupying every habitable nook and cranny within Grand Canyon.

The Prehistoric Pueblo culture declined at Grand Canyon after A.D. 1190, and speculation concerning their complete withdrawal less than twenty years later focuses on adverse environmental conditions. Overpopulation may have depleted arable soils, plants, and game animals. Immigrants of other cultures may have hastened

9

Hopi village of Walpi on First Mesa, 1918. Some Hopi villages have been continuously occupied since the twelfth century and, like Prehistoric Pueblo counterparts, perch in nearly inaccessible locations. The Hopi are among the only successful dry farmers in the American Southwest, planting fields in the flatlands beneath reservation mesas. This cultural landscape is little changed from the sixteenth century when Spaniards first arrived in the Grand Canyon region.

GRCA 11329

Petroglyphs (etched) and pictographs (painted) cover mineral-stained canyon walls throughout the Colorado Plateau. These images were photographed in Glen Canyon in 1913.

NAU.PH.568.2324

tenures. American Indians who replaced these people, however, arrived from many compass points with differing lifeways to settle limited portions of the canyon area. Despite extensive trade, shared survival traits, and significant cultural borrowings during centuries of interaction, these separate bands and tribes retained, and still retain, important aspects of their individuality.

Hopi Indians, who live east of Grand Canyon, have occupied mesas within their present reservation for nearly a thousand years. The *Hopituh Shi-nu-mu*, or peaceful people, descend from the Prehistoric Pueblo and have used canyon resources for many centuries.[5] Traditional Hopis believe, in fact, that their ancestors emerged from the *Sipapuni*, a mineral spring located along the Little Colorado River gorge, and that its waters and those of the Colorado River are the source of their rainfall. Well into the twentieth century, Hopis annually visited this holy place and the river below today's Beamer Trail to collect salt. For five hundred years or more they have crossed the Coconino Plateau along the ancient Moqui Trail to trade with traditional friends, the Havasupai Indians. Although the Hopi have never lived at the canyon as a tribal unit, individuals have traded, worked, and lived with European Americans at the South Rim since arrival of the first pioneers.

Navajo Indians have also long used canyon resources and lived seasonally upon both rims. The *Diné*, meaning "the people," Apachean Athabascans from Canada, arrived east and northeast of Grand Canyon by the year 1500. A hunting-raiding society when they entered the Southwest, prolonged exposure to Pueblo cultures and European Americans influenced them to take up animal husbandry, weaving, and silver work by the 1870s. The Navajo today

their departure. Droughts which gripped the Southwest in the twelfth and thirteenth centuries perhaps scattered the remainder. The more than 2,500 Prehistoric Pueblo cultural sites documented within Grand Canyon National Park, probably a fraction of the total, attest to their once-prominent presence.[4]

Paleo-Indians, Archaic peoples, and Prehistoric Puebloans as far as we know lived within fairly uniform cultures which touched occasionally and then enveloped the entire Grand Canyon region during their respective

occupy the largest Indian reservation in the
United States, including the far southeastern lip
of Marble Canyon. Some individuals continue
to hunt deer, collect pinyon nuts, trade, live,
and work at both canyon rims.[6]

The Southern Paiute are among the earliest
American Indians to establish permanent homes
at and within Grand Canyon. Their ancestors
migrated from the western Great Basin after
A.D. 1000 and may well have mingled briefly
with North Rim Prehistoric Puebloans before
the latter's exodus. Families of the Uinkarets
and Shivwits bands west of Kanab Creek and
the Kaibabits band to the east lived for centuries
along the Arizona Strip and within Colorado
River tributaries as far east as the Paria River.[7]
These people led seminomadic lives prior to
the arrival of Mormon pioneers, combining
agriculture with hunting and gathering to
eke out an existence. Today, members of the
Kaibabits band cultivate fields and raise livestock
on their small reservation adjacent to Pipe
Spring National Monument north of Grand
Canyon National Park.[8]

Hualapai and Havasupai Indians are closely
related residents who have inhabited Grand
Canyon's South Rim, southern plateaus, inner-
canyon terraces, and Colorado River tributaries
since perhaps the twelfth century. Common
ancestors emigrated from the lower Colorado
River, and the tribes have always considered
themselves members of the same Pai culture.
Only misunderstandings of the first European
Americans to northern Arizona resulted in
separate tribal names and reservations by the
late nineteenth century. Pai territory at one
time extended from the Grand Canyon south to
Bill Williams Mountain and the lower Colorado
River east to the Little Colorado River.[9]

*Navajo Indians photographed by
Thomas O'Sullivan of the Wheeler
Survey near Fort Defiance, New
Mexico, 1873. O'Sullivan and other
early western photographers carefully
framed their subjects to fit European-
American stereotypes of western tribes,
but here he accurately portrays the
weaver's art and people's dress.*
GRCA 9903

*Below: Navajo medicine men
preserving the ancient ritual of sand
painting at Gallup, New Mexico, 1923.*
GRCA 15247

Chief Manakadja beside a transitional cut-lumber home, 1938. One hundred and fifty tourists visited Supai in that year as tribal members began to develop a tourist industry, today's major economy. Havasupai packers have since led tens of thousands down the Hualapai Trail, through Supai, to informal campsites below Bridal Veil Falls.

GRCA 190

The Hualapai, or pine tree people, traditionally occupied the Coconino Plateau south of Grand Canyon and east of the Grand Wash Cliffs, as well as Colorado River tributaries like Peach Springs and Diamond Creek canyons. They subsisted on small game, fruit, berries, and nuts, supplemented by limited agriculture along the few perennial water sources found in their territory. The United States government set aside a half-million-acre reservation within Hualapai traditional lands in 1883, which doubled in size in 1947 when Atlantic and Pacific Railroad Company grant lands (odd-numbered sections within the original reservation) were returned to the tribe. Most Hualapais make a living today through ranching, lumbering, and wage labor.[10]

Until the twentieth century, the Havasupai, or *Havsuw 'baaja* (people of the blue water), led a migratory lifestyle similar to the Hualapai. They moved seasonally between upland plateaus in winter and inner-canyon springs in summer, occupying every tributary canyon descending from the South Rim to the Colorado as far east as the Little Colorado. Most Havasupai families preferred a summer home in the village of Supai where the entire population irrigated as many as fifty fertile acres along Havasu Creek. A few family units preferred solitary sites to the east and west, including Indian Garden, Fossil Bay, Dripping Springs, Santa Maria Spring, National Canyon, and Mohawk Canyon. In winter, the Havasupai returned as a unit to the plateau, where they hunted, collected plant foods, and travelled to trade and socialize with Hualapai relatives and Hopi friends.[11]

The Havasupai found their lifestyles curtailed when the federal government reduced traditional lands to a sixty-square-mile reservation in 1880. Responding to Havasupai concerns about white miners invading even this small domain, federal surveyors pared the reservation in 1882 to a mere 518 acres along Havasu Creek. Boundaries meant little at first, but bureaucratic enforcement of land-use regulations from 1910 through the 1920s pressured the people to remain year round within flood-prone Havasu Canyon. In 1975, the tribe reacquired more than 200,000 acres of traditional canyon and plateau lands bordering Grand Canyon National Park, offering hopes for a more diverse economy and amenable living conditions. Most Havasupais today earn their living from tourism, ranching, and wage labor.[12]

Although this history now turns its attention to people of European descent who arrived to dominate Grand Canyon life by the late nineteenth century, it is worthwhile to consider the much longer period of human occupation. Paleo-Indians and Archaic peoples traversed and lived at the canyon long before classical civilizations arose in Europe. Prehistoric Puebloans developed an advanced culture that eventually enveloped nearly all of the Colorado Plateau and lasted six times longer than our present United States government. Four of today's tribes lived here long before Columbus stumbled upon the New World.

Longevity at Grand Canyon led to adaptation to difficult country and limited resources. Consideration of how native peoples approached the land instructed the first

European-American explorers and later pioneers on regional transportation routes and survival strategies. Without exception, early white people crossed the region with few difficulties when guided between scarce water holes by native guides; those who went it alone always suffered. All but a few of today's inner-canyon trails were first developed by Prehistoric Puebloans and later American Indians, then improved by pioneer prospectors and tourist guides, as often as not with native labor. Successful early settlers identified later, like William Bass, Sanford Rowe, and the Hull brothers, sustained their enterprises with the direct assistance of Havasupai Indians or by mimicking their development of check dams, water tanks, gardens, and camp structures.

When white settlers first came to the Grand Canyon region, Havasupai, Hualapai, and Southern Paiute Indians had yet to be consigned to reservations. The Hopi and Navajo had only recently been so constricted, and paid little attention to mandates as they continued to follow traditional travel routes in pursuit of natural resources. Persistent mingling occurred among native and immigrant peoples—most of it friendly, some of it violent—until, by the end of the pioneer period, there remained no question of political and economic dominance. This continuing interaction is identified where appropriate in the following stories of European-American exploration, exploitation, and settlement.

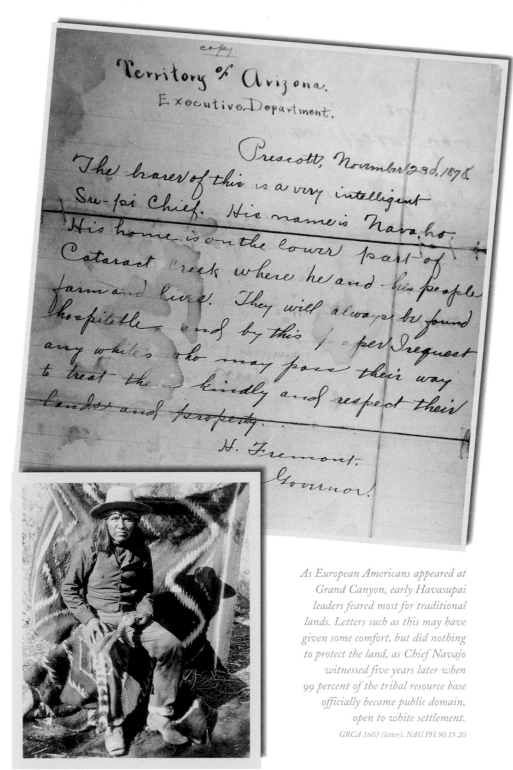

As European Americans appeared at Grand Canyon, early Havasupai leaders feared most for traditional lands. Letters such as this may have given some comfort, but did nothing to protect the land, as Chief Navajo witnessed five years later when 99 percent of the tribal resource base officially became public domain, open to white settlement.
GRCA 1603 (letter); NAU.PH.90.15.20

CHAPTER TWO
Ephemeral Contacts

John Wesley Powell, 1874.
GRCA 17228

ADVENTURERS, MISSIONARIES, EXPLORERS, AND SETTLERS SWEPT ACROSS THE AMERICAN SOUTHWEST FOR MORE THAN THREE HUNDRED YEARS before the last of these chose to remain within the Grand Canyon region. Arrogant armor-clad men arrived first to pursue a folktale of riches, but settled for a few meager outposts of Spanish civilization. Missionaries who accompanied the first conquistadors, bent on turning Indian souls to Christian beliefs, ranged even farther than their gold-seeking companions, but also fared worse than they initially hoped. Buckskin-clad mountain men appeared briefly to trap along southwestern streams, then remained long enough to lead government surveyors east to west across a newly won empire. Surveys led to wagon roads and finally a railroad that fueled the modern economy of northern Arizona and brought easterners to settle towns astride a few well-spaced railroad depots. Residents of these towns would inevitably gaze across the broad Coconino Plateau to ask how the great chasm to the north might turn a profit.

Opposite:
A storm over
Vishnu Temple in
Grand Canyon.
GRCA 9788

THE SPANISH

In 1519, decades before English colonists landed at Jamestown, Spanish conquistador Hernán Cortés stepped ashore at Vera Cruz, Mexico, to begin his personal conquest of mainland America. Following a two-year struggle to subdue the Mexicas, Cortés's lieutenants fanned out to seek the fabled Seven Cities of Antilia.

Pursuit of the mythical cities of gold quickly faded while Spaniards turned to the mundane yet lucrative business of exploiting New World minerals, lands, and people. Before surrendering the dream, however, one of the last and greatest of the Spanish military entradas penetrated far to the north and touched the mile-high banks of the Colorado River at Grand Canyon.[1]

The far-reaching expedition of 1540-42 was led by Francisco Vásquez de Coronado, an ambitious young nobleman in partnership with New Spain's viceroy, Don Antonio de Mendoza. It was an expensive and well-equipped affair, boasting three hundred Spanish cavalry and infantry; nearly a thousand Indian auxiliaries; hundreds of horses; thousands of cattle, sheep, and goats; and one Marcos de Niza, a Franciscan friar and imaginative liar who claimed to have seen the first of the fabulous seven cities. After a long march through New Spain's unsettled northern territory, Coronado arrived at the first of the Zuni pueblos in today's western New Mexico. Here, and along the way, he found nothing that would turn a *marevidi* back in Mexico City.[2]

Dismayed at the poverty of the immediate area, and understandably irked at Fray Marcos whom he sent home in disgrace, Coronado listened attentively to Zunis who claimed that pueblos to the west held far greater riches. Duped by this misdirection—a hopeful survival strategy practiced by southwestern Indians on many white interlopers during the first years of contact—he sent Pedro de Tovar with a score of cavalry to the west. The Spanish lieutenant attacked and defeated the Hopi, but found nothing to excite his interest other than reports of a great river even farther west. Coronado sent another officer, García López de Cárdenas, to find the river, which Spaniards hoped would serve as a waterway to the Gulf of California.[3]

Arriving among the Hopi, Cárdenas found guides eager to lead his party ever westward. After a twenty-day trip that should have taken half that time, the Spaniards arrived at the canyon's South Rim in late September 1540, most likely in the vicinity of Moran and Lipan Points. They spent several days looking for water, scratching their helmets, and searching for a way to the river, which they misjudged from their lofty angle to be a mere six feet wide. Several of the party scrambled a third of the way down, gained a better understanding of the awful chasm's dimensions, and guessed correctly that the river within would not afford a navigable path to the sea.[4]

In all probability, the Hopis successfully pulled the wool over these first European eyes to view Grand Canyon. They knew of far easier and shorter routes from their homes to the Colorado River, which was what the Spaniards sought, after all, not a mile-high scenic view. Even after leading the Spaniards to the South Rim, the guides could have shown them down a variation of today's Tanner Trail which led to traditional Hopi salt mines at river level. They also could have anticipated the Spaniards' desire to find a water route to the sea and led them farther west along the Hopi-Havasupai-Mohave trade trail (Moqui Trail) to the navigable lower Colorado River. Hopi leaders very likely advised their men to guide the unwelcome sojourners along an exaggerated path to the highest point above the river and to volunteer no information of value.

If this was the Hopis' intent, the ruse worked. The Spaniards left the region convinced that a near-waterless wasteland lay west of the Hopi pueblos, difficult to traverse and to no purpose. They could view the canyon only as an impenetrable barrier prohibiting Spanish exploration to the northwest. The party returned to Zuni with these assessments and no Spanish military force ever again approached Grand Canyon. Coronado returned to Mexico City in 1542, discredited for having found nothing of value and bankrupt for having tried.

Although judged an immediate failure, this last of the great entradas had lasting regional effects. As the sixteenth century neared its end, other expeditions aided by the first conquistadors' information nudged the Spanish frontier northward. Expeditions led by Francisco Sanchez Chamuscado, Francisco de Ibarra, and Antonio de Espejo returned to the Zuni and Rio Grande pueblos. In 1581, Chamuscado brought Catholic missionaries who would attempt to establish a permanent foothold among the pueblos. In 1582-83, Espejo's party prospected for minerals within Hopi lands and Arizona's Verde Valley. These efforts revealed opportunities for mining, ranching, agriculture, and converts that led to permanent Spanish settlement within the Rio Grande pueblos in 1598 under the leadership of the Basque nobleman, Juan de Oñate.[5]

Spaniards had lived among the New Mexico pueblos for 170 years before officials in Seville, never quick to authorize costly New World initiatives, got around to the settlement of Alta California. By 1776, Franciscans led by Fray Junípero Serra and military men like Juan Bautista de Anza established the Presidio of Monterey and a number of other forts and missions as far north as San Francisco.[6] By this same year, it had become clear that an overland route between the Rio Grande pueblos and California missions could tie together northern extremes of empire. To this end, two expeditions led by Spanish priests passed south and north of Grand Canyon.

The journal detailing Father Garcés's 1776 solitary expedition from the lower Colorado River to the Hopi pueblos is the earliest written record of travel immediately south of the canyon. It recounts the journey of one man negotiating a semiarid landscape, not a wilderness, but a land alive with Indian communities and individuals treading well-developed paths. A succession of Hopi, Hualapai, and Havasupai Indians guided the affable priest to his destination. Without interpreters he and those he met communicated through friendly gestures and maps drawn in the sand.[7]

Garcés's journey began at the Mohave Indian villages along the western segment of the Moqui Trail which brought him to the vicinity of Peach Springs. He detoured to the northeast by a spur trail—likely a variation of today's Hualapai Trail—which led him deep within tributary drainages to the village of Supai. Here the priest found thirty-four Havasupai families at their summer residence and noted cattle and horses with Spanish brands that had been obtained in trade from the Hopi. He also observed with approbation fine irrigation dams and canals along Havasu Creek and the people's successful farming efforts. After feasting for five days with these receptive canyon residents,

Garcés left Havasu Canyon by way of the Topocoba Trail, then regained the Moqui Trail east and southeast to the canyon rim.[8]

Although he knew that the Colorado River flowed parallel to his path somewhere to the north, his first glimpse of the river within Grand Canyon impressed him deeply. In the vicinity of Grandview Point, he gazed beyond the rim and

… halted at the sight of the most profound canyons which ever onward continue; and within these flows the Rio Colorado. There is seen a very great sierra … and there runs from southeast to northwest a pass open to the very base, as if the sierra were cut artificially to give entrance to the Rio Colorado into these lands. I named this singular (pass) Puerto de Bucareli.[9]

Zuni Pueblo, 1870s. Marcos de Niza with the Moorish slave, Estevan, "discovered" Zuni in 1539 while searching for the fabled Seven Cities. Estevan was killed by the pueblo's occupants; Niza dared only glimpse the pueblo from afar, assumed it was the first of the golden cities, and reported the find to the viceroy in Mexico City, which launched the entrada of Francisco Vásquez de Coronado.
Photograph by Jack Hillers, Powell Survey photographer. GRCA 11339

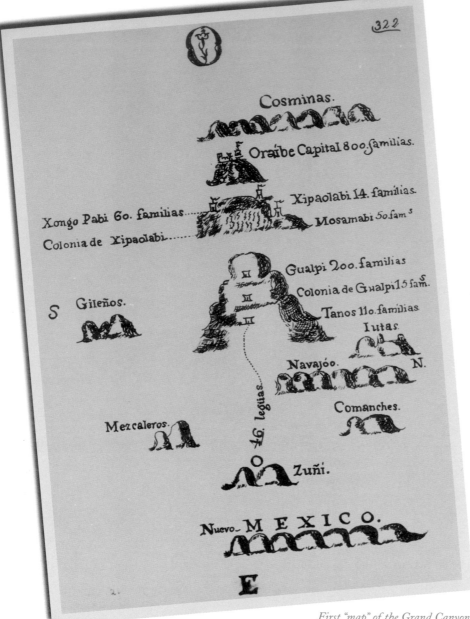

First "map" of the Grand Canyon region, a 1775 illustration by Fray Silvestre Velez de Escalante who seemed more concerned with the number of potential souls to save than intervening terrain. "Cosminas," lettered at the top, was one of several variations of the Spanish name applied to the Havasupai.

Hayden Library, Arizona Collection

Thus, 236 years after Cárdenas, Garcés made the second European visit to the Grand Canyon and bestowed upon it one of its more picturesque names. He continued to the Hopi pueblos, but residents, ambivalent at best to Spanish visitors, sent him packing soon after his arrival. En route back to the Mohave villages, he paused once again at Supai to visit the friendlier Havasupai.[10]

Garcés had set out to blaze a trail from the Mohave villages to the Rio Grande pueblos. He achieved this objective in less than three weeks by treating regional residents with respect; they in turn provided guides and revealed their well-trodden trade trail. In completing his journey he had actually accomplished New Spain's goal to find a land route from California to New Mexico, since he had recently crossed California mountains and deserts from Monterey to reach the Mohave Indians. The remaining distance from the Hopi mesas to Santa Fe was also known to the Spanish, if not to Garcés, as it had been travelled in the prior year by Father Silvestre Velez de Escalante, mission priest at Zuni. Before leaving the Hopis on 4 July 1776, Garcés sent a letter to the Zuni mission presumably describing his success. By that date, however, Escalante was in Santa Fe, called by his superior to participate in the second ecclesiastical exploration of 1776.[11]

Fray Francisco Atanasio Dominguez had arrived in Santa Fe in March 1776 to inspect the Rio Grande missions and to investigate a route to Monterey. For the latter task he recruited nine New Mexicans, including the twenty-six-year-old Escalante as diarist and unofficial co-leader. When the Zuni missionary had visited the Hopi in the summer of 1775, he found them to be on the surly side of accommodating.

Thus, even though he had been informed by the Havasupai and perhaps by Garcés of the Moqui Trail, he was inclined to avoid the Hopis, Mohaves, roving Apaches, and aridity of northern Arizona. Dominguez agreed, and the party set out on 29 July 1776 to find a second route to the Pacific coast, this time far to the north of Grand Canyon.[12]

The Dominguez-Escalante Expedition travelled northwest to the approximate latitude of Monterey, then angled across central Utah with the help of Ute Indian guides. The priests dawdled to preach their faith to everyone they encountered, however, thus took too long to traverse the Wasatch Mountains and reach the Great Basin to have any hope of making the west coast before winter snows closed California's high sierra. Low on provisions and without their Ute guides, the party veered south from the area of today's Cedar City, Utah, intending to cross the Colorado River and return to Santa Fe by way of the Moqui Trail.[13]

The priests had a celestial idea of where they were as they turned back for Santa Fe, but no knowledge of intervening terrain.[14] Fortunately, they encountered Southern Paiute bands as their southward journey led them beside the western escarpment of the Colorado Plateau to the Virgin River. The Paiutes proved reluctant to guide the party—this was probably their first encounter with whites—but helpfully warned them to turn east since the Colorado River south of here flowed within mile-high cliffs. Heeding this advice, the retreating party surmounted the Hurricane Cliffs then travelled the entire length of the Arizona Strip.[15]

Although they crossed the strip without guides, the priests encountered Uinkaret and Kaibabits Paiute Indians along the way who directed the travellers to the nearest waterpockets; sold them dried mountain sheep meat, prickly pear cakes, seeds, and pinyon nuts; and even kept them abreast of current events with news of last year's trip along Grand Canyon's South Rim by Garcés. Native residents kept pointing eastward toward the nearest river crossing as the party rounded the north side of the Kaibab Plateau and glimpsed Marble Canyon to the south. Terrain and the location of springs funneled the men along the base of the Vermilion Cliffs to the confluence of the Paria and Colorado Rivers. Here the priests ran into an apparent dead end, unnerving them enough to name the site *San Benito de Salsipuedes*, which translates, "let the errant brothers get out if they can."[16]

The party spent several days at this site that nearly one hundred years later would be settled by a fugitive and named Lees Ferry. After several unsuccessful attempts to swim, then raft, the swift current, the men discovered an escape route over the cliffs and made their way northeast into Glen Canyon, passing the site of today's Wahweap Marina at Lake Powell. At last they reached an old Ute ford of the Colorado, known ever since as the Crossing of the Fathers, and fired a musket volley to celebrate their safe passage. They continued south and east to the Hopi pueblos, tried again to convert its residents without success, and tramped off along the known route to Zuni and Santa Fe.[17] Dominguez and Escalante were the last colonial Spaniards known to have visited the Grand Canyon region.

● ● ●

Tenuous Spanish control of its northern provinces ended in 1821 with the revolution that secured Mexican independence. Despite nearly three hundred years of military incursions and colonization efforts, goals along the northern frontier had not been achieved. Native residents had no stockpiles of precious metals for the taking. Mining and trade in animal skins had not enriched the Spanish economy. Agricultural and pastoral pursuits remained little above subsistence levels. The two prongs of colonization reaching north along the Rio Grande and Pacific coast remained isolated despite exploratory efforts of missionary priests. No great numbers of souls turned to the Catholic faith.

At first glance, Spanish influence in the Grand Canyon region appears even less. Judged in the context of events, this is true enough. Only brief forays of Cárdenas, Garcés, and Dominguez touched the canyon at all, and their visits merit description only as a series of "firsts." In a larger sense, however, the Spanish presence forever altered lifestyles of regional American Indian tribes. Contact started the first Grand Canyon residents on a long path of cultural

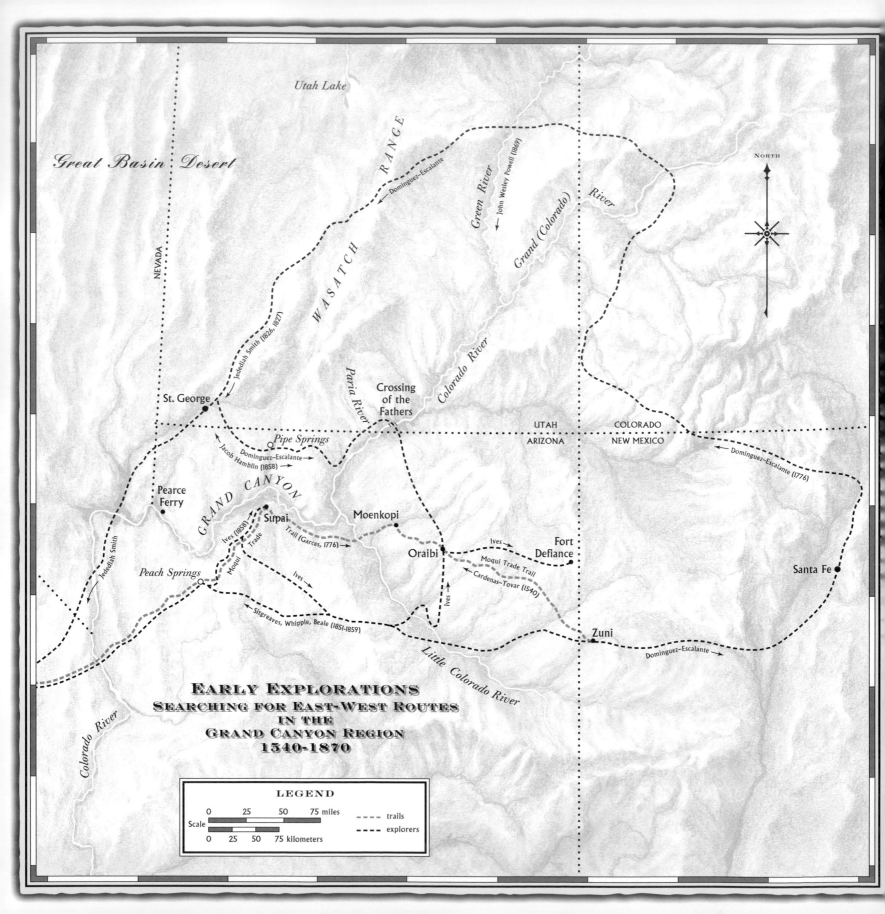

Utah Lake

Great Basin Desert

NORTH

NEVADA

WASATCH RANGE

Dominguez–Escalante

Green River

John Wesley Powell (1869)

Grand (Colorado) River

Jedediah Smith (1826, 1827)

Paria River

Colorado River

St. George

Crossing of the Fathers

UTAH
ARIZONA

COLORADO
NEW MEXICO

Pipe Springs

Dominguez–Escalante

Dominguez–Escalante (1776)

Jacob Hamblin (1858)

Pearce Ferry

GRAND CANYON

Supai

Moenkopi

Ives (1858)

Moqui Trade Trail (Garces, 1776)

Jedediah Smith

Ives (1858)

Moqui Trade Trail

Oraibi

Ives

Fort Defiance

Santa Fe

Peach Springs

Ives

Moqui Trade Trail

Cardenas–Tovar (1540)

Ives

Sitgreaves, Whipple, Beale (1851-1859)

Zuni

Colorado River

Little Colorado River

Dominguez–Escalante

EARLY EXPLORATIONS
SEARCHING FOR EAST-WEST ROUTES
IN THE
GRAND CANYON REGION
1540-1870

LEGEND

| 0 | 25 | 50 | 75 miles |

Scale

| 0 | 25 | 50 | 75 kilometers |

- - - trails
- - - explorers

exchange with European Americans that would become more tumultuous with the arrival of United States citizens in the 1850s. Some changes, such as the acquisition of guns, horses, and steel knives, would have a direct effect on those who followed the Spanish explorers.

THE TRAPPERS

With the overthrow of Spanish rule, fur trappers of varied nationalities who had been prohibited from operating in New Spain's northern frontier took advantage of relaxed regulations under Mexican administrators. With or without official permits issued at the provincial capital at Santa Fe, these men continued to trap beaver along the Rio Grande, Gila, and Colorado Rivers and their tributary streams.[18] Speculatively, dozens in the ensuing quarter century set their traps within Grand Canyon, since beaver thrived along inner-canyon perennial tributaries like Bright Angel Creek, and trappers—who never missed a stream in their incessant search for pelts—would have had few problems following Indian paths down to and along the river.

Such men certainly probed the Colorado River upstream of the canyon, starting from New Mexican bases at Santa Fe and Taos or from the gateway to the West, St. Louis, Missouri. Joe Walker, probably one of those who trapped illegally before Mexico assumed control of New Mexico, continued to trap, guide, and prospect throughout the West until the late 1860s, and is known to have visited

southern Utah streams, the Little Colorado River gorge, and northern Arizona just south of the canyon's South Rim between 1837 and 1840. In 1824, William Wolfskill and Ewing Young led a party which trapped the San Juan River and other Colorado tributaries. In the same year, William Becknell with a party of nine men set trap lines within the upper Green River as did Etienne Provost along the Green and Colorado.[19] The enigmatic French trapper Denis Julien scratched his name and the year "1836" all along the lower cliffs of the Green and Colorado as far downstream as Cataract Canyon. Trapping companies of the 1820s and 1830s employed hundreds of these men who crossed and recrossed a territory that would become the states of Wyoming, Utah, Colorado, Arizona, and New Mexico.

William Henry Ashley, partner in the Rocky Mountain Fur Company with Andrew Henry, illustrated trappers' willingness to build boats or rafts to float southwestern rivers in pursuit of pelts. In April 1825, Ashley and six men launched a bullboat of wooden frame and buffalo skins on the Green River, fifteen miles above the Sandy River in western Wyoming, then trapped several hundred miles of riverbank to the later site of Green River, Utah. Here they abandoned their boats, traded for a few horses with a passing party of Utes, and continued on their way to try inland tributaries.[20] Ashley etched his name and the year in the cliffs within Red Canyon, to be found forty-four years later by a more famous river runner,

John Wesley Powell, who dubbed the rapid at this point Ashley Falls.[21]

Trappers also worked the Colorado south of Grand Canyon, often starting from Santa Fe and following the Rio Grande south to the Gila headwaters in southwestern New Mexico, thence west beside the Gila and north along the Colorado probably as far as the Grand Wash Cliffs. The Ewing Young party of 1826-27 fully illustrates this circular route as well as often violent encounters with native residents and the lucrative, yet unpredictable, nature of fur trapping.

Young left Santa Fe in the autumn of 1826 in charge of a colorful collection of vagabonds including George Yount, Tom "Pegleg" Smith, and James Ohio Pattie. They trapped south along the Rio Grande to the Gila where they engaged in a brief hand-to-hand skirmish with Apache Indians, then moved west along the Gila where they found the remains of eight French trappers who had fared worse than they in a dispute with Pima Indians. Young's crew attacked the Pimas in random retribution, then casually worked the Gila to the Yuma villages on the lower Colorado River where they turned upstream into territory of the Mohave Indians.[22]

The Mohave had inhabited many miles of Colorado River shoreline below today's Lake Mead since long before the first Spanish entradas. They were sometimes receptive to white visitors like Garcés and other times hostile, depending on mood and prior encounters. When the trappers arrived loaded down with pelts, the Mohave demanded payment for extraction of their natural resource. Young's refusal led to a pitched battle and lesser skirmishes as the harried men retreated upstream. Free at last of Indian problems but exhausted from months of work, hard travel, and fighting, the men quarreled, and Pegleg Smith with a few others left the party. Young, Pattie, Yount, and the rest headed east for Santa Fe.[23]

Ewing Young's return to New Mexico in early spring 1827 provides the only known records of early trappers passing alongside the Grand Canyon. Considering the vague journals of Yount and Pattie, the men appear to have left the Colorado near Black Canyon, surmounted the Black Mountains, then made their way east-northeast beside Grand Canyon's southern edge.[24] They likely traced or closely paralleled Garcés's footsteps of half a century earlier—the journals are too sketchy to say for sure—but travel without guides resulted in an entirely different kind of trip.

By Pattie's account it was a horrible experience, with the river in sight but unattainable deep within its gorge. His thoughts no doubt reflected those of Cárdenas nearly three centuries earlier. Pattie described the canyon and river within as "… these horrid mountains, which so cage it up, as to deprive all human beings of the ability to descend to its banks.…"[25] Suffering badly from thirst, and near starvation because they refused to eat the horses that carried their pelts, the men managed to reach Zuni where they eventually recovered from the ordeal.

They moved on to Santa Fe only to have twenty thousand dollars' worth of furs confiscated by Mexican authorities for failure to obtain a trapping permit.[26]

In 1826, twenty-seven-year-old Jedediah Strong Smith made a more valuable contribution to southwestern exploration when he completed the overland route from Santa Fe to the Pacific coast begun by Dominguez. Smith left the annual trappers' rendezvous at Bear Lake, Utah, with eighteen men in August 1826, crossed the Wasatch Mountains, and turned south along the exact path followed by the Spanish priests to the later site of Hurricane, Utah. Instead of turning east in retreat as the missionaries had, Smith continued down the Virgin River through its narrows to the Muddy River, thence to the Colorado and the Mohave villages where he arrived six months before Ewing Young's party. He then crossed the southern California desert to the Mohave River and continued to the Mexican town of Los Angeles.[27]

Smith repeated his trip in the following year and trappers Ewing Young, William Wolfskill, and George Yount came along the route soon thereafter. Others followed, until a thriving business in pelts, mules, horses, and Indian slaves sprang up along what became known as the Old Spanish Trail in the 1830s and 1840s. In 1844, United States Army Captain John C. Frémont described the path as a well-defined western segment of a larger trans-western trail, travelled by annual caravans between St. Louis and Santa Fe along the eastern leg known

as the Santa Fe Trail, then west to Los Angeles. In 1848, the western caravan numbered two hundred traders and stretched in a dusty line for more than a mile. Mormon pioneers during the 1850s used Smith's segment as a vital supply link between their settlements at Salt Lake and San Bernardino, California. The same trail would develop into U.S. Highway 91 in the early 1900s and Interstate 15 by the 1970s.[28]

Joe Walker, William Ashley, Ewing Young, George Yount, James Pattie, and Jedediah Smith were but a few of many who trapped streams to make a living and in the process haphazardly revealed the region as something less than a wilderness. Each of these men passed their knowledge on to others, but only a few remained active in the Southwest for more than a decade or stayed to guide the next wave of European Americans. One who arrived early and stayed the remaining forty years of his life to guide others deserves special mention.

Joaquin Antoine Leroux came west from St. Louis with William Ashley in 1822 and began his long career as a Taos trapper in 1824.[29] During the 1820s and 1830s, Leroux trapped from the Mexican border north to the Rocky Mountains and just about every stream in between before retiring to his wife's half-million-acre hacienda at Taos, New Mexico.[30]

With the onset of the Mexican-American War in 1846, Leroux began an illustrious second career as a guide for United States military and exploring parties. His first assignment found him in the employ of Colonel Stephen W.

Kearny's Army of the West. Along with fellow trapper-guides Pauline Weaver and Baptiste Charbonneau, he led Captain Philip St. George Cooke's Mormon Battalion in 1846-47 as it blazed the first wagon road from Santa Fe to San Diego, California. After the war, Leroux guided numerous punitive expeditions against Navajo, Ute, and Apache Indians, then led the Sitgreaves, Gunnison, and Whipple expeditions in search of wagon and railroad routes from 1851 to 1854.[31]

By 1853, Leroux had become so famous as a southwestern guide that the United States Congress formally requested his advice on a route for a transcontinental railroad. From among the four east-west paths he had travelled —that of the Mormon Brigade, a Salt River route, the Old Spanish Trail, and Sitgreaves' route— Leroux recommended the latter, which was soon selected as the path of the Beale Wagon Road and by the Atlantic and Pacific Railroad in 1866 for its line across northern Arizona. He continued to guide military columns, including General Albert Sydney Johnston's army that marched into Mormon Utah in 1858 and punitive strikes against Comanche and Kiowa Indians, until his death in 1861. His passing was attributed to "asthma complicated by spear wounds," an understandable end for one who travelled so often among southwestern Indian tribes.[32]

GOVERNMENT SURVEYORS

Two coincident events in 1848 significantly altered southwestern history and indirectly accelerated European-American settlement at Grand Canyon. In May of that year, Mexican and United States senators ratified the Treaty of Guadalupe Hidalgo ending the Mexican-American War. Essentially a war of United States expansion in an era when citizens and government officials fervently embraced Manifest Destiny, its conclusion required Mexico to cede her northern lands to the United States. Thus, with a few strokes of the pen, a territory that would one day form the states of California, Nevada, Arizona, Utah, Colorado, and New Mexico joined another former Mexican province, Texas, to complete the outline of the American Southwest.[33]

The concurrent event of 1848, discovery of placer gold at Sutter's Mill, California, incited a rush of gold seekers that threatened to tip the continent on its western end. To accommodate the forty-niners and explore a newly won empire, the United States Government began to survey wagon roads across a wilderness expanse known only to American Indians and a few trappers. One important goal was to locate a central route between Cooke's road south of the Gila River and the Old Spanish Trail far to the north of Grand Canyon.[34]

The U.S. Corps of Topographical Engineers ordered Captain Lorenzo Sitgreaves to explore for such a path across the thirty-fifth parallel in 1851. Since virtually nothing was known of Grand Canyon in that year, Sitgreaves proceeded from Zuni pueblo down the Zuni and Little Colorado Rivers, apparently hoping to effect a crossing at or near the latter stream's confluence with the Colorado. Terrain and guide Antoine Leroux dissuaded him of that impossible notion. Instead, the experienced trapper-guide, despite his ignorance of the country to be crossed, led the party around the north slope of the San Francisco Peaks and west past the later sites of Williams, Ash Fork, and Peach Springs,

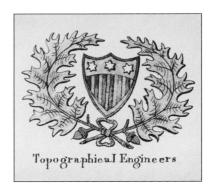

Congress created the U.S. Army Corps of Engineers in 1802 to carry out limited federal road construction. By 1838, the separate Corps of Topographical Engineers consisting entirely of officers evolved from the earlier group. Under its chief, Colonel John J. Abert, the Topographical engineers became responsible for all federal works of civil improvement, including far western road surveys, topographical mapping, and much road construction. The Corps included noteworthy and capable western explorers like Captain Amiel Whipple, Captain William Raynolds, Lieutenant James Simpson, and Lieutenant Joseph Ives. GRCA 17263

Lt. Joseph Christmas Ives of the U.S. Army Corps of Topographical Engineers. Ives's death in 1868 saved him later embarrassment for labeling Grand Canyon a region that "shall be forever unvisited and undisturbed."

thence west to the Colorado and downstream to Camp Independence near the temporarily abandoned army post at Yuma. This proved one of the more arduous of the 1850s army explorations, as Hualapai Indians shot a few more arrows into guide Leroux, Mohaves wounded the party's physician-naturalist, Dr. Samuel W. Woodhouse, Yuma Indians killed one army private, and many suffered from scurvy because of a mule-meat diet by journey's end. For his efforts, Sitgreaves had pointed the way for others but failed to locate a definitive wagon road.[35]

In 1853-54, Captain Amiel Weeks Whipple explored a railroad route that roughly paralleled Sitgreaves' path as far as the San Francisco Peaks before veering southwest to the Needles along the Colorado River. He concluded that both a wagon road and railroad could be built along his line of march. Armed with the information of Sitgreaves and Whipple, the United States Congress authorized fifty thousand dollars to construct a wagon road from Fort Defiance, New Mexico Territory, to the lower Colorado River and assigned the task to another of the Southwest's remarkable explorers, Edward Fitzgerald Beale.[36]

Beale first came west in 1846 as a young naval officer of the Mexican-American War and before his ultimate retirement made six transcontinental treks, the second of which brought an official report of the California gold discovery to Washington, D.C. Beale left the navy in 1850 to settle in California where he became Superintendent of Indian Affairs and a brigadier general of the state's militia. At some point in his multifaceted career, he developed an unlikely fascination for camels and a fervent belief that they could be used as pack stock in southwestern deserts.

Beale's appointment as wagon road superintendent along the thirty-fifth parallel coincided with the government's willingness to indulge his fantasy for camel trains. Seventy-six of the gangly beasts were shipped to Texas in 1856, and in June 1857 Beale set forth from San Antonio along existing roads to Albuquerque and Fort Defiance. Leaving the latter post in August, he moved slowly west along the line of Whipple's march, occasionally leading his men from his favorite white camel, Seid. He roughed out a road, little more than wagon tracks, which touched at Leroux Springs and Lewis Springs, just north of the future sites of Flagstaff and Williams, before continuing west along Sitgreaves' path to the Colorado River above today's Needles and on to Los Angeles. In 1858 and 1859, Beale returned to improve the road's alignment and grades.[37]

Immigrants to the fertile valleys and gold fields of California put Beale's wagon road to good use for the next several decades. After arrival of the railroad in the early 1880s, portions of his road combined with access roads along the tracks to form the western segment of the National Old Trails Highway, a transcontinental path that served into the early automotive era. With better alignments, grades, surfacing, and bridge crossings it would become United States Route 66 in 1926 and Interstate 40 by the 1970s.[38]

And the camels? They proved their worth as pack animals able to carry heavier loads longer distances between waterholes than standard pack mules. Extremes of temperature and terrain did not bother them. They ate anything and thrived. Yet despite superior performance and Beale's enthusiasm, more pressing concerns of the American Civil War and muleskinners' aversion to their unusual odor prohibited further military service. Many of the animals and a few of their Middle Eastern handlers roamed Arizona's deserts for decades, popping up at unlikely places to brighten local desert lore. Some served admirably as pack stock among southern Arizona mining camps, while startled desert dwellers shot a feral few on sight. All disappeared from the southwestern scene by the early years of the twentieth century.

Beale's road cut in half the shadowy region which lay between the Gila River and Utah's Rocky Mountains and opened northern Arizona to immigrant wagon trains, but the territory hugging Grand Canyon and its north-eastern tributaries remained a mystery during the 1850s and 1860s. Survey parties moved laterally across central Utah in efforts to refine the Old Spanish Trail while Mormon colonizers from the Great Salt Lake began to penetrate southern Utah, but maps still labeled the expansive region "unexplored." The Colorado River within Grand Canyon split this wilderness in two, and no one beside its banks at any given point knew exactly where it came from or where it went.

The first government party sent to correct this deficient knowledge of Grand Canyon country was led by Army First Lieutenant Joseph Christmas Ives in 1857-58. Ives approached his assignment to find the head of Colorado River navigation by travelling upstream from the Gulf of California in a fifty-foot-long sternwheel steamboat named the *Explorer*. He found what he believed to be the "practical" head of navigation when his craft slammed into a submerged rock in mid-channel, somersaulting several men into the river. The mishap occurred just below Black Canyon and a long way short of the Grand Wash Cliffs.[39]

After exploring in a skiff another thirty miles upriver to confirm that a wagon road could be built to the Old Spanish Trail near Las Vegas, Ives sent part of his force back to Yuma and equipped the rest for an overland journey to explore alternative routes north into Mormon Utah. The "multinational" remnant chosen to persevere included Ives, Prussian naturalist-artist H. Balduin Möllhausen, Bavarian artist-topographer Baron Friedrich W. von Egloffstein, American physician-geologist John Strong Newberry, eleven Mexican and Californian muleskinners, three Mohave guides—Iretaba, Kolhokorao, and Hamotamaque—and two dozen soldiers. With these men and 150 mules, Ives started west in March 1858 along Edward Beale's wagon tracks, angling northeast along a path that also traced Whipple's route and almost certainly that of Garcés.

Nearing Peach Springs, Ives decided to descend to the Colorado in search of a crossing, and with the help of Hualapai guides in early April 1858 he and his men became the first European Americans known to reach the river within Grand Canyon. Spending only a couple days near the mouth of Diamond Creek, Ives left by a different route without his Mohave

H. Balduin Möllhausen, Prussian artist-naturalist who accompanied the Ives expedition. This steel engraving, drawn from an 1850s photograph and published in Mollhausen's Pictures from the Kingdom of Nature *(1904), depicts the young man in "trapper's garb." He completed dozens of field sketches that served as guides for his watercolors, some of which illustrated Ives's official reports. Mollhausen returned to Europe after this trip and wrote numerous memoirs of his western adventures before his death in 1905.*

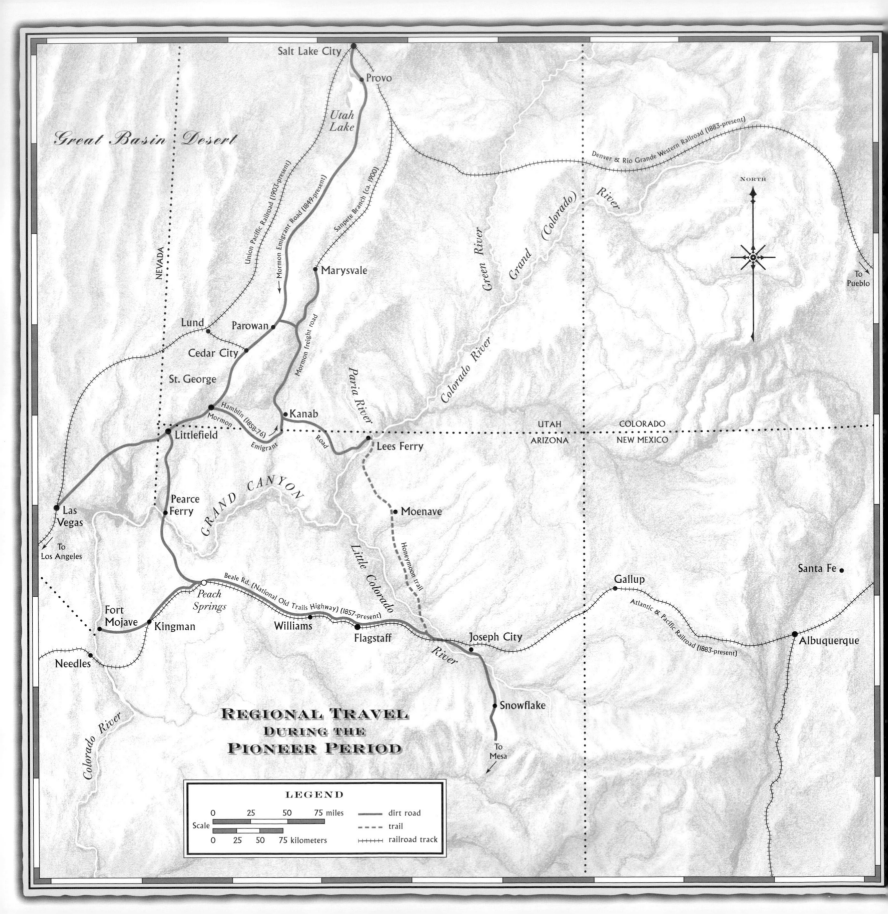

Salt Lake City

Provo

Utah Lake

Great Basin Desert

NEVADA

Union Pacific Railroad (1903–present)

Mormon Emigrant Road (1849–present)

Sanpete Branch (ca. 1900)

Marysvale

Denver & Rio Grande Western Railroad (1883–present)

Green River

Grand (Colorado) River

NORTH

To Pueblo

Lund

Parowan

Cedar City

Mormon freight road

St. George

Paria River

Colorado River

Hamblin (1858–76)

Mormon

Littlefield

Kanab

Emigrant

Road

Lees Ferry

UTAH
ARIZONA

COLORADO
NEW MEXICO

Moenave

GRAND CANYON

Pearce Ferry

Little Colorado

Honeymoon trail

Las Vegas

To Los Angeles

Santa Fe

Beale Rd. (National Old Trails Highway) (1857–present)

Gallup

Peach Springs

Fort Mojave

Kingman

Williams

Flagstaff

Joseph City

Atlantic & Pacific Railroad (1883–present)

Albuquerque

Needles

River

Colorado River

Snowflake

REGIONAL TRAVEL
DURING THE
PIONEER PERIOD

To Mesa

LEGEND

0	25	50	75 miles	——— dirt road

Scale

0	25	50	75 kilometers	- - - trail
				++++ railroad track

guides, who had returned home, and promptly got lost with the "aid" of two reluctant Hualapais. He regained his bearings after emerging from the canyon and continued northeast as close to its south rim as the rugged tributary canyons of Cataract Creek allowed.

Ives tried once more to descend to the river along a trail leading to the Havasupais but was stymied at a forty-foot cliff within a side canyon. When the men discovered a decrepit ladder, perhaps used by Garcés eighty-two years earlier, beneath this ledge, Egloffstein, the stoutest member of the party, tried to climb down first. His descent surely resembled a slapstick comedy as the rotund topographer clung for his life to one vertical pole while each rotted rung snapped beneath his weight. At the bottom and with no way for the rest to follow, the baron ambled down to Supai, soon returning with one of its residents. This man watched (amused, one imagines) as the party hauled Egloffstein out with a musket sling rope then retreated by the way they had come in.

With his large party, thirsty mules, and no guides to point the way to infrequent springs, Ives had as much difficulty as Ewing Young finding sufficient water on the Coconino Plateau. Commenting that a "more frightfully arid region probably does not exist upon the face of the earth," he discontinued his canyon

reconnaissance well west of Cataract Creek's principal gorge and turned south for the Beale road. The men reached the site of Williams on 25 April 1858, then moved on to the Hopi villages and Fort Defiance.[40]

Ives was the first European-American explorer to produce a detailed and widely read report of the "Big Cañon." Admitting that the region offered "natural features whose strange sublimity is perhaps unparalleled in any part of the world," he quickly added that "most of it is uninhabitable, and a great deal of it impassable."[41] While camped high among the pines of today's Hualapai Reservation, Ives summarized Grand Canyon's dubious potential for future settlement:

Lithograph depicting one of Lt. Ives's camps on the Coconino Plateau south of Grand Canyon, 1858.
GRCA 16242

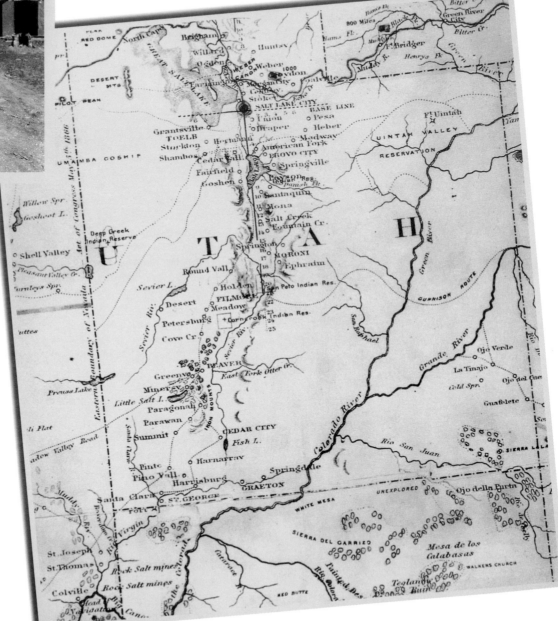

Major Powell headed his own topographical survey, then served as chief of the U.S. Geological Survey and Bureau of Ethnology. One of the finest federal bureaucrats in U.S. history, Powell worked hard but in vain for the orderly settlement of the arid West, proposing the creation of western states along watershed boundaries. He died in 1902, the year the Newlands Act created the Bureau of Reclamation which belatedly implemented some of his ideas. Lake Powell is named for him.
GRCA 17230

Map carried by Powell on his 1869 river expedition. Note the many Mormon settlements along the Wasatch Range and Sevier and Virgin Rivers, but little other settlement in the canyon region. Comparison with any modern map reveals many inaccuracies, such as Cataract Creek flowing into the Little Colorado, the latter stream's misplacement, and other relational errors. Powell's river trips and surveys corrected the mistakes and filled in the blanks. NAU.PH.268-35

The region last explored is, of course, altogether valueless.... Ours has been the first, and will doubtless be the last, party of whites to visit this profitless locality. It seems intended by nature that the Colorado River, along the greater portion of its lonely and majestic way, shall be forever unvisited and undisturbed.... The deer, antelope, the birds, even the smaller reptiles ... have deserted this uninhabitable district.[42] These words would not please modern chambers of commerce, nor did they prove a very astute appraisal of real estate that within a few decades would be crawling with cattlemen, miners, and tourists.

• • •

Egloffstein's maps accompanying Ives's report are masterful works, depicting topographical features in shaded relief and identifying the entire route, campsites, and known springs. A peculiar aspect, however, is omission of the Colorado River upstream of its confluence with the Little Colorado (itself geographically misplaced), an indication of how little white men knew of the larger region. The remainder of the river and a more accurate depiction of its passage through Grand Canyon awaited the voyages of the most celebrated of canyon explorers, John Wesley Powell.

Powell, a self-educated teacher from Illinois and amateur naturalist of the Colorado Rockies, ventured west in 1869 determined to float the Colorado River, but as an unknown civilian at the onset of the second era of federal explorations that included more prominent men like

Clarence King, Lieutenant George M. Wheeler, and Ferdinand V. Hayden, he had to scramble for financing. The only government support he could muster consisted of military rations for his men: mostly ex-trappers, mountain men, and Civil War veterans like himself. Powell had to make do with a few thousand additional dollars and scientific instruments from the Smithsonian Institution, Illinois Natural History Society, and Illinois Industrial University.[43]

The makeshift crew of ten men launched four wooden boats of Powell's design from Green River, Wyoming, in May 1869. As they left the banks of the Green River, echoes of the first locomotive to steam over the recently completed transcontinental railroad rang in their ears.[44] Rails had joined east and west coasts at Promontory Point, Utah, far to the north of Grand Canyon country. Powell intended to complete the task of exploration which would reveal reasons to do the same in the Southwest.

What started out as a well-equipped scientific expedition quickly slipped into a journey of survival. At first the party floated the placid waters of the upper Green, taking notes and barometric readings, charting the river's course, describing the surrounding wilderness, and getting a tan. But as the river began to churn, the expedition started to lose pieces of itself. Three weeks into the voyage, a rapid Powell named Disaster Falls splintered one of his boats, the *No Name*, and washed most of its contents downstream within the canyon of Lodore. Five weeks later at

the confluence of the Grand and Green Rivers, only nine men (one had walked out at the Uinta River) with musty apples, spoiled bacon, and coffee, remained. On 4 August, they passed the uninhabited mouth of the Paria River, hungry, tired, and mentally askew from nearly three summer months spent within ghastly, ovenlike canyons. As they plunged into the last and greatest of these, the Grand Canyon, thoughts of science had been replaced by a keen desire for escape.[45]

The remainder of the first Powell expedition unfolded with escalating hardships, crises, and dramatic denouement. The leader's own account reveals a nearly unbroken series of rapids run, lined, or portaged; men hungry and heated, then rain-drenched, shivering, and sleepless on riverside benches; and hopes focused on a merciful end to the ordeal. On 27 August, they came to a cataract Powell described as "worse than any we have yet met in all its course." Here, at Separation Rapid, three members of the party could take it no longer. Bill Dunn and brothers Seneca and Oramel Howland climbed out of the canyon in an effort to reach the Mormon settlements to the north, only to be killed by Shivwits Paiute Indians. The remaining six emerged from Grand Canyon just two days later and floated easily to the mouth of the Virgin River where several Mormons sent to look for the expedition or its remains facilitated their return to civilization.[46]

Powell's first journey down the Green and Colorado Rivers proved little more than another ephemeral contact in Grand

Canyon settlement history. True, significant exploration had been accomplished, and maps could be redrawn with the correct courses of the Green and Colorado Rivers connecting the dots of already known river crossings. All would henceforth know for certain what Cárdenas and Ives had surmised: this was not a navigable river in the normal sense. Granted these achievements, Powell himself recognized the need to return and complete the scientific work his first exploration had begun. His second and far more fruitful expedition of 1871-72, concerned for the most part with the history of the Arizona Strip, is recounted later.

Although Powell's exploration had limited immediate influence on Grand Canyon settlement, it did spark two movements which have added greatly to canyon history. The first derived from national exposure to the "romantic" adventure. Newspapers reported Powell's supposed death then resurrection through the imaginings of editors, hyperbole of some who claimed to know of the party's progress, and Powell's own accounts sent out from several points along the river. Powell was interviewed a number of times soon after both voyages, and in 1874 published an account in the popular *Scribner's Monthly* magazine. In 1875, the federal government printed his report, which was widely read, and in 1895 Flood and Vincent published this romanticized, none-too-accurate version of the journey.[47] The widespread publicity would attract visitors from the East by the end of the century who in turn would contribute to pioneer developments at Grand Canyon.

The second movement is owed to others who followed Powell down the river and wrote about their discoveries and adventures, creating an entire genre of Grand Canyon history focused narrowly on the Colorado River. Robert Brewster Stanton made the trip in 1889-90 to survey a railroad route near river level. His detailed geologic reports of the Green and Colorado Rivers influenced pioneer history by sparking a rush of prospectors to Grand Canyon in the early 1890s. Frederick S. Dellenbaugh, youngest member of Powell's second expedition, published *A Canyon Voyage* in 1908 which contributed much to North Rim settlement history as well as to the river's romantic lore. After Stanton, river runners multiplied and either published their accounts, like Ellsworth Kolb's 1914 *Through the Grand Canyon from Wyoming to Mexico*, or left journals for others to discover and bring to print.[48]

THE RAILROAD

Grand Canyon history would have unfolded in a far different manner had Robert Brewster Stanton's railroad been built. The engineer argued that a line running no more than a few hundred feet above river level was eminently practical given advanced construction techniques. In 1890, when the canyon enjoyed no more protection than any other "worthless" piece of public domain, the only obstacle to its construction would have been the indifference of venture capitalists. That proved to be the case, as the advantages of a river route would not overcome the costs nor the fact that a regional railroad had been in place since 1883.[49]

The railroad south of Grand Canyon resulted from the early efforts of Sitgreaves, Whipple, and Beale, who first explored and reported on the feasibility of travel across the thirty-fifth parallel during the 1850s. The American Civil War slowed the progress of western road building, but after 1865 congressional attention turned from the issue of national unity to development of the western territories. Amid the rush of a new generation of government explorations and hastily formed corporations eager for federal land grants, Congress approved the charter of the transcontinental Atlantic and Pacific in 1866. Following a survey in 1867-68, tracks crept slowly west along the proposed line until arriving at Albuquerque, New Mexico, by 1880.[50]

A snail's pace, chronic financial problems, and congressional threats to revoke the Atlantic and Pacific charter jeopardized completion of the line to the Pacific coast. In 1880, however, the Atchison, Topeka and Santa Fe Railroad Company acquired half interest, injected new money, and sent engineer Lewis Kingman to complete a location survey to the Colorado River. Crews of Irish, Mexican, Chinese, and American Indian track layers followed until August 1883 when rails met with those of the Southern Pacific Railroad Company at Needles, California. Northern Arizona was at last joined with the rest of the nation.[51]

The importance of the Atlantic and Pacific to the economic development of northern Arizona and Grand Canyon's pioneer history cannot be overestimated. As the railroad established workers' camps and railheads at favorable points along the line, enterprising men as quickly erected tent and shanty businesses to service work gangs. The railroad chose to locate permanent stations at many of these sites, and some businessmen remained to develop towns beside the tracks. All major towns along today's Interstate 40—Holbrook, Winslow, Flagstaff, Williams, Ash Fork, Seligman, and Kingman—trace their development, if not their origin, to the railroad and the years 1881-83. Without exception, these towns became the jumping-off points for canyon exploration and exploitation which immediately followed.[52]

The railroad created not only towns but the means by which families could settle and earn livings. Aside from employing hundreds of men who created a demand for goods and services, the railroad brought rapid and efficient transportation. Prior to 1883, freight arrived in Arizona by wagon train from Albuquerque and Los Angeles or by steamboat from the Gulf of California along the lower Colorado River, and cost from three hundred to three hundred sixty dollars per ton.[53] After that year, goods which formerly took weeks or months to reach destinations could be shipped in days at a fraction of the cost.

Economic effects were instantaneous. Population and property values doubled in Yavapai and Mohave Counties between 1880 and 1884. Livestock, which had grazed northern Arizona plateaus and valleys in small herds since the 1860s, multiplied, with Yavapai County alone boasting one hundred thousand cattle and three

Atlantic and Pacific Railroad crews laying track across northern Arizona, ca. 1882. Kansas State Historical Society

hundred thousand sheep in 1884. Companies like the Aztec Land and Cattle Company brought in huge Texas herds to graze miles of railroad grant lands. Box cars carried meat and wool to eastern markets. Miners, who had worked rich gold and silver lodes of Mohave County and filed more than two thousand claims since the 1860s, had formerly shipped only high-grade ore to distant refineries by wagons, steamers, and ocean vessels. Rails now tied northern Arizona mines to a smelter at El Paso, making lower-grade deposits attractive and inducing prospectors to consider far more abundant minerals than gold and silver.[54]

As the economies of fledgling northern Arizona towns exploded in the early 1880s, easterners made their way into the territory to get in on the ground floor. New people brought new energies, ideas, and perspectives to Grand Canyon, only twenty to seventy-five miles north of the tracks.

CHAPTER THREE
South Rim

THE ATLANTIC AND PACIFIC RAILROAD'S ARRIVAL ACROSS NORTHERN ARIZONA AND CONSEQUENT INVIGORATION OF REGIONAL TOWNS PROMISED THAT GRAND CANYON'S SOUTHERN EDGE WOULD BE DEVELOPED BEFORE TOO MANY YEARS ELAPSED. Enterprising men and families for the ensuing two decades left these gateway towns and followed the paths of American Indians and a few early prospectors to find rimside locations amenable to homesteading, mining, or simple tourist facilities.

Opposite: Early motorists venturing north from the railroad towns often followed their imaginations rather than their roads. Motorized transport, then as now, ended at the canyon edge.
GRCA 16412

Once they had proven that tourism held the greatest promise of financial reward, others with more capital moved in, wrested control, and joined with nascent federal land agencies to create over time the blueprint for centralized visitation experienced today at the Grand Canyon National Park's South Rim. Centralization was not the way things began, however, nor was it inevitable that the site of today's Grand Canyon Village would become the focus of attention.

SOUTHWEST

Initial developments southwest of Grand Canyon are owed to several events dating back to California's gold rush. Many of the first forty-niners chose southern routes across Arizona to reach the gold fields, and whether they followed Cooke's wagon road along the Gila River or Juan Bautista de Anza's parched desert route to Monterey known as El Camino del Diablo, nearly all ended up at a Colorado River crossing just south of its confluence with the Gila. Here in 1849, United States dragoons established Camp Calhoun (known as Fort Yuma by 1852) to protect travelers from the several Yuman tribes in the region. Prospectors inevitably paused to pan sands of the Colorado upstream of the military installation and found both placer and hard-rock gold sufficient to spawn mining districts along the lower river. These in turn begat a flourishing steamboat business connecting riverside mining camps with the outside world via the Gulf of California.[1]

In 1858, Mohave Indians attacked one of the first California-bound emigrant trains to use

Troops, Indians, and immigrants at Ft. Mohave. Alexander Gardner, a noted Civil War photographer, accompanied the 1867–68 Kansas Pacific Railroad survey along the route that would later be used by the Atlantic and Pacific, capturing along the way some of the first photographs taken of northern Arizona. Boston Public Library 23602, 53725

the Beale Wagon Road.[2] In response, Lieutenant Colonel William Hoffman led a detachment up the Colorado River from Fort Yuma to punish the recalcitrant Mohaves, then left Major Lewis A. Armistead to establish Camp Colorado near Beale's Crossing. Within a few months the army renamed the post Fort Mohave, which for the next several decades protected the thirty-fifth parallel road from Indian attack and doubled as a port for immigrants who steamed upriver from the Gulf of California, then transferred to wagons to penetrate Arizona Territory's northern and central interiors.[3]

Between infrequent patrols, bored Fort Mohave soldiers prospected the nearby Black and Cerbat Mountains and soon uncovered rich deposits of gold and silver. Men who had been unlucky panning California's sierra streams and the lower Colorado joined the new rush and formed mining districts in the new boom region by 1863. Meanwhile, former trapper-guide

turned prospector Joe Walker discovered even richer placer gold deposits at Lynx Creek in the Bradshaw Mountains of northcentral Arizona, leading to the settlement of Prescott in the same year. Several thousand hungry men operating from the two centers of mining activity attracted ranchers who ranged cattle north of the Beale road to feed a fast growing Mohave County populace. In 1864, William H. Hardy established a ferry named Hardyville ten miles upstream of the fort, and in the following year constructed a toll road east to Prescott, capital of the recently created Arizona Territory.[4] By 1865, people, freight, and mineral ore flowed briskly southwest of Grand Canyon.

The influx of miners, ranchers, freighters, and supporting military ignited conflicts with Hualapais who often exacted tribute for travel through their territory in the form of sheep, cattle, and mules. Isolated incidents erupted into the Walapai War in 1865, a long series of Hualapai raids and United States Army retaliations that enfeebled the tribe and, by 1874, forced survivors onto the Colorado River Reservation far south of their traditional range. No one seemed to care when the Hualapais bolted the reservation and returned to Mohave County in 1875-76, because in their brief absence ranchers had already usurped the best springs and grasslands. Unwilling to leave their homeland again, and recognizing the futility of continued fighting against white immigrants who never seemed to diminish, many chose instead to work for the interlopers who eagerly employed them as wage laborers and cowboys.[5]

Warfare slowed settlement during the late 1860s, but promise of mineral wealth continued to lure prospectors northward to tributary canyons of the Colorado River. Disregarding Havasupai occupational rights, these men followed the path of Garcés into Havasu Canyon where they discovered ample lead and silver deposits surrounding three waterfalls below Supai and staked some of Grand Canyon's earliest mining claims. William Hardy reportedly worked the first of these as early as 1866. In 1873, another local prospector named Charles Spencer located the Moqui Claim below Bridal Veil Falls, and in 1879, men led by W.C. Bechman and H.J. Young opened a lead mine beneath Mooney Falls: the two-hundred-foot-high lower cataract named for miner Daniel Mooney who fell to his death in 1880 while descending a nearby cliff face.[6]

The A.A. Coupland surveying party near Cataract Canyon, ca. 1893. Coupland was agent for the Consolidated Gold and Copper Mines Company of Williams, one of several concerns interested in mineral deposits within Havasu Canyon. The base map identifies contiguous claims along Havasu Creek below and overlapping the reservation. NAU.PH.663-1-55

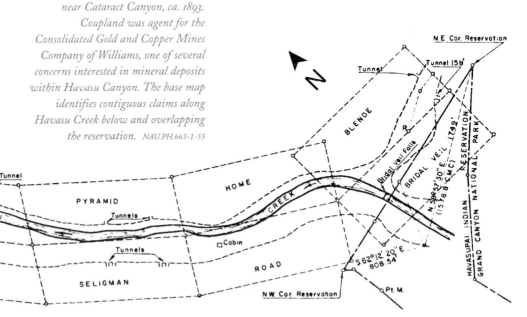

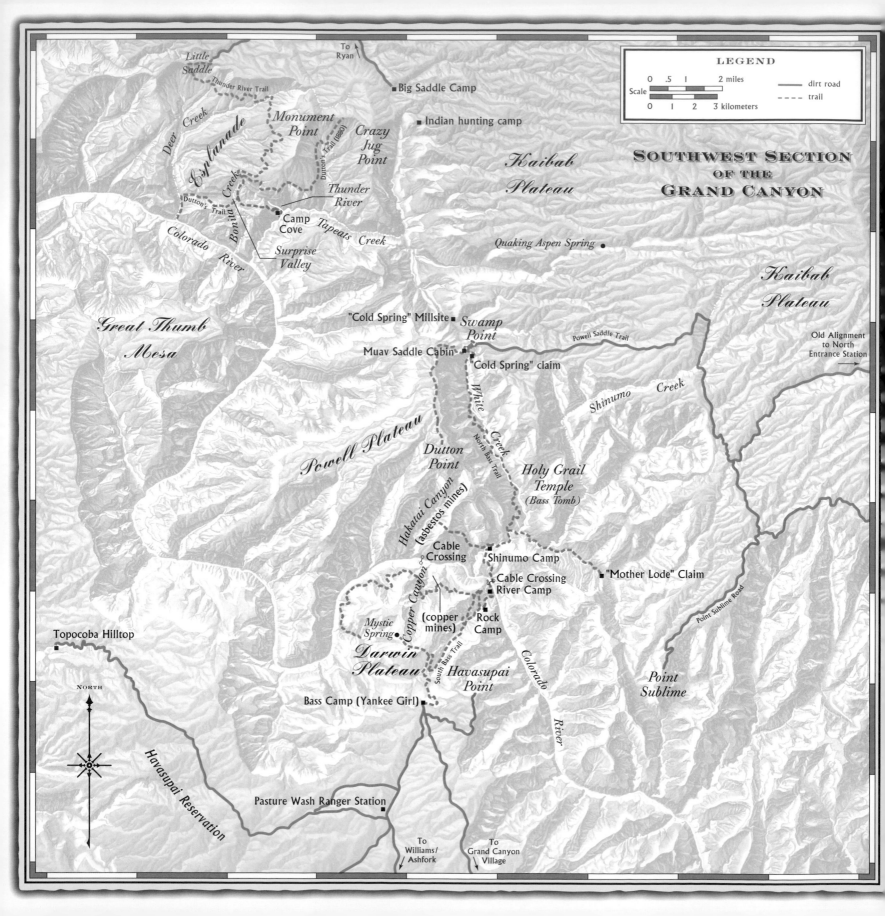

SOUTHWEST SECTION
OF THE
GRAND CANYON

LEGEND

Scale
0   .5   1   2 miles
0   1   2   3 kilometers

—— dirt road
- - - trail

*Kaibab
Plateau*

*Kaibab
Plateau*

To Ryan

*Little
Saddle*

Deer Creek

Thunder River Trail

Esplanade

*Monument
Point*

Dutton's Trail (1880)

*Crazy
Jug
Point*

■ Big Saddle Camp

■ Indian hunting camp

*Thunder
River*

Dutton's Trail

Bonita Creek

■ Camp
Cove

*Surprise
Valley*

Tapeats Creek

Colorado River

Quaking Aspen Spring ●

*Great Thumb
Mesa*

"Cold Spring" Millsite ■

*Swamp
Point*

Muav Saddle Cabin ■

Powell Saddle Trail

Old Alignment
to North
Entrance Station →

"Cold Spring" claim

White Creek

Shinumo Creek

Powell Plateau

*Dutton
Point*

North Bass Trail

*Holy Grail
Temple
(Bass Tomb)*

*Hakatai Canyon
(asbestos mines)*

Cable
Crossing

Shinumo Camp ■

■ "Mother Lode" Claim

Cable Crossing
River Camp

(copper
mines)

*Mystic
Spring* ●

Copper Canyon

Rock
Camp ■

Point Sublime Road

Topocoba Hilltop ■

*Darwin
Plateau*

South Bass Trail

*Havasupai
Point*

Colorado River

*Point
Sublime*

NORTH

Bass Camp (Yankee Girl) ■

Havasupai Reservation

Pasture Wash Ranger Station ■

To
Williams/
Ashfork ↓

To
Grand Canyon
Village ↓

Only the wistful drive of early prospectors or hopes for an extraordinary strike can explain mining activity deep within Havasu Canyon before arrival of the Atlantic and Pacific. In these years, miners had to hoist ore-laden mules over Mooney Falls by derrick, then drive them ten miles or more along hazardous paths earlier described by Ives and Garcés to the canyon rim, two thousand vertical feet above.[7] After another hundred miles by trail and the Beale road to Hardyville or Fort Mohave, ore was transferred to steamers for a several-hundred-mile float to the Gulf of California, then reloaded onto ocean-going vessels at Puerta Isabel and carried another fifteen hundred miles or so to reduction mills at San Francisco. Only middlemen made money under these transportation conditions.

Havasu Canyon mining claims proliferated after the Atlantic and Pacific arrived, such that the constant parade of miners through the center of Supai prompted a Havasupai chief, who was named Navajo, to insist in 1882 that reservation boundaries secure the tribe's summer home. Government surveyors either misunderstood or took advantage of the Havasupais' request when they subsequently reduced the reservation to a few acres comprising only the village and nearby fields. Definitive boundaries did nothing to protect the residents, however, as the only good path to the mines led through the village, and at least one claim overlapped the minuscule reservation's southern boundary. For the next forty years, Havasupais could do little but hope

that all this interest would not lead to their removal.

The Bridal Veil Mines Association of New York City worked the largest group of Havasu claims from 1885 to 1901, shipping one hundred tons of high grade lead and silver ores.[8] In 1902, another eastern consortium, the Grand Canyon Gold and Platinum Company, staked claims and built trails throughout Havasu Canyon as far as the Colorado River. Others went so far as to apply for a congressional charter to build a railroad from Williams to the waterfalls via the Topocoba Trail, but settled for a wagon road along the same route which they failed to complete despite an investment of seventy-five thousand dollars. The road grade has served as a new alignment to the ancient Indian trail ever since.[9]

W.I. Johnson staked claims and water rights within Havasu Canyon in 1906 and later erected a lead concentrator plant. He ran a ditch from Bridal Veil Falls for water power and processed several hundred tons of ore. Others started to build a hydroelectric plant near the falls in 1909, but one of the devastating floods which frequent Havasu Canyon answered native prayers by flushing the incomplete works down to the Colorado River in January 1910. Most mining activity at Supai ended about the time Johnson sold his interests in 1919, but these and other unpatented claims totalling ninety-five acres remained in private hands until E.F. Schoeny sold them to the National Park Service in 1957 for fifteen thousand dollars. The park service developed and maintained a tourist

campground on these claims until the tribe regained them, and another two hundred thousand acres of traditional lands, in 1976 with the Grand Canyon National Park Enlargement Act.[10] All in all, Havasu Canyon between 1866 and 1919 experienced some of the longest lasting and most intensive mining activity ever undertaken within Grand Canyon.[11]

In January 1883, Atlantic and Pacific work gangs reached the vicinity of Peach Springs, well to the west of Havasu mines and just twenty miles south of the Colorado River. The ample water source had served the Hualapai for centuries and refreshed explorers, surveyors, and soldiers since 1776. Although the federal government included the springs within the Hualapai Indian Reservation, created in 1883, the Atlantic and Pacific retained rights to pipe water to its station facilities four miles to the south.[12]

An early visitor described the typical railroad town which grew up surrounding the depot as

… an Arizona village consisting of five saloons, six dwelling houses, a "stage" office, and an Indian camp in the background. It is so called, apparently, because no peach grows within a hundred miles.[13]

This cynical traveler apparently overlooked nearby peach trees but accurately portrayed or underestimated the saloon-to-residence ratio. In 1883, photographer Ben Wittick wandered through town and identified twenty buildings and tents, all but one of which sold whiskey. Perhaps the one business that did not peddle booze was Sam Sing's wash house. Or it

Farlee Hotel in its latter days, probably after abandonment by the Farlees ca. 1915 (left) and in use by local explorers ca. 1920 (right).

Mohave County Historical Society 682, 683

may have been the small hotel operated by Julius H. and Cecilia M. Farlee.[14]

Little is known of the Farlees before they came to Peach Springs, but the couple arrived soon after the first locomotive pulled into the station. By his own account, Julius fought for the Union during the Civil War and spent time in the notorious Libby prisoner-of-war camp at Richmond, Virginia. He carried a rifle ball in one leg for the rest of his life as a reminder of the conflict, and when he ventured west following the war, suffered badly from lung disease likely brought on by his prison stay. Nothing has been uncovered of Cecilia prior to 1883, but it is known that she worked in the family restaurant and hostelry in town and remained until her death about 1919.[15]

By March 1883 the Farlees had opened their small establishment and a blacksmith shop in Peach Springs as well as a stage line to their tourist hotel near the Colorado River along Diamond Creek.[16] These businesses earned them the distinctions of having the first hotel of any type at or within Grand Canyon,

the first canyon tourist business, and the first stage line to run from a railroad town to the scenic chasm. Ironically, this hotbed of activity centered in the very vicinity where Joseph Ives, only twenty-five years earlier, had sworn that no one would ever again approach and the inner-canyon hotel itself stood hardly more than a stone's throw from Ives's camp beside Diamond Creek.

The Farlees' stage line and canyon hotel in many ways cast the mold for pioneer tourist enterprises that soon followed from Ash Fork, Williams, and Flagstaff to South Rim locations farther east. With the help of Hualapai laborers, Farlee upgraded the ancient Hualapai trail down Peach Springs Canyon to something resembling a wagon road. Although he claimed to have invested thousands of dollars on the road, early visitors remarked that it was a rough path for a stage and that it required anywhere from three to ten grueling hours to negotiate its twenty-three-mile length. One visitor, Mary Wager Fisher, wrote that her gloves were "torn into tatters from efforts to hang on to the buckboard," a hurried trip perhaps as it required only three and one-half hours. A demanding schedule and likely the nature of the ride prompted Farlee to hire drivers for his regular thrice-weekly run, including early resident and later deputy sheriff John Nelson and a Hualapai man named Honga.[17]

Tourists on the Farlee line descended more than three thousand vertical feet within ever-constricting cliffs to reach the Grand Cañon Hotel, alternately known as the Farlee or Diamond Creek Hotel, a little less than a mile from the Colorado River. The hotel, a two-story wood frame structure, offered eight bedrooms (four on each floor) in the main building, and a lobby, kitchen, and dining room in two attached wings. Visitors agreed that it was a "very primitive hut" or a "rude little house, roughly boarded," but clean, comfortable, and airy.[18]

Once ensconced in the resort hotel, guests had little to do but stroll down to the river at the limited sandy mouth of Diamond Creek, walk back, amble up the creek a ways, or climb a fifteen-hundred-foot-high precipice called Prospect Point where custom demanded they add a rock to the peak's monument cairn and slip a visiting card into the bottle on top. Farlee led customers to these destinations and of course, like all early canyon guides, had unofficial names for geologic features worth noting, preferring biblical titles such as Solomon's Temple, Babel's Tower, and the Pyramid. Guests had little reason to stay at the hotel to enjoy its amenities, since there were few of these, and no opportunity to sit back and admire the canyon's grand vistas, as there are none to speak of at Diamond Creek's mouth. If they visited in summer, the normal tourist season then as now, guests might just sit in the shade and pant, since

Advertisement in the Mohave County Miner, *5 March 1887.*

the heat is particularly oppressive at this elevation and worse still for the reflective cliffs. Like Joseph Ives, most left soon after they arrived.[19]

The Farlees kept a regular stage schedule to their creekside hotel during the years 1883 to 1889 and served seventy-five to one hundred guests per season, although the hotel remained open into the 1890s and perhaps as late as 1901 to accommodate special groups. After abandonment, anyone who happened into the area like hunters and river runners used the building, but it steadily deteriorated after 1901, until by 1923, only the foundation and portions of its wood frame remained. Briefly in 1919, Colonel John C. Greenway used it as a headquarters and some of its lumber to build a raft and a riverside shanty called "Camp Powell" while drilling for a dam site in the vicinity. Greenway, who had interests in a mine at Ajo, dreamed of building a hydroelectric dam to power his mine equipment as well as an electric tram from Ajo to the Gulf of California. Although core samples promised a solid foundation in the river's granite bottom, Greenway died, the Hoover Dam project got underway downstream, and this one of numerous early

WHAT'S IN A PLACE NAME?

Place names should give us a sense of history and a means to communicate geographical knowledge to others through conversation, manuscripts, and maps. At Grand Canyon, however, variable place names bestowed upon prominent features by American Indians, explorers, geologists, map makers, river runners, early prospectors, tourist operators, and federal employees, among others, hamper the historical writer's ability to connect the past with the present. Despite the best efforts of the United States Board on Geographic Names which has acted as arbiter since 1890, the plethora of names over centuries, their individual whimsies, and especially latecomers' penchant for "layering" names for features that already carried a handle resulted in some confusion.

Aside from inconsistencies between what Indians called places and what European Americans did with the translations, spellings, and their own imaginings, an understandable lapse between cultures, I wager that far more than half of today's labels between Lees Ferry (Pahreah Crossing) and Colorado Crossing (Pearce Ferry, or is it Pierce?) have been called something else. Take Bright Angel Creek, for example. Powell first named it Silver Creek. In fact, all regional creeks and rivers had earlier Spanish and trapper

names as did the Colorado itself, which had half a dozen including my favorite, *El Rio del Tison* (the Firebrand River). And Grand Cañon? Ives called it Big Canyon, about as imaginative.

The Bright Angel Trail? Nope, it was the Bright Angel Toll Road then Cameron's Trail before its modern appellation, and in the very early days it ended at Angel Plateau (Plateau Point). Nearly all of the canyon's trails had former names, in fact, as did most scenic viewpoints. If you had enjoyed a surrey ride along the South Rim in 1900 from Rowe's (Hopi) Point eastward to Desert View, your guide might have stopped at Sentinel, Eternity, Grant, O'Neill's, Ashurst, Cremation, Morton, Orient, Castle, Sunset, and Ripley Points, passing along the way Cape Horror and Cape Split, none of which appear on modern maps. If you employed Bill Bass's services out to Camper's Paradise (Bass Camp), your view to the northeast would take in Le Conte (Darwin) Plateau with its three fingers named Mystic Spring Plateau (Spencer Terrace), Observation Plateau (Huxley Terrace), and the Grand Scenic Divide. Across the way you would espy Point Sublime (Sublime Point?) and you would reach it via the Mystic Springs (South Bass) Trail down Trail (Bass) Canyon and the Shinumo and White (North Bass) Trails.

And another good-natured historical swipe at canyon place names: if there's room for Isis, Horus, Shiva, and Osiris temples, not to mention Cheops Pyramid and dozens more eastern-geologic metaphors, why have some of the more prominent pioneers been forgotten? Ralph Cameron, for example. Sure, he has a town in the Painted Desert and still causes chills in official backbones, but nothing within the park? Pete Berry*, certainly more politically acceptable, deserves a butte, not enough certainly, but alliterative at least. David Rust and Uncle Dee Woolley are high on the list for North Rim recognition. The Kolbs have an arch and a river rapid (there were two of them after all), but Big Jim, the Verkamps, Babbitts, Ferralls, and a dozen other deserving folks still stand in the shadows of Mencius Temple et al.

*The National Board of Geographic Names has just recently named the Coconino summit just north of Grandview Point "Berry Butte."

Recommended Reading:
Nancy Brian, *River to Rim: A Guide to the Place Names along the Colorado River in Grand Canyon from Lake Powell to Lake Mead* (Flagstaff: Earthquest Press, 1992).

Above: Trail sign at Grand Canyon National Park. GRCA 10227

dam-building schemes at Grand Canyon never rose from the riverbed.[20]

The town of Peach Springs thrived during the early pioneer period with a railroad round-house and maintenance shops, a Fred Harvey hotel, several smaller hotels, and service businesses. The town acquired a post office in 1887 and its school enrolled as many as twenty children through the remainder of the nineteenth century. Happy days ended abruptly in 1907, however, when the railroad moved its facilities to Seligman and the Harvey hotel soon followed. Peach Springs recovered from near ghost town status after the National Old Trails Highway was improved for automobiles in 1916-17, and U.S. Route 66 came along on the same alignment in the late 1920s, but declined again when Interstate 40 bypassed it far to the south in the 1970s. The town survives today as the seat of Hualapai government and a service center for tourists on their way to the Havasupai Reservation.[21]

* * *

Williams also blossomed with the arrival of the Atlantic and Pacific in September 1882, figured prominently in Grand Canyon pioneer history, and has since experienced ups and downs through shifting tourist tastes and altered road alignments. It was described in the early 1880s, much like Peach Springs, as a

… typical frontier town, with a few wooden buildings and a long row of tents strung out parallel with the railroad [and] over thirty saloons … not a Salvation Army Camp, by any means.[22]

It, too, existed as a principal supply point for the Atlantic and Pacific, but by 1892 had acquired the Grand Canyon Hotel; drug, hardware, and general merchandise stores; ice

Williams, Arizona, ca. 1890 (top) as a stop along the railroad main line, and ca. 1905 (center) as a hub for Grand Canyon tourism. Note the same ponderosa pine in both photos. For many years Williams and Flagstaff competed for prominence along the railroad. Though Williams won the best roads and spur railway to Grand Canyon, Flagstaff became Coconino County seat (1891) and the largest town in northern Arizona. U.S. 66 would later parallel this row of buildings.
Museum of New Mexico, Seaver Center 87-31 160-A

Peach Springs, 1897. Mohave County Historical Society

Captain Billy Burro, long-time friend, guide, and employee of Bill Bass.
NAU.PH.568.6289

Bill Bass's Rock Camp, about one mile from the river immediately below several bedrock tanks, looking up Bass Canyon. Today's South Bass Trail skirts this site to the right center of the photo.
Huntington Library

houses, meat markets, liveries, poolhall, restaurants, and several Chinese laundries, all within a platted townsite just south of the railroad tracks. As tourism picked up between 1892 and 1901, town population increased from six hundred to four thousand and several industries moved in like the Williams Brewing Company and Bottling Works, the Saginaw Lumber Company, a planing mill and box factory, and the Lombard, Goode and Company mineral smelter. The town's economy and population remained healthy throughout the pioneer period servicing miners, ranchers, lumbermen, railroad workers, and especially tourists.[23]

William Wallace Bass found Williams as earlier described when he followed the freshly laid rails into town in July 1883. Like so many of the early pioneers to Arizona and Grand Canyon, he was born in the Midwest, in Shelbyville, Indiana, on 2 October 1848. Bass

worked as a carpenter, telegrapher, railroad conductor, and dispatcher in New Jersey and New York before failing health urged him west in 1880. After wandering about northern Mexico, New Mexico, and southern Arizona for several years, he arrived in Williams a thirty-four-year-old man, 5 feet 6 inches tall, a wiry 145 pounds, unmarried, and broke. On the positive side, he had regained his health and seemed eager to begin a new life.[24]

Besides severing home ties to start anew in the West, Bass shared other traits with Grand Canyon pioneers. Most contemporaries described him as opinionated, strong-willed, confident, competent in a number of trades, and clearly willing to take on any employment until he found a steady line of work. Through the 1880s he labored for the railroad, dabbled in a ranch near town, exercised his carpentry skills, hauled ice, served as clerk of the Williams justice court, deputy sheriff, and constable, and played fiddle at local dances. While juggling this array of jobs, he began to explore economic possibilities at Grand Canyon.[25]

A number of apocryphal stories recount how and why Bass first came to the South Rim, but most likely he combined a curiosity to visit the Havasupai Indians with a desire to prospect for mineral wealth. His keen interest in the tribe developed into life-long friendships with many of its members, while prospecting led less to mineral wealth than an appreciation of Grand Canyon's scenic rewards. His abiding love for the canyon would result in a forty-one-year relationship, during which time he built more roads and inner-canyon trails than any other individual in canyon history and enjoyed an unofficial monopoly over tourist activities in its southwestern and northwestern sections.[26]

Bass's early years at Grand Canyon proved busy as he built roads, trails, and camps adequate for his prospecting trips and early forays into tourism. In 1885 he put together a crude tent camp at its very edge, twenty-five miles west of today's Grand Canyon Village. Because the only other white men living or working in the vicinity were a few ranchers, Bass did not bother to homestead the site or make any other legal claim to the camp until 1900, when he filed on the five-acre property as the Yankee Girl mining claim and associated millsite. Earlier than that year, however, Bass dubbed the site Camper's Paradise, and with improvements by 1894 it became known as Bass Camp, his primary base of mining and western tourist operations until 1923.

From 1885 to 1891, Bass, Captain Billy Burro, and several other Havasupai friends improved an old Indian trail to the inner-canyon Esplanade nearly two thousand vertical feet below Bass Camp. He named it the Mystic Spring Trail after an elusive water source that he had long sought in vain until Captain Burro led him to it in exchange for a side of beef. By 1891, Bass extended his trail from the spring to the Colorado River and roughed out a wagon road from Williams to his rimside camp. He filed on this overall seventy-seven-mile linear property as a toll road to establish proprietary rights, though he apparently never charged for its use. Bass offered tourist trips from Williams to his camp and into the canyon as early as 1885, but did so on an informal basis until he completed

road, trail, and camp improvements by the early 1890s.[27]

Bill Bass developed his early mining and tourism businesses slowly for reasons common among the first canyon entrepreneurs. He had arrived penniless and could make improvements only as he earned money from odd jobs. With little cash to pay others, he often worked alone to build, prospect, mine, advertise, and guide. Each autumn as tourist traffic dissipated he retreated to the inner canyon to prospect along Mystic Spring Trail, Trail Canyon (renamed Bass Canyon), and across the Colorado into White, Shinumo, Hakatai, and Hotauta Canyons, but never made a dollar at mining during these early years. He did earn enough to survive guiding fewer than thirty people per year, but hardly saved the capital needed to make dramatic improvements.[28]

Another factor contributing to slow growth was the universal pioneer need to develop water sources. With few dependable springs and no perennial creeks between the rim and Williams, Bass had to construct cisterns and check dams along his trails and wagon roads to catch snowmelt and runoff from summer thunderstorms.[29] A close friend and writer at the turn of the century, George Wharton James, wrote in his romantic prose that Bass with

... drill and hammer, brain and muscle ... assisted by powder and dynamite, and, later, by cement, has blasted out and made water tight vast rock cisterns, which store the rain-water, storm flows, and melted snow ... all through the heated months.[30]

George Wharton James, prolific southwestern author of the 1890s–1920s and good friend of William Wallace Bass, sitting at River Camp directly across from the fire pit seen today along the South Bass Trail.
Huntington Library 9788

Mrs. Gayler and George Wharton James roughing it on the rim. Huntington Library 9841

Ada on the front porch of the Bass Camp cabin, some-time between 1894 and 1904. GRCA 3633

One might consider James's assessment so much hyperbole without knowing that Bass operated the sole tourist business over a nearly waterless forty-five-hundred-square-mile area throughout the pioneer period and needed water for stock and tourists at many strategic points. As evidence of his efforts, Grand Canyon National Park superintendent J.R. Eakin wrote in 1924 that Bass's improvements were worth thousands of dollars and represented the only dependable water sources in the entire southwestern portion of the park.[31]

Having exercised "brain, muscle, and dynamite" to overcome South Rim aridity, Bass directed what energy and money remained to his budding tourism business. His operation essentially paralleled that of the Farlees, but offered a richer canyon experience. Guests wrote ahead with details of their trip so Bass could gather necessary supplies. On the assigned day he drove to the Williams train station in a six-passenger wagon once used by General Nelson Miles during the Apache Indian wars. A long haul north from

town brought parties to the Caves, a large limestone sinkhole near the seventh and final crossing of Cataract Creek.[32] James described this remarkable campsite as a

… tent over a wood floor used for sleeping and warmed by a sheet iron stove, when firewood was available. The kitchen and dining room combined was reached by going down a ladder into the cave. An old cook stove had been installed and the stove pipe emerged through a natural opening in the roof of the cave. A rough table of pine boards and dry goods boxes for seats and also for cupboards were the main furnishings of this underground kitchen.[33]

After 1894 when Bass completed an all-weather road from Ash Fork, passengers reached the Caves earlier in the day, ate lunch, then continued to the rimside camp by late afternoon. The wagon road traced reasonably level terrain but was subject to washouts that required finely dressed patrons to get out and push.[34]

After a jolting two-day jaunt from Williams or an equally bumpy if briefer ride from Ash Fork, guests arrived at the "very brink of the Great Abyss" at a location that James called Surprise Outlook. Views obtained at Bass Camp are spectacular, indeed breathtaking, after travelling blind through dense pinyon pine and juniper immediately before the rim. Arriving on a late summer afternoon, the broad view across to the North Rim often was bathed in pastel colors with cliff faces, spires, and monuments magnified in bold relief. Bass advertised this panorama as the most beautiful obtained

from any point along the South Rim, and it is useless to argue the claim.[35]

Like the Farlees' inner-canyon hotel, the camp itself defied precise architectural description but might be termed "pioneer vernacular." For style and comfort it could not compete with hotels that developed farther east along the rim, but early Grand Canyon tourists desiring a week-long wilderness experience found it comfortable enough. In 1894, Bass upgraded from the initial configuration of shack and storage tents to include

… a large circus tent partitioned off into six bedrooms with a dining hall through the center. The kitchen was a small cabin adjacent to one entrance of the tent through which food was carried to the dining hall. It was within a stone's throw of the Rim, and among the scrubby junipers and pinyon trees surrounding the tent were six wooden-floored tent houses.[36]

The camp by this year also included several cisterns, corrals, and a four-by-four-foot darkroom formed by placing limestone slabs and a wooden door in front of a small niche in the cliffs immediately below the rim. Bass used the darkroom for his own amateur photographic efforts, but professionals like Frederick Maude, A.F. Messinger, Henry G. Peabody, and Oliver Lippincott used it as well.[37]

Early visitors to Grand Canyon's South Rim who spent one and sometimes two days in uncomfortable buckboards or stagecoaches were not about to glance into the scenic abyss then turn for home. They often stayed a week and sometimes lingered for a month or more to justify the round-trip effort. Before automobiles and concentrated services at the Grand Canyon village area produced the congestion endured today, visitors looked forward to solitary walks along the rim and long inner-canyon saddle trips, and many remained until they had their fill. Those who came to Bass Camp enjoyed the widest selection of guided trips available during the pioneer period and a man who appreciated their presence enough to lead them anywhere for an all-expense rate of five dollars per day.[38]

Upon arrival and on any morning or evening during their stay, guests strolled out to Sunset Point north of camp or east along the rim toward Havasupai Point to obtain inspiring views. More durable visitors hiked a mile or so down the Mystic Spring Trail to poke around Prehistoric Pueblo ruins at the base of the Coconino Sandstone, or perhaps all the way down to the Esplanade in a day trip. Most got around to taking a one- or two-day mule ride down to Mystic Spring where they could wander upon some forty miles of informal paths or climb nearby Mt. Huethawali. The most adventuresome after 1896 might spend a week or more continuing to the river, crossing in one of several small boats, and venturing as far as Point Sublime on the North Rim.

Another favored trip required a fourteen-mile wagon ride west to Topocoba Hilltop overlooking Lee Canyon and another thirteen miles by muleback to the village of Supai. The early trail dropped from the hilltop in a electrifying descent, but after the turn of the century the incomplete freight road noted earlier served as a gentler though still difficult route to the bottom. Once within Lee Canyon's

intermittent creek bed, the trail easily followed the drainage to its confluence with Havasu Canyon, then downstream to Havasu Springs and another mile to the Indian village. Bass enjoyed a good relationship with many of the tribe, often bringing them mail, medicine, and whatever money he had in his pockets in return for occasional meals and the right to use their trails and campsites near the falls. Paying customers loved the trip as they had a chance to learn something of another culture "up close and personal" while secure in the company of a man who held the Havasupais' respect.[39]

After 1894, Bill Bass accelerated his efforts to expand his tourism enterprise. He and George James prepared lantern slides which they showed throughout the United States. These advertisements brought influential people to his camp like western writer Zane Grey, artist Thomas Moran, and Colorado River historian Frederick Dellenbaugh.[40] He also recruited a few long-term employees like Captain Burro, R.M. "Dad" Bleak, John Waltenberg, and Hubert Lauzon to make improvements and help with operations. Bleak came to work in 1897 and helped for many years as a wrangler, stage driver, and trail worker. Waltenberg, who arrived about 1900 and remained twelve years before moving on to California, was Bill Bass's most consistent prospecting companion and partner in ten or more mining claims. Hubert Lauzon, who accompanied the Kolb brothers on the last leg of their 1911-12 river trip and married Bass's daughter Edith, was a regular camp employee. George James, brother Duncan James, and Frederick Maude took time out from their professions to build trails and occasionally guide tourists during their extended visits.[41]

Tourists at Topocoba Hilltop, the start of the Topocoba Trail, 1901. Note that they are using the hair-raising old trail segment on the north side of the dropoff.
GRCA 11312

Hubert Lauzon, Grand Canyon pioneer who worked for Bill Bass, married Edith Bass, and accompanied the Kolb brothers on the second half of their 1911 river trip, 1920. *GRCA 5562*

From 1898 to 1901, these men and a few wage laborers completed Bass's inner-canyon travel network comprising more than fifty miles of primary and secondary trails with a few overnight camps along the way. The arterial path from South to North Rims continued from the base of the Mystic Spring Trail by descending Bass Canyon to the Colorado River below Bass Rapid, the entire segment from rim to river known in later years as the South Bass Trail. A mile from the river, Bass established Rock Camp beneath an intermittent fifteen-foot-high waterfall near a series of bedrock water tanks where he kept food, a small forge, and other supplies for overnight stops when darkness caught parties along the trail.[42] Nearer the river where the trail crosses Precambrian schist he developed River Camp, a wide spot in the path with a tent and stacked-stone fireplace, used when the Colorado was in flood.[43]

In 1906, Bass overcame the uncertain river crossing with a two-strand cable system installed sixty feet above the river just below Bass Rapid. He upgraded to a four-strand rig in 1908, and added an enclosed cage large enough to carry a pack animal and several people.[44] Once across the Colorado, the north trail led parties to perennial Shinumo Creek where Bass established Shinumo Camp about 1899. James described it as

… part tent, part wood, part indoors, part outdoors. The fireplace is of stone and out of doors, and the table is a great slab of red sandstone resting on two heavy rock supports …. There are two good beds. Across the stream a little way down is the Shinumo garden [with] excellent melons, cantaloupes, radishes, onions, corn, squash, beans, and with a fair-sized peach and other trees … [45]

This camp along the most beautiful segment of the trail corridor proved an important inner-canyon site for the remainder of Bass's tenure at Grand Canyon. He used it as an overnight stop for multiday trips and in some years spent long winter months here with his family.

From the campsite, the Shinumo Trail (renamed the North Bass Trail years later) generally traced Shinumo then White Creeks west of the Powell Plateau. The most difficult portion climbed a steep talus ramp some six hundred vertical feet in tight switchbacks to the top of the Redwall Limestone. Mrs. James B. Gayler of Ridgewood, New Jersey, one of the first to ride over Bass's improved north side trail in 1901, described the Redwall segment as

… a tremendous climb which I accomplish by clinging to the coat tails of the guide with one hand and sometimes with both hands, he holding tight to the burro's tail ahead of him. Belshazzar [her burro] accepts this—to me—novel situation with accustomed cheerfulness and does his best to haul us up the mountain, stopping occasionally to recover his breath. [46]

Once atop the Redwall, the trail continued its ascent up the White Creek drainage to the base of the Coconino Sandstone where it passed a Prehistoric Pueblo ruin and a perennial

spring before reaching Muav Saddle. From the saddle, Bass built trails up to the isolated Powell Plateau and to Swamp Point on the North Rim, completing Grand Canyon's first transcanyon tourism corridor used by hunters, sightseers, surveyors, and rangers for the next quarter century.[47]

As Bass completed his trail network at the turn of the century, he began to employ the illegal mechanism used by many settlers in the American West and nearly all Grand Canyon pioneers to protect hard-won business interests: staking mining claims to strategic points within his sphere of influence.[48] Some of Bass's claims were clearly legitimate, such as those to extensive copper deposits near the mouth of Copper Canyon and to high-grade asbestos ore downriver within Hakatai Canyon. Several of Bass's spur trails ended at these locations and he later shipped ore from mines developed in both tributary canyons. But he also filed numerous bogus claims to protect strictly

tourism-related interests at Rock Camp, his cable and ferry sites, Shinumo Camp, and Muav Saddle. It was no coincidence that he protected most of these sites during the few years preceding creation of Grand Canyon National Monument in 1908—after which year mining entries were disallowed—and no surprise that these mineral-barren claims never passed into private hands through the patenting process.[49]

One might attribute Bass's success after 1895 to an amazing burst of personal energy and an astute business sense combined with good luck, good health, fortunate partnerships, and friendly relations with Havasupai neighbors. All this is true, but close examination of Grand Canyon's pioneer tourist enterprises reveals that the most durable and successful, with few exceptions, belonged to families. Bill Bass secured his most "fortunate partnership" in January 1895 when he married Ada Lenore Diefendorf, an educated

Left: Mining asbestos the old-fashioned way. Bill Bass and helpers in Hakatai Canyon filled ore sacks which they loaded on mules for the long trip to Bass Camp. A later cable system crossing the river below Copper Canyon provided the most direct route via the Tonto Trail to the South Bass Trail, but an earlier path ran from Hakatai Canyon to Shinumo Camp where it picked up the North Bass Trail to the river and crossed by Bass's 1906 cable system to the south side trail. GRCA 13682

Right: Rock cabin on the North Bass Trail below Muav Saddle. Prospectors and cattlemen built this cabin with stones from a nearby Prehistoric Pueblo site at the turn of the century. Cabin ruins are found today beside the six-foot-high totem at the spring.
Arizona Historical Society

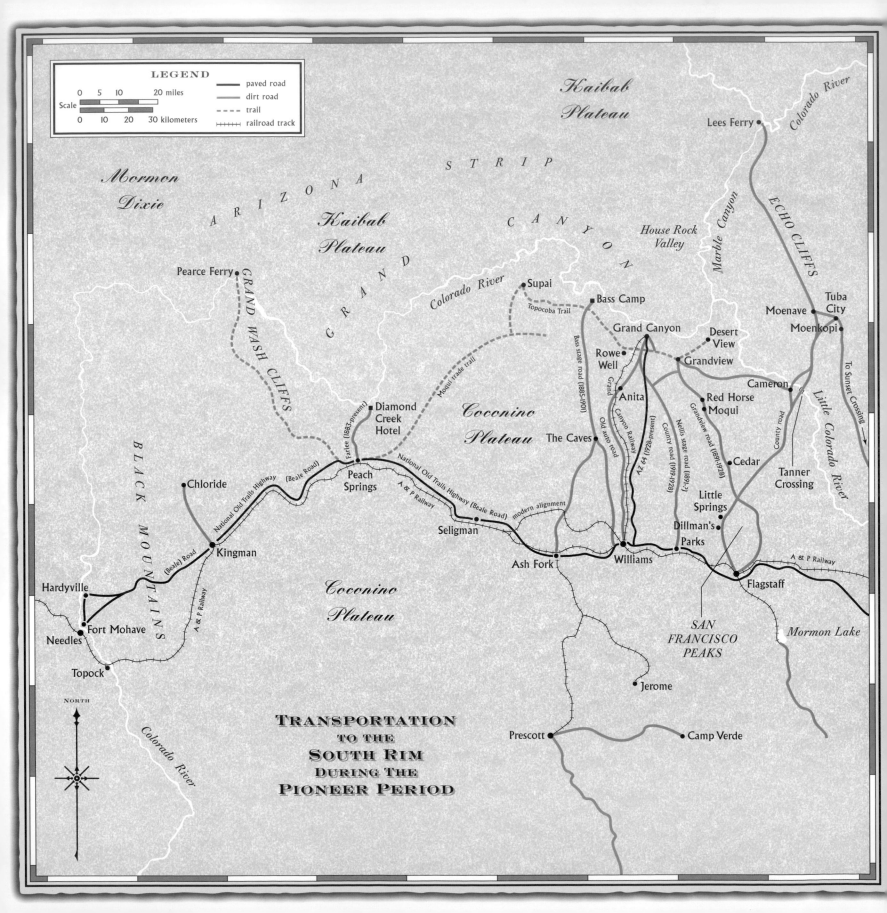

LEGEND

Scale
0 5 10 20 miles
0 10 20 30 kilometers

— paved road
— dirt road
- - - trail
+++ railroad track

Mormon Dixie

ARIZONA STRIP

Kaibab Plateau

Kaibab Plateau

Kaibab Plateau

GRAND CANYON

House Rock Valley

Colorado River

Lees Ferry

Marble Canyon

ECHO CLIFFS

Colorado River

Pearce Ferry

GRAND WASH CLIFFS

Supai

Bass Camp

Topocoba Trail

Grand Canyon

Desert View

Grandview

Moenave

Tuba City

Moenkopi

Moqui trade trail

Diamond Creek Hotel

Farlee (1883–present)

Coconino Plateau

Rowe Well

Bass stage road (1885–1901)

Anita

Red Horse

Moqui

Cameron

Little Colorado River

To Sunset Crossing →

BLACK MOUNTAINS

Chloride

The Caves

Grand Canyon Railway

Old auto road

AZ 64 (1928–present)

County road (1919–1928)

Nellis stage road (1892–?)

Grandview road (1891–1928)

Cedar

County road

Tanner Crossing

National Old Trails Highway (Beale Road)

Peach Springs

National Old Trails Highway (Beale Road)

A & P Railway

Little Springs

Dillman's

(Beale) Road

Kingman

Seligman

modern alignment

Parks

Williams

A & P Railway

Ash Fork

Flagstaff

Hardyville

A & P Railway

Coconino Plateau

SAN FRANCISCO PEAKS

Mormon Lake

Needles

Fort Mohave

Topock

Colorado River

NORTH

Jerome

Prescott

Camp Verde

TRANSPORTATION TO THE SOUTH RIM DURING THE PIONEER PERIOD

and enduring woman who would become a full partner in her husband's enterprises.

Ada was born in Charlottesville, New York, on 29 August 1867, and grew up in the East where she studied piano and violin, attended the New England Conservatory of Music, and later earned her living as a teacher. She moved to Prescott in the early 1890s, and in 1894, vacationed at the South Rim with an aunt. After spending seven days in the company of Bill Bass and another five months thinking about what she might be getting into, she married him and moved to Bass Camp to become the first white woman to raise a family at the rim.[50]

For the remaining years of the nineteenth century, Ada helped immeasurably with the family's widespread operations, her days filled with duties typical of frontier wives like cooking, cleaning, sewing, and a thousand other household chores men manage to overlook. But life at Bass Camp in the 1890s, when the nearest town lay seventy miles to the south and the nearest neighbor twenty miles to the east, proved anything but typical. She had to wrangle horses, retrieve and care for footloose livestock, and occasionally make an incredible fourteen-mile round trip to the Colorado just to do the wash, while otherwise looking after guests as camp proprietress. These duties were interrupted and in early years complicated by the birth of her first two children: Edith Jane in 1896, and William Guy in 1900.

An educated woman with more options than most during the late nineteenth century, Ada seemed to wrestle with the life she had chosen. When she travelled east to deliver Edith, she did not return until a year and a half later, and then only after her husband came to visit and perhaps used personal persuasion.

Artifacts at Bass's camp near his Hakatai Canyon asbestos claims.
GRCA 5298

Life as a pioneer tourist operator, mother, and wife to a man who spent weeks away from their isolated home must have been enervating, and she very likely questioned the relationship more than once. After returning to the rim from Williams following the birth of her son, however, Ada determined to remain at Grand Canyon and assumed even more responsibilities as their business continued to prosper.[51]

Of course, life at the very edge could never be all work and drudgery. There were incomparable natural scenes, interesting guests, help from camp workers—especially John Waltenberg, a personal favorite—and occasional surprise visits that forced a smile. One such visitor arrived at Bass Camp in April 1904, a government surveyor who stood shivering on her doorstep, naked but for an old quilt draped around his shoulders. As the man thawed inside the cabin, he explained that he had lost his clothes while swimming to the south bank of the Colorado River. He had

The White House at Bass Siding, ca. 1925. The desperado with the pistol appears to be William G. Bass.

scrambled in bare feet to Rock Camp where he luckily found the quilt and a burro to carry him the remaining six miles to the rim. With the only cabin for many miles around, the Basses likely received many such transient visits.

Ada dispelled some of the tedium herself by improving accommodations at Bass Camp with new furniture, a piano which she played well for guests and family, a small library, and other niceties. After giving birth to her third child, Hazel Canyonita, in 1903, she helped tear down the circus tent that had stood for ten years and expand the frame cabin. When the family completed renovations in 1904, the camp consisted of the cabin with three bedrooms, a large living room, dining room, kitchen, and pantry; tent-cabins along the rim; corrals, outbuildings, and several cisterns.[52]

Bill Bass had campaigned with others for a railroad from Williams to the South Rim since 1894, but as one finally inched its way toward the rim twenty-five miles to the east instead of toward his rimside camp, the family had to scramble to retain customers. When tracks reached the Anita copper mines in early 1900, Bass all but abandoned his wagon road from Ash Fork and built a new one from Anita to Bass Camp. Soon after the Grand Canyon Railway reached the South Rim, Bass claimed a five-acre millsite beside the tracks five miles south of the rim at Milepost 59. In 1902 he

arranged for a flag stop there called Bass Siding, and built yet another road to carry passengers to Bass Camp.[53] When Ada returned in 1906 following the birth of her fourth and last child, Mabel Melba, she found a new two-story frame house awaiting her at the siding. Called the White House, it doubled as a second home and tourist hotel for the family's remaining years at the canyon.[54]

The Bass family ultimately had no choice but to join in the burgeoning tourist trade that developed at Grand Canyon's railway terminus, and did so by offering buggy, and later automobile, trips along the southcentral rim. To get closer to this business, they leased two and one-half acres from the United States Forest Service within a mile of the railroad terminal in 1912 and built their third tourist facility, a two-story building sheathed in decorative pressed tin, appropriately dubbed the Tin House. They did well in the mad scramble for dollars at the new tourist center, but continued to control the western trade as well, operating Bass Camp and leading a few trips along their inner-canyon trails. Bass also retained his monopoly on mining operations along his trail network for the remainder of the pioneer period, shipping twenty-five tons of high-grade copper ore in 1908, and in 1917 selling at least six tons of long-strand asbestos to buyers in China, France, and the eastern United States for fifteen hundred dollars per ton.[55]

Although the Basses continued to make a good living until about 1920, the evolving nature of Grand Canyon tourism warned of the eventual demise of their western enterprises. Railroad facilities at the developing Grand Canyon Village better suited more affluent visitors who arrived by rail with only a few hours or days to

spend. Developmental controls initiated by the Department of Forestry about 1897, tightened by the renamed United States Forest Service in 1905, and diligently enforced by the National Park Service after 1919, favored the railroad, which could invest huge sums of money to cope with an exploding tourist population.

As Bass operations wound down between 1919 and 1926, the National Park Service entered into on-again, off-again negotiations with Bass to obtain rights to his camps, roads, trails, and mining claims within Grand Canyon National Park. The park service believed Bass had no legal rights to his improvements, but could not be sure of its position since he had kept up assessment work on a few mineral-bearing claims and had actually shipped some ore. Park superintendent Eakin summarized the situation in 1924 in a letter to Senator Carl Hayden: *You will note that Mr. Bass' mining claims and mill sites are not ... patented. It is my opinion, however, that if the land office were to investigate the validity of these claims that some of them at any rate would be held to be valid claims. As Bass Camp is filed as a millsite, if any of these claims in the canyon were declared valid, it would automatically make Bass Camp Mill Site valid ... As stated before, Mr. Bass will give a quitclaim deed to all these structures and all his mining and mill sites claims in Grand Canyon National Park for the sum of $25,000.*[56]

Park service personnel from rangers on up to Director Stephen Mather took a personal interest in Bass's properties. They recognized the roles he and Ada had played in development of the park and wanted to do something for them toward retirement, but unfortunately did not have the money to buy them out. Mather finally convinced the Santa Fe Land Improvement Company to pay the price, even though the railroad subsidiary had not the slightest interest in the properties. The Santa Fe had earlier intimated that they might be willing to do the deal for a lesser price, but Mather proved a fair man

Left: Shep, Ada, Mabel, and Hazel in front of the Tin House, ca. 1915. Pressed tin was commonly used for decorative interiors at the turn of the century, but rarely used as an exterior surface.
Arizona Historical Society

Right: Partial Bass family portrait on the White House porch, ca. 1920. Left to right: Ada; Mabel; Edith's son, Bert Lauzon; Edith Bass Lauzon, pregnant with Loren "Tiny" Lauzon.
Arizona Historical Society

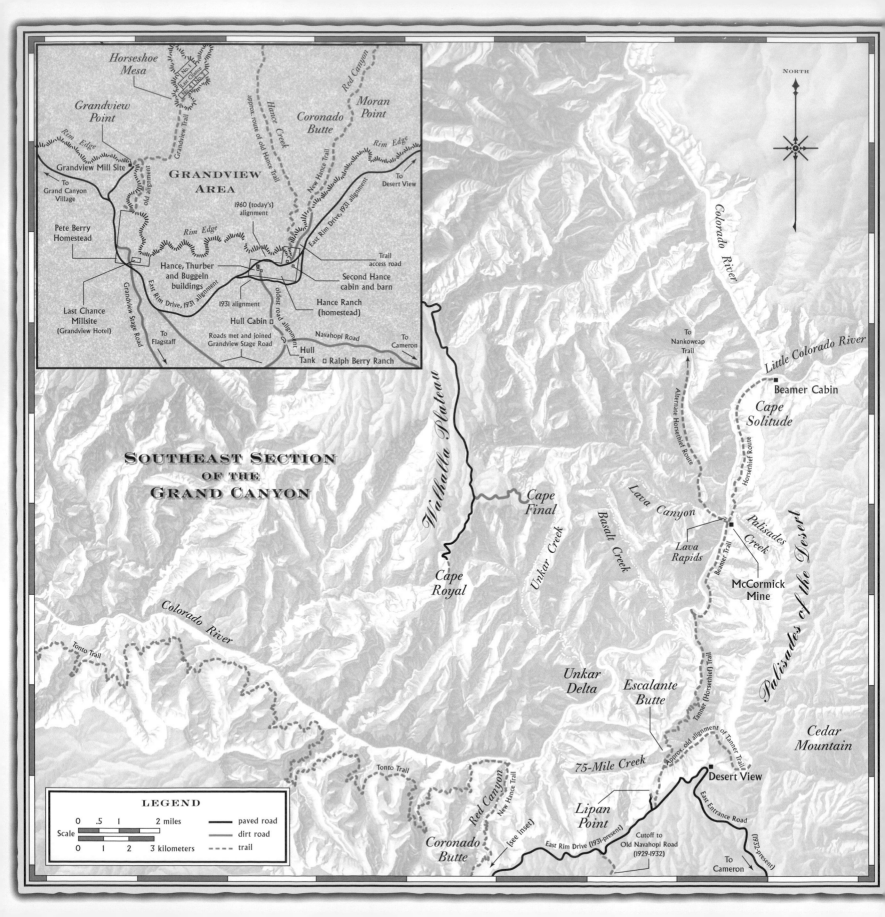

NORTH

GRANDVIEW AREA

Horseshoe Mesa

No. 1
Last Chance Mine No. 1

Grandview Point

Rim Edge

Grandview Trail

old alignment

Hance Creek

approx. route of old Hance Trail

Red Canyon

Coronado Butte

Moran Point

Rim Edge

Grandview Mill Site

To
Grand Canyon
Village

New Hance Trail

To
Desert View

Pete Berry
Homestead

Rim Edge

1960 (today's)
alignment

East Rim Drive, 1931 alignment

Trail
access road

Last Chance
Millsite
(Grandview Hotel)

Grandview Stage Road

East Rim Drive, 1931 alignment

Hance, Thurber
and Buggeln
buildings

1931 alignment

oldest road alignment

Second Hance
cabin and barn

Hance Ranch
(homestead)

To
Flagstaff

Hull Cabin

Roads met and joined
Grandview Stage Road

Navahopi Road

To
Cameron

Hull
Tank

Ralph Berry Ranch

Colorado River

To
Nankoweap
Trail

Little Colorado River

Beamer Cabin

*Cape
Solitude*

Alternate Horsethief Route

Horsethief Route

SOUTHEAST SECTION
OF THE
GRAND CANYON

Walhalla Plateau

*Cape
Final*

Unkar Creek

Basalt Creek

Lava Canyon

Lava
Rapids

Beamer Trail

*Palisades
Creek*

McCormick
Mine

*Cape
Royal*

Colorado River

Palisades of the Desert

Tonto Trail

*Unkar
Delta*

*Escalante
Butte*

Tanner (Horsethief) Trail

*Cedar
Mountain*

Tonto Trail

Approx. old alignment of Tanner Trail

Red Canyon

New Hance Trail

75-Mile Creek

Desert View

[see inset]

*Lipan
Point*

East Entrance Road

LEGEND

0	.5 1	2 miles

Scale

0	1 2	3 kilometers

——— paved road
——— dirt road
- - - - trail

*Coronado
Butte*

East Rim Drive (1931-present)

Cutoff to
Old Navahopi Road
(1929-1932)

To
Cameron

(1932-present)

despite his determination to eliminate small commercial operators and land owners from national parks. He wrote that while

… the Bass properties may not be worth $25,000 to the Atchison Company or Fred Harvey, Superintendent Eakin has placed a valuation on them of that amount, which he considered a very fair one, both to Bass and to the Government. Personally, I would not approve of getting the properties for less value, even if Mr. Bass would consent to their sale under the immediate need for ready funds.[57]

The railroad succumbed to Mather's persuasion and paid the full amount, writing equal checks to wife and husband in recognition of Ada's essential contributions. They signed a quitclaim deed in February 1926, ending seven decades of combined involvement at Grand Canyon. The properties passed from the railroad to the Fred Harvey Company in 1955 then to the United States government on 29 June 1956.[58]

The Basses moved to Wickenburg, Arizona, where Bill, not about to retire at the tender age of seventy-seven, did some prospecting, mining, and farming while running a gas station and campground. He died of a cerebral hemorrhage on 7 March 1933 and his cremated remains were dropped by airplane over Bass Tomb (renamed Holy Grail Temple), a rock spire beside Shinumo Creek. Ada remained in Wickenburg near her children and grandchildren until her death in 1951. She was buried in Grand Canyon Cemetery near her daughter, Edith Bass Lauzon, who died of appen-

dicitis in 1924. William Guy Bass worked for the Fred Harvey Company as an automotive stage driver from 1917 until 1926, then moved to Wickenburg to be near his aging parents. In later years, he ran the town's La Siesta Motel, became a noted desert photographer, and entertained motel guests with slide shows of Grand Canyon until his death in 1981.

Today, there is little evidence that mining and tourism once thrived west of Grand Canyon Village. One can still descend from Peach Springs along Farlee's old road to Diamond Creek, but nothing but a few nails are found at the site of Grand Canyon's first hotel. The paths of Garcés, Ives, and miners along the Topocoba and Hualapai Trails can be traced to the travertine waterfalls below Supai, but only debris and a few glory holes witness this long ago hotbed of mining activity. Evidence of Bass's presence remains only in disintegrating wagon roads off the beaten path; his network of trails, most of which are still used by backpackers; remnants of cable crossings below Bass Rapid and Copper Canyon; debris below the rim at Bass Camp, which the park service demolished in 1937; and scanty remains at each of his inner-canyon camps.

SOUTHEAST

After Mohave County miners began to exploit mineral deposits within Havasu Canyon, but before the Farlee and Bass families developed tourist enterprises, a few solitary prospectors

penetrated southeastern portions of Grand Canyon. Like their counterparts to the west, they initially hunted for gold and silver, settled for less valuable metals, and earned little until the Atlantic and Pacific brought cheap and timely transportation across the thirty-fifth parallel. Consequent developments at Flagstaff sent a greater number of men and a few families to the southeastern rim who, like Bill Bass, would earn a little money from copper and asbestos mines while securing their developments through permissive land laws. A few of these soon realized that Grand Canyon's wealth lay in visitors'—not ore—pockets and redirected their camps, trails, and intimate knowledge of local geology toward tourism.

Pioneers to southeastern Grand Canyon prior to the railroad's arrival did not follow a clearly delineated settlement path as had those who travelled a navigable river to developed Mohave County mining districts. Relatively poor mineral deposits and a formidable Hopi-Navajo cultural shield kept European Americans from approaching the southeastern rim for many years. By 1876, however, vanguards of Mormon expansion had streamed south from Lees Ferry to settle among the tribes at Moenave, Moenkopi, Tuba City, and sites astride the Little Colorado River. Non-Mormon miners and ranchers had also moved north about the same time from Prescott and Camp Verde to live alongside the Beale road.

The town of Flagstaff, which would become the debarkation point for south-

*Flagstaff immediately after the rail-
road's arrival, 1882. NAU.PH.433-1*

"Flag Staff" about 1880. The territorial census in that year counted only sixty-seven people in the Flagstaff vicinity, most of whom earned a living through cattle and sheep ranching.[59]

Flagstaff's growth through the early 1880s resembled that of Peach Springs and Williams, as all three owed their prosperity to Atlantic and Pacific work gangs. With tracks on their way by 1881, town population swelled to two hundred with the predictable high percentage of rowdies. One observer made the all too familiar assessment that *Flagstaff has one store and five deadfalls [saloons] and is situated seven miles south of San Francisco Mountain on the railway line. They sell water and whiskey.*[60]

eastern Grand Canyon development in the 1880s and 1890s, was settled in 1876 by the Arizona Colonization Company of Boston, Massachusetts. Company leaders, excited by Amiel Whipple's promising report for a regional railroad and somewhat misled by territorial boosters, mistakenly set their initial sights for the barren Little Colorado country. To the Boston company's good fortune, however, four companies of Mormon colonizers who would endure years of hardship at the unpromising site beat them to it by just a few days. The disgruntled party of fifty easterners continued to the base of the San Francisco Peaks where they laid out a townsite called San Francisco Mountain, then quickly renamed it Agassiz before scattering by the end of the year. Agassiz thereafter grew by a few immigrants at a time until residents renamed the settlement

Saloons, gambling halls, and shootings led to early vigilance committees, but after road crews moved on down the line, the town gained relative peace and continued to grow toward regional prominence. Fueled by the Ayer lumber mill which began cutting trees in 1882, population reached 500; then, 600 in 1884; 1,000 in 1887; and 1,500 by 1891.[61]

Most settlers and part-time developers at Grand Canyon's southeastern rim would arrive from Flagstaff, but a few prospectors from other locales preceded them. Seth Tanner is the first European American aside from García López de Cárdenas and Francisco Tomas Garcés known to explore this end of the canyon, although in the two decades he

spent combing the area for mineral wealth he never built a nearby home. Tanner, as scout and guide for some of the earliest Mormon immigrants ranging south from Utah, reached Moenkopi in December 1875, then built a cabin along a Little Colorado ford which became known as Tanner's Crossing. After 1911, a trading post and small Navajo population developed a short distance downstream into the town of Cameron along today's U.S. Highway 89.[62]

In 1877, Tanner located several claims beside the Colorado River within Grand Canyon at a highly mineralized deposit known as the Tanner Ledge. In 1880, he organized the Little Colorado River Mining District, which did not touch the canyon itself but led others to prospect along the Colorado downstream of the Little Colorado confluence. He filed claims to copper deposits between Lava and Basalt Canyons, some of which he sold to another long-time regional resident, George McCormick, in the 1890s and

1900s. McCormick along with his brother and son Melvin worked at least one of these claims, the McCormick Mine at the mouth of Palisades Creek, through the First World War.[63]

Ben Beamer came to Grand Canyon later than Seth Tanner, but was another who prospected the banks and side canyons of the Colorado River downstream of the Little Colorado. In 1890, Beamer remodeled a Prehistoric Pueblo ruin he found near the mouth of the latter stream into a cozy cliffside cabin and base camp.[64] Remnants of a plow found near the cabin suggest that he tilled the adjacent narrow bench much as the Prehistoric Puebloans had seven hundred years earlier. Beamer's contribution to canyon development and his legacy is the trail bearing his name which hugs the Colorado River atop the Tapeats Sandstone from his cabin to Palisades Creek, and from the McCormick Mine along Dox Sandstone cliffs to the base of the Tanner Trail.

Left: Beamer Cabin, photographed in 1968 was much as it appears today. The cliff face serves as the back wall and part of the ceiling. GRCA 5173B

Right: Frame construction trading post at Cameron, near the 1911 BIA suspension bridge, ca. 1920s. Replaced by today's stone structures alongside U.S. Highway 89. NAU.PH.632-6

Seth Benjamin Tanner: Mormon scout and guide to the Little Colorado River area, horse trader, early Grand Canyon prospector and miner. GRCA 7060A

Franklin H. French and sons Charles and Frederick. French prospected with Seth Tanner, occasionally guided regional visitors like George Wharton James, married Emma Lee after the execution of her husband in 1877, and settled with Emma near Winslow in later years. NAPHS 666-22

During the 1880s, Seth Tanner and another prospector, Franklin French, reconstructed a path which had been used for centuries by the Hopi, Navajo, and perhaps Prehistoric Puebloans from a point east of today's Desert View to the Colorado River. Tanner, Lewis Bedlins, and Fred Bunker further improved the trail about 1889, and it was known at least for a short while as the Bunker Trail. By 1890, French built the upper portion along today's alignment from Lipan Point to the Redwall Limestone and the entire ten-mile route to the river became known as the Tanner-French Trail, but since the turn of the century it has been called simply the Tanner Trail.[65]

These pathfinders and others used the Moqui, Tanner, and Beamer Trails along with the Hopi Salt Trail within the Little Colorado River gorge to form a circular prospecting route tying the southeastern canyon to Mormon and Indian villages to the east. Beamer and Tanner improved their trails to facilitate prospecting and to transport what little ore they extracted. Later, these connecting trails south of the river combined with the north side Nankoweap Trail, built by John Wesley Powell and geologist Charles D. Walcott in 1882, to form a rugged transcanyon route known at times as the Horsethief Trail. The route gained its disreputable title from outlaws who drove stolen horses down the Tanner segment, paused long enough to alter brands, then continued along the Beamer to ford the Colorado above the Little Colorado confluence. They reached the Arizona Strip and southern Utah by way of the Nankoweap, sold their stolen merchandise in the Mormon settlements, swiped others from their customers, and repeated the drive in the opposite direction. As a river-bottom

alternate, the thieves may have used a low-water ford below Lava Canyon Rapids near the McCormick Mine, ascended Lava Canyon, and continued west of Temple Butte to the Nankoweap Trail.[66]

• • •

Despite the romantic ambience of western horse thieves, or perhaps because of it, developments at Lipan Point, Desert View, and the relatively roomy inner canyon below never advanced beyond trails, claims, mines, and a few temporary shelters during pioneer days.[67] The few miners who frequented this side of the canyon abandoned their efforts by the end of the First World War or were compelled to leave soon after the National Park Service arrived in 1919. Permanent settlement and extensive development did occur along the southeast rim about a dozen miles west, however, and again began through the exploratory efforts of prospectors.

William Henry Ashurst appears to have been the first of dozens to examine the inner canyon downstream of the Tanner Trail during the 1880s and 1890s. Ashurst and his large family settled at Anderson Mesa south of Flagstaff in 1876, and by 1880 he began to winter in Grand Canyon, driving horses down to pasturage at Indian Garden and other points. In early 1893, Ashurst and others who had been prowling about the chasm's depths since the late 1880s met to organize the Grand Canyon Mining District.[68] They defined the district to include the entire gorge from rim to rim between Red Canyon and a line three miles west of the Bright Angel Fault. These boundaries included most of the easily accessible portions of Grand Canyon other than those travelled by Seth Tanner and Ben Beamer to the east and Bill

Bass to the west. District rules allowed each claim to measure a maximum fifteen hundred feet in length straddling a body of ore to a width of six hundred feet (about twenty acres) and placed no limit on the number of claims an individual might hold. Annual assessment work of one hundred dollars required by federal law could be met by manual labor valued at five dollars per day, which applied to all work done on approach trails, buildings, mills, adits, or any other form of improvements made to extract or transport ore.[69]

These rules illustrate the legal flexibility accorded miners during the pioneer period, and help explain why they made improvements and the process by which they came to control Grand Canyon prior to the arrival of federal regulators. Often working together in groups of three to six, they completed a claim's assessment work in several days then moved on to others, all along enjoying each other's company, sharing heavier tasks, and witnessing improvements, in the event of later questioning by the General Land Office. The number of sites one man claimed depended solely on his inclination to work, what he could afford to pay others to keep up his assessments, or his willingness to lie about improvements. After 1890, when reports of Robert Brewster Stanton's railroad survey sparked something of a mineral rush, other hopefuls joined William Ashurst and John Hance within the Grand Canyon Mining District, including brothers Niles, Ralph, and Burton Cameron, Pete Berry, John Marshall, C.H. McClure, T.C. Frier, and Dan Hogan. These men, along with dozens of lesser known area residents, formed an amazing combination of mining partnerships recorded with Coconino County between 1891 and 1908.[70]

J.A. Pitts in 1947 recalled a prospecting trip he and others made in the winter of 1891-1892 that reveals sincere if unsuccessful mining efforts of the 1880s and 1890s as well as the basic reason all miners turned to tourism or left the area. In late autumn, Pitts, William Ashurst, John Marshall, C.H. McClure, and Merrit Fisher left Flagstaff for a winter-long trip to the canyon bottom. Within several days they reached the southeastern rim where John Hance joined the party and all continued down a precipitous trail Hance had improved to the Tonto Platform. Leaving beef cattle and a few horses to graze at Indian Garden, the men descended to the river and crossed in Ashurst's rickety rowboat. They trekked another three miles up a tributary on the north side, probably Bright Angel Canyon, where they spent the winter hacking away with shovel and pickaxe at several copper claims. During their stay, Buckey O'Neill, a pivotal character in later developments at the South Rim, happened by for a few days to break the tedium and obtain options on some of Ashurst's asbestos claims.[71]

When the men had piled up "a nice little bunch of ore," they sent Pitts back to Flagstaff for supplies. Reaching town after two days of "awful rough riding," Pitts ran into Charles Babbitt who, with four brothers, had extensive cattle holdings, trading posts, and general stores in the Grand Canyon region. Babbitt, who was known to finance ("grubstake") more than one hopeful prospector, succumbed to Pitts's account of rich ore deposits and joined the partnership with two hundred dollars cash, supplies, and a new four-mulepower Studebaker wagon. On his return to the rim,

William Henry Ashurst family, 1890s. Henry Fountain Ashurst in left rear would become Arizona's first U.S. senator following statehood and would introduce one of several bills to create Grand Canyon National Park. William Ashurst died in a landslide within the canyon in 1901; his good friend John Hance found his remains weeks after the accident occurred. NAPHS 335-4

Ruins of cabin that stood near the McCormick Mine (note mine talus in right background), 1968.

GRCA 5167

This camp at the mouth of Red Canyon at the base of the New Hance Trail could be considered standard for pioneer era prospectors as well as tourists who rode inner-canyon trails before permanent inner-canyon camps existed.

Arizona Historical Society 63541

Stage to Grand Canyon along the Grandview road with San Francisco Peaks in the background.

Huntington Library PF23, 088

Pitts happened into Pete Berry and the Cameron brothers who helped him pack the supplies down their new Bright Angel Trail to Indian Garden where Pitts established a camp.

After lugging supplies and driving burros down to the river along an essentially trail-less route and then making multiple hazardous crossings to get the goods to the north side, Pitts and the others strapped two hundred pounds of ore to each burro for transport back to the river. They had to unpack and reload everything into the minuscule rowboat, making untold numbers of crossings in the shallow-draft craft before repacking the burros and struggling up to the Tonto Platform. Fletch Fairchild and Burton Cameron helped get the ore from Indian Garden to the rim where the men reloaded it into the Studebaker then hauled it nearly ninety miles to the railroad station in Flagstaff. Here it dawned on them to assay the ore and when they found it would pay only twenty dollars per ton—less than the cost to ship it to El Paso for reduction—they dumped the entire winter's labor and wandered away shaking their heads.

Pitts married one of William Ashurst's daughters, prospered in the cattle business, ran large merchandise stores in Ash Fork and Seligman, then retired to Upland, California, where he lived to a ripe old age. Nearly sixty years after his brief encounter with Grand Canyon mining he recalled that he had

… *spent four months in the canyon that winter. Since my mining adventure I haven't been seized with a desire to travel those trails again. Charlie Babbitt and I never mention mines when we meet.*[72]

Other noteworthy characters he worked with and met on that trip, however, continued to stake claims into the 1900s and to hope that some would produce copper or asbestos ore

worth shipping. It will be worthwhile to recall this months-long, grueling, and profitless experience when considering later why Grand Canyon pioneers argued so heatedly against corporate takeovers and federal regulators after the turn of the century.

Along with prospectors whose sole purpose was to find and develop mineral deposits, others with differing entrepreneurial spirits came to the southeastern rim in the 1880s. Philip and William Hull arrived southeast of Grandview Point about a mile from the rim some time between 1880 and 1883, established a sheep ranch, and helped start one of the region's best-loved tourist businesses. The youthful Hull brothers along with their part-time employee and informal partner, John Hance, are usually credited with leading the earliest paying tourists into Grand Canyon, although Julius Farlee could rightfully take exception to the claim. In February 1884, William Hull drove early sight-seers Flagstaff lumber magnate Edward E. Ayer and his wife to the South Rim by wagon where Hance took over to lead the couple over the brink along his recently completed trail down Hance Canyon.[73]

By 1885, the Hulls, Hance, Silas Ruggles, and likely others roughed out a seventy-three-mile wagon road from Flagstaff to Hull Ranch and on to Hance's cabin at the rim near Grandview Point. In the same year, the brothers and their father, Philip Hull Sr., established a rest stop at East Cedar Ranch, thirty-four miles northwest of Flagstaff, which served infrequent early travelers along the wagon road. Flagstaff residents who offered transportation services during the 1880s included A.C. Morse, who ran a livery and drove or rented light passenger wagons; E.S. Wilcox, who owned the Grand Canyon Livery and Feed Stables and advertised teams, guides, and drivers; and James W. Thurber, who also rented teams and wagons.[74]

The Hulls remained active in this very early tourist trade through the 1880s. They also lured eastern capitalists in one of several failed efforts to finance a railroad from Flagstaff to the southeast rim, and continued to transport visitors along the stage road they helped build. In 1888, they constructed Hull Cabin at their sheep ranch which stands today as the oldest log home within many miles of Grand Canyon, and in the same year spent

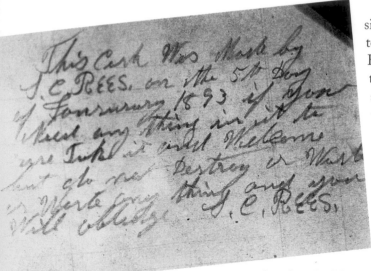

Cowboys of the CO Bar spread, in front of East Cedar Ranch stage station, ca. 1910. NAU.PH.93.25.8

Mining claims and notes like this were left throughout the canyon by early prospectors, usually encased in tobacco tins, occasionally found even today. "This cache was made by J.C. Rees on the 5th day of January 1893. If you need anything in it to use take it and welcome but do not destroy or waste any thing and you will oblige. J.C. Rees."
GRCA 8118

sixteen hundred dollars to build a nearby reservoir. Hull Tank afforded plentiful water for livestock and early tourists, and was valued far more than the buildings and four hundred acres which comprised the ranch.[75]

Philip Hull Jr. died in November 1888 at the age of forty-one, but William remained active in the area for another decade. He sold the sheep business in 1893, but continued to guide tourists to the southeast rim and joined the prospecting boom with Ashurst and others in the 1890s.[76] He also died young, at Prescott, Arizona, in 1904 at the age of thirty-nine.

• • •

The Hulls' partner, Captain John Hance, survives in Grand Canyon lore as its most colorful resident, a lifelong bachelor who dabbled in mining but made his living from tourism. More is written about Hance than any other canyon pioneer and for good reason. He was the first person and one of only a handful before 1900 to take up full-time residence at the very edge of the abyss and remained the rest of his life. Much of what is written about the man is folklore, however, or muddled because early writers used Hance, one of the great prevaricators of the Southwest, as their source of information.

Hance was born the third of fifteen children to John and Rachel Leight Hance at Cowan's Ferry, Tennessee, about 1838 and moved with his family to Missouri in 1852 and to Kansas by the 1860s. Although his younger brother George served as a messenger for Union officers during the Civil War, neither his niece nor nephew could later recall "Captain" John Hance joining either side during the war. They did remember that he had worked as a muleskinner for Lorenzo Butler "Tame Bill" Hickok (Wild Bill's brother) hauling supplies between western military forts, which may as close as he got to the fighting. Civilian ranks of captain, major, colonel, and even general proliferated in the late nineteenth century, and although some reflected permanent or brevet ranks achieved during the Civil War, others were assumed by well-liked or respected men who never experienced military service.[77]

John and George Hance arrived in Prescott, Arizona, by way of Fort Union, New Mexico, in November 1868. They were among a party of twenty-three to make the wagon trip, and it is testament to dangerous times in central Arizona Territory that Yavapai Indians killed eight of the original party within a year of arrival. In 1869, George and John along with younger brother James moved to Camp Verde where John hauled supplies for the military, mined, farmed, and raised livestock. The brothers witnessed fierce skirmishes between the United States Cavalry and Yavapais, Hualapais, and Tonto Apaches in the late 1860s and early 1870s, and knew well the famous Indian fighter, General George Crook. When the army herded Camp Verde Reservation Indians south to the San Carlos Reservation in 1873, they hired the eight teams of John and George Hance to carry the baggage and infirm.[78]

John Hance drifted north from Camp Verde after 1876 and first visited Grand Canyon some time before 1881. He lived occasionally in

Williams, but worked for the Moroni Cattle Company which had its headquarters at Fort Moroni, the Mormon lumber camp built about 1881 by John W. Young in Fort Valley (north Flagstaff).[79] By most accounts, Hance moved to the southeast rim three miles east of Grandview Point by 1883 and soon improved an inner-canyon trail to facilitate prospecting and later access copper and asbestos claims. After leading Mr. and Mrs. Ayer along this trail in 1884, he decided that tourism might earn an easier meal ticket than mining and filed for a 160-acre homestead, built a cabin near the head of his trail, and in September 1886 placed this advertisement in the Flagstaff newspaper:

Being thoroughly conversant with all the trails leading to the Grand Canyon of the Colorado, I am prepared to conduct parties thereto at any time. I have a fine spring of water [Glendale Springs] near my house on the rim of the canyon, and can furnish accommodations for tourists and their animals.[80]

Hance's accommodations actually resembled those of Bill Bass or something a little worse. Although he kept a log cabin near the rim and a rock cabin along Hance Creek for his own use, visitors stayed in tents and, later, tent-cabins with board floors, beds, tables, chairs, and few other comforts. On the bright side, he charged guests only a dollar for dinner and a night's lodging, and otherwise provided "excellent meals." He also rented camping outfits, pack and saddle horses, and durable trail clothing, and sold sundry supplies.[81]

Visitors clearly did not come to Hance Ranch for the meager accommodations, but for the scenic views and opportunity to spend a few days with their host and guide. Between 1883 and 1894, Hance led guests down the old Havasupai trail along Hance Creek which he had rediscovered and improved. His guests, like earlier Indians, had to descend the precarious narrow path on foot as it zig-zagged steeply down to the Tonto Platform. Here the terrain

Left: Outfitting at Flagstaff for a prospecting trip to Grand Canyon, 1890. The scene is Front Street near the new railroad depot as the town begins to flourish. NAU.PH.433-6

Right: Prospectors who had accidents often had to wait a while for rescue! This skeleton was found by Ralph Cameron employee Clarence Spaulding in 1906 and photographed by the Kolb brothers, who left it to be rediscovered in 1923 by this party of the Birdseye dam-site expedition. NAU.PH.568.8203

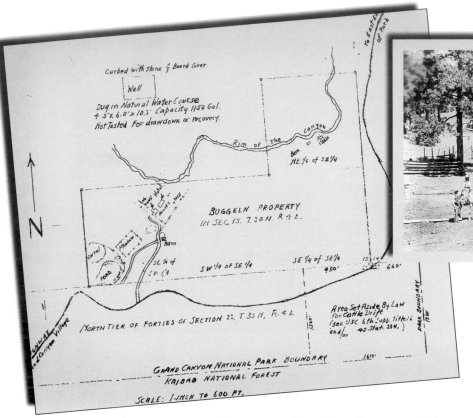

Left: This sketch map of the Hance Ranch property was made in 1941.
Fred Harvey Company

Right: The Hance Ranch evolved from the pioneer's modest log cabin (on the left) to include Thurber and Tolfree's larger log structure and the Buggelns' frame residence, just out of sight on the right, ca. 1908. Fred Harvey Company

flattens considerably and guests could remount to ride around Horseshoe Mesa upon an informal prospectors' path—the Tonto Trail—or scramble on foot down intermittent Hance Creek to the Colorado River with the help of rope ladders at occasional waterfalls. When rockslides obliterated the old trail in 1894, Hance built a better one, known today as the New Hance Trail, suitable for pack stock down Red Canyon east of his ranch.[82]

Guests stayed with Hance not only for his expert guidance but to listen to the canyon's premier storyteller. By all accounts the man had little regard for the truth but a lively imagination, quick wit, and an amazing ability to tell any one of several hundred stories with variable punch lines. As one visitor noted in 1897:
Anyone who comes to the Grand Canyon and fails

to meet John Hance will miss half the show. I can certify that he can tell the truth, though it is claimed by friends that he is not exactly like George Washington in that particular as he can do the other thing when necessary to make a story sound right.[83]

To offset his reputation as a liar, it is only fair to add that contemporaries described him as a thoroughly polite and gentle man, genuinely fond of animals and most everyone he met, who never tired of interacting with guests. Nonetheless, he had a practical reason for telling whoppers, as he revealed to one of his oldest friends, Mrs. Elizabeth B. Heiser of Flagstaff:
I've got to tell stories to them people for their money; and if I don't tell it to them, who will? I can make these tenderfeet believe that a frog eats boiled eggs; and I'm going to do it; and I'm going to make 'em believe that he carries it a mile to find a rock to crack it on.[84]

Hance was able to hoodwink listeners because of his credible appearance and straight-faced delivery. Numerous photographs confirm contemporary descriptions of a "weathered, hard-bitten, hard-boiled" man, about five feet eleven inches tall, 155 pounds, and ramrod-straight posture. He typically sported a full goatee and mustache and was seldom seen without a hat. Dressed in buckskin with cradled rifle and holstered pistol, or in the sturdy wear of turn-of-the-century prospectors, he appeared the soul of blunt western honesty.[85] Picking up on statements or questions of a guest—and most guests were first-timers, ignorant of the region's natural history—he would respond with feigned sincerity. For example, when guests inevitably asked whether there were snakes in the area, he replied:

Snakes? [pause to compose] No, there's no snakes in the Grand Canyon any more. Used to be, though. Millions of 'em. One day down at Indian Gardens, I must have seen four hundred snakes at once. They were all in a big ring, single file, just going around in a circle ... when I looked again, the ring was smaller, just about half size. I couldn't see where any snakes had left, so I looked closer; and do you know, every snake had swallered the tail of the snake ahead of him and they were all crawling and swallering just as steady as a twenty-one-jewel Swiss movement. By evening they were all gone. They'd eaten each other all up![86]

Local yarn spinning was not Hance's exclusive domain. Bill Bass, although a somewhat more serious fellow, was known to tell a few improbable stories and certainly other of the early tourist guides, as some today, entertained their guests in this way. It was part of the western experience, and a vacationing audience has receptive ears. No one did it better or more often than John Hance, however, and guests showed their appreciation by tipping generously. By the end of each summer season, he had enough stashed away to winter below the rim at his rock cabin and work his copper and asbestos claims along the river.[87]

Hance sold his ranch, trails, and tourist business to James Thurber and J. H. Tolfree in 1895 for fifteen hundred dollars, but kept his mining claims and stayed nearby to regale vacationers along the southeastern rim. When the first Grand Canyon post office of "Tourist, Arizona" opened at the ranch in 1897, Hance became its first postmaster. He patented and sold his asbestos claims near the river in 1901 for $6,250, but stayed to manage the Hance Asbestos Mining Company for its new Massachusetts owners.[88]

In 1906, Hance accepted a Fred Harvey Company offer to live free and clear at the Bright Angel Hotel in exchange for his services as canyon commentator and public relations man. Here he remained doing the job he loved best until illness in late 1918 prompted friends to move him to the Weatherford Hotel then to the indigent hospital in Flagstaff where he died in January 1919, just a few weeks before the United States Congress created Grand Canyon National Park. He had been a trend setter during his entire thirty-five-year canyon tenure, so it was only fitting that he be the first person buried in Grand Canyon Cemetery, with dozens of old friends on hand to mourn the loss of a true canyon pioneer.[89]

The sale of the Hance tourist enterprise to Thurber and Tolfree in 1895 coincided with Thurber's purchase of a stage line from E.S. Wilcox, who had expanded service since the

James Thurber family, ca. 1890.
NAPHS 401-14

The Atlantic and Pacific's Grand Canyon Stage Line formalized tourist travel to the Grandview area during 1892–1901. NAPHS 56

1880s over the Flagstaff wagon road. As the number of cross-country passengers wanting to pause to see Arizona's scenic wonder increased, the Atlantic and Pacific in 1892 initiated their thrice-weekly Grand Canyon Stage Line along the same road. In 1895, or soon thereafter, Thurber arranged to operate the railroad's line and by 1898 owned it outright. In July 1899, probably a peak month for southeastern rim tourism, some three hundred visitors rode his stage from Flagstaff to Hance Ranch and Grandview Point.[90]

The stage during the years 1892–1901 left Flagstaff from the Bank Hotel near the train station at the corner of Leroux Street and Santa Fe Avenue. In summer, it covered the seventy-three-mile distance to Hance Ranch in ten to twelve hours with three relay stations providing rest stops, meals, and fresh teams. The first of these lay eighteen miles from town at Fern Mountain Ranch and was operated by homesteaders Mr. and Mrs. Augustus Dillman. The second stop thirty-four miles along the road at East Cedar Ranch had begun with the Hulls in the 1880s and continued as a midway stop, owned by John W. Young's Arizona Cattle Company and by the Babbitt family after 1899. The third relay was called Moqui Station, located about sixteen miles from the rim. The stage also ran in winter, but sporadically and along a different initial road segment that climbed counterclockwise around the San Francisco Peaks before joining with a county road then returning to the summer route.[91]

Several accounts reveal that the stage ride was similar to that offered by Bill Bass in distance, duration, and discomfort, though the business seemed better organized. The stage left for Grandview on Mondays, Wednesdays, and Fridays; returned to Flagstaff on Tuesdays,

Thursdays, and Saturdays; and usually kept its schedule. Thurber employed several eclectic conveyances, including a four-horse Concord coach; a six-horse "stage train" of connected coaches, surreys, or spring wagons; and an eighteen-passenger mud wagon. Most were equipped with canvas flaps to keep out rain and some of the dust. Passengers stretched their legs at the three relays, and again when walking up steep grades and helping to pull their vehicle out of the muck. They otherwise enjoyed pinyon, juniper, and ponderosa forests and cinder cones blanketing the vast volcanic field which surrounds the San Francisco Peaks as the stage bumped along at seven to ten miles per hour. Round-trip fare over the years ranged from fifteen to twenty dollars per person.[92]

Thurber and Tolfree also brought some organization to Hance's former ranch and camp. They added a multiple-room log building used as a kitchen and dining room, converted the adjacent one-room Hance cabin into a stage station (and some suggest, a tavern), replaced simple canvas tents with sturdier tent-cabins, and raised the daily fare to three dollars. They moved the aging storyteller himself to the head of his old trail and built him a cabin and barn from which he guided guests along the rim and the New Hance, Tanner, and Rim Trails, the latter a scenic path just beneath the canyon lip which connected the Old Hance and New Hance trailheads. Tolfree, his wife, and two daughters ran the camp while Thurber managed the business and drove the stage, calling himself the "gentlemanly driver of the Grand Canyon Stage." Thurber also built the Bright Angel Hotel fourteen miles to the west at the site of today's Bright Angel Lodge and extended the stage line to that point in 1896.[93]

Thurber sold his Flagstaff stage line and Bright Angel Hotel to Martin Buggeln in 1901. Buggeln, whose early history is more closely associated with the southcentral rim, retired in 1906 from conflicts being waged at the head of the Bright Angel Trail and in the next year purchased Thurber's 160-acre Hance Ranch for five thousand dollars. Buggeln built a seventeen-room, two-story frame hotel beside the existing log kitchen/dining room in 1907, intending to expand upon the operation begun by Hance, Thurber, and Tolfree, but never reopened the tourist facility.[94]

Martin Buggeln, wife Emma Walker Buggeln, and daughters Edna and Deletta instead turned Hance Ranch into a cattle operation which remained active through the 1930s, much to the park service's chagrin. After Emma died in 1923, Buggeln renewed his interest in converting his ranch, by that year an inholding within the four-year-old national park, into a tourist hotel. He gave up the idea in 1925, however, when park service administrators who, along with the Fred Harvey Company, were intent on channeling tourism to the southcentral rim, denied him commercial use of park roads and disallowed any form of advertising within the park.[95]

Martin Buggeln died at Phoenix, Arizona, in 1939. Three years later, second wife Eva Moss Buggeln extended a purchase option on the 160-acre parcel to the federal government. The National Park Service scraped together the money to exercise the option in 1948, eliminating the last private inholding east of Grand Canyon Village other than Hance's patented asbestos claims above the north bank of the Colorado River, which still remain in private hands. In 1957, park rangers razed the intact but

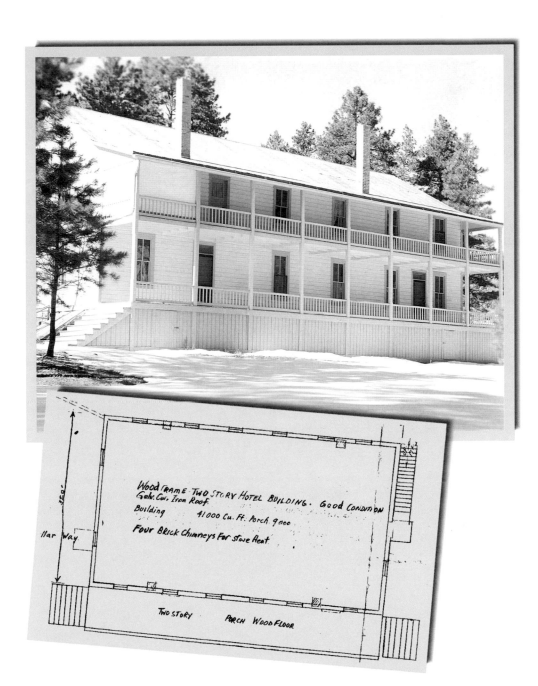

Above: The Buggeln residence at Hance Ranch. GRCA 679 Below: Architectural drawing from 1941. GRCA

MORE JOHN HANCE

One day when the canyon was fogged from rim to rim, Hance told a party of dudes that it was almost heavy enough for him to ski across. "I do it every once in a while," he told the disbelieving party, "but the last time I tried it, I got about half way across when the fog began to lift. I hurried around from one patch to another, but I just couldn't make it. I finally hit a hole in the fog, and wound up right over there on top of Zoroaster Temple. I was marooned for four weeks

Captain John Hance, 1910.
Arizona Historical Society 16160

before there was enough fog again for me to get out! It was a light fog, but I was lots lighter by that time, too!"

John Hance was approached by a stranger to the canyon rim who asked him about deer hunting in the vicinity.

"Why, it's fine," he replied. "I went out this morning and killed three all by myself." "That's wonderful," exclaimed the stranger, "do you know who I am?" "No, I don't," admitted John. "Why, I'm the game warden, and it looks to me like you've broke a few of the game laws!" "Do you know who I am?", asked John Hance. "No, I don't," replied the warden. "Well, I'm the biggest liar in Arizona!"

As John Hance was pointing out the scenery to a number of visiting dudes, one asked him how he lost the end of his finger. "My finger?" he asked, star-

ing at the abbreviated end of his right index finger, apparently never having considered what gain he could make out of the slight deformity. "Why, ma'am, I wore it off in thirty years of standing here on the rim of the Grand Canyon, pointing to the scenery!" Appreciatively received by his listeners, Hance ambled off to try it again on the next dude he met.

Above: Hance Ranch in its earliest configuration with Hance on horseback in front of his cabin and tourists beside a guest tent, 1880s.
Sharlot Hall Museum 1703P

deteriorating Buggeln frame hotel, Thurber/ Tolfree log building, and outbuildings.[96] East Rim Drive passes through the old homestead today in the vicinity of Buggeln Hill, but nothing remains of the extensive Hance, Tolfree, Thurber, and Buggeln operations except a few foundation outlines, dirt road grades, and bits of building debris.

• • •

While tourism thrived at Hance Ranch between 1883 and 1907, entirely separate developments took place just three miles west at Grandview Point. Here a number of early prospectors under the leadership of Peter D. "Pete" Berry claimed and developed one of the few paydirt mines ever opened within Grand Canyon. Like John Hance, Berry decided to juggle tourism and prospecting for a while before focusing on sightseers at the turn of the century. Unlike Hance, he built something that actually resembled a hotel and remained to compete with railroad interests nearly to the end of the pioneer period.

Pete Berry was born in Cedar Falls, Iowa, in 1858, but moved with his family to Missouri in 1866 and ended up in the mining town of Pitkin, Colorado, by 1879. In early 1887, Pete learned that his older brother John, who ran a Flagstaff saloon, had been shot to death by brothers George and Billy Hawks while trying to break up a barroom brawl. He hurried to Flagstaff to settle his brother's affairs and perhaps seek revenge, but found upon arrival that a vigilance committee of John's friends had broken into the local jail and beaten him to the latter task.[97]

Pete stayed to manage his brother's saloon and marry his widow, May Hill Berry, an Irish woman of great beauty but apparently free spirit.

A few years after the birth of their son, Ralph, in 1889, May left Pete—her third or fourth husband—and skipped town with their son in the company of a travelling salesman. One story relates that Pete paid Niles Cameron one hundred dollars to go to Tucson and kidnap Ralph. In any event, the boy returned, Pete divorced May in 1894, and some years later married his housekeeper, Martha Thompson. Another story goes that Pete woke up in a Flagstaff hotel after a drunken binge and was "shocked" to find Martha in bed with him. She showed him a marriage certificate, however, and despite the bawdy beginning they stayed together happily for the rest of their long lives.[98]

Although Pete was reportedly a heavy drinker in his youth, a trait by no means rare among canyon pioneers, nearly everyone who knew him during his forty-four years at the southeastern rim agreed that he possessed many fine traits. He was an exceptionally hard worker and perfectly honest, though "when starting to tell a little story it always took him

Pete Berry (far left) and stepson Sam Parker with others in front of Pete's saloon, Flagstaff, 1896. Berry, like many Grand Canyon pioneers, maintained a residence and business in one of several nearby towns as well as at the canyon. Most pioneers spent the summer tourist season at the canyon rim, and some remained through the winter to prospect the inner canyon while their families returned to town. GRCA 8995A

FAMILIES INTERTWINED

As Flagstaff began to shed its wild and wooly image by 1886, David and William Babbitt disembarked from the westbound train in search of a cattle herd and grazing land. Dr. D.J. Brannen helped them find what they wanted: nearly one thousand prime Herefords and 160 acres at Lockett Meadow beside the San Francisco Peaks. By June, brother Charles (C.J.) joined the pair and the following year brother George joined them at their new spread at "Babbitt Park," near today's Lake Mary. By the time the fifth brother, Edward, arrived in 1891, an economic empire surpassing all in northern Arizona had begun to emerge: the Babbitt Brothers Trading Company.

Everyone living in the northern half of Arizona Territory knew the Babbitts, who quickly expanded from their CO Bar spread to make them the largest ranching family in the region, then diversified into Indian trading stores, merchandising, and a hundred other ventures. If you did not do business with the family, which was hard to avoid, you knew them through their community involvement or political office. They have always supported the arts, and at one time or another have been leaders of the Democratic Party, mayors of Flagstaff, Coconino County supervisor, judge, territorial legislator, state senator, and more recently, governor, presidential candidate, and United States Secretary of the Interior. They were good people to know, committed to fair dealing and patient when it came to debts owed them during hard times.

The Verkamps are as well known as the Babbitts in northern Arizona but the families' close relationship is perhaps less familiar. Both came from Cincinnati, Ohio, where in 1882 David and George Babbitt opened a grocery across the street from the wealthy Gerhard Verkamp, his wife, Anna, and their nine children. Over the years, the five Babbitt brothers became well acquainted with the four Verkamp sisters and Emma married David; Mary wed C.J.; and Matilda, Edward. Beyond these family unions, Papa Verkamp remained a supporter of the Babbitt enterprises until his death in 1897, often giving money to his sons-in-law, bailing them out of financial scrapes, and once offering a million-dollar guarantee when creditors came knocking at their doors.

Verkamp brothers John, Leo, and Oscar followed the Babbitts to Arizona and were at times partners in various Babbitt cattle ranches and other enterprises. Leo was an early mayor of Flagstaff at age twenty-five and once head of the county Republican Party while John ended up at Grand Canyon selling Babbitts' and others' curios at the turn of the century. The Verkamps have retained their presence at the South Rim since 1905, John's family moving here full time in 1936. Early Babbitt ventures at the canyon included C.J.'s effort to buy Pete Berry's rights to the Bright Angel Trail and to lease the Grandview Hotel in 1902; David's incorporation of the Grand Canyon Electric Company in the same year, with plans to dam Bright Angel Creek to produce hydroelectric power for Flagstaff; and numerous mining ventures, all ending in uncharacteristic failures. The Babbitts' canyon successes since 1910 have been in general stores at the South Rim and later at Tusayan.

Recommended Reading:
Dean Smith, *Brothers Five: The Babbitts of Arizona* (Tempe: Arizona Historical Foundation, 1989)

Above: The five Babbitt brothers after arrival at Flagstaff, Arizona, in the 1880s. The brothers were always ready to try something new and became one of the most prominent business families in northern Arizona. At Grand Canyon, they grubstaked prospectors and established a store and campground. Charlie (left) in 1902 tried to buy Pete Berry's interest in the Bright Angel Trail and his Grandview Hotel and trail. NAU.PH.112

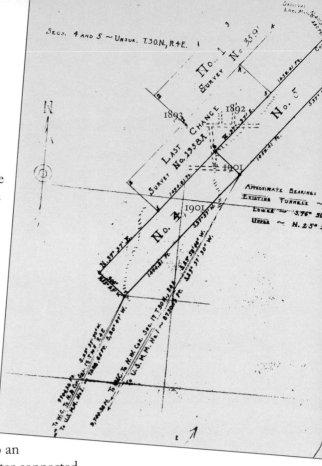

half an hour or more to get it out." Others described him as a well-educated man with an inquisitive mind, of large stature but quiet, soft-spoken, sensitive, and sensible. He judged harshly those who did not pull their weight and became embittered in later years as he perceived the United States Forest Service and railroad interests joined to destroy his business, but was remembered most as the mild "solid citizen" type.[99]

Almost immediately after arriving in Flagstaff, Berry began prospecting with three brothers of somewhat greater fame, Ralph, Niles, and Burton Cameron, with whom he remained long-time friends and formed many formal and informal partnerships through the years. Berry filed a claim and built a temporary cabin at Grandview Point as early as 1888, but not until 1890 did the partners make dozens of claims on and alongside the Redwall Limestone at Horseshoe Mesa, 2,500 vertical feet below Grandview Point.[100] They performed mandatory assessment work in 1890 and 1891, then in 1892 Pete noted in his daybook that *Ralph struck the Bonanzi. We worked on it till 6 PM and Dug it all out. at 4 PM We were raged assed millionaires [.] at 6 PM No millionaire but ragged assed all the same.*[101]

The "bonanzi" was the Last Chance claim, one of four at Horseshoe Mesa later patented by the partners and decidedly more productive than Berry's 6:00 P.M. assessment, as it contained high-grade copper sulfide ore well worth extraction and transport to reduction mills. Berry's claim on the rim near Grandview Point was also patented as an associated millsite and used between 1892 and 1907 as a supply point for the mines as well as a hotel site.[102]

Pete Berry, Ralph and Niles Cameron, Ed Gale, Dave Von Needa, and Bob Ferguson went to work on a three-and-one-half-mile trail from the millsite to the mines in July 1892. Working dawn to dusk, six and seven days per week, they completed the substantial, if frightening, "Grand View Toll Trail" in February 1893. The early trailhead dropped off the rim just north of the original rimside millsite, about a mile southeast of today's trailhead at the Grandview Point parking lot, and in places near the top consisted simply of logs chained to a cliff face. About 1902, the partners built today's upper trail to an inner-canyon millsite and Berry later connected the new upper segment to the old lower trail at the top of the Coconino Sandstone to allow a safer descent for tourists. It is the route taken by today's hikers.[103]

Berry and the Camerons did not become millionaires, but earned some money from their Horseshoe Mesa mines in the early and middle 1890s since ore in upper levels averaged 30 percent copper and contained fair amounts of gold and silver. These rich veins produced a seven-hundred-pound nugget of over 70 percent copper which the partners sent to the Chicago World's Columbian Expositioin in 1893. On a more mundane level, the men led eight to ten ore-laden mules from mesa to rim each day, then drove one-ton wagon loads over the stage road to Flagstaff for railroad shipment. In 1895, Berry and the Camerons organized their claims into the Grand Canyon Copper Company

Above: Contiguous copper claims atop and alongside Horseshoe Mesa, including the "bonanzi" Last Chance claim, ca. 1905. GRCA 14075
Below: Note the mule train (upper left) about to start up the Grandview Trail, and various bunk houses and cook shacks scattered on the mesa. Page Spring is at the base of the leftmost trail.
Seaver Center 84–4 (8596) P–4142

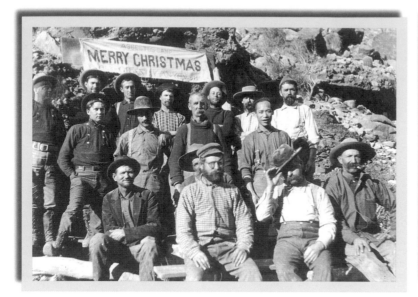

Miners at Asbestos Camp, ca. 1903. Very few mines within Grand Canyon could support large payrolls but some, like those owned by the Canyon Copper Company on Horseshoe Mesa, 1902-07, employed several dozen miners and muleskinners.
NAU.PH.568-3360

Pete and Martha Berry in the modestly decorated interior of the Grandview Hotel. Huntington Library 9744

and stepped up production, ultimately shipping 140 railroad carloads during their ownership. In 1902, they sold the mines, trail, and millsite while the selling was good to Henry P. Barbour of Chicago, who turned around and sold everything to John H. Page and a similarly named concern, the Canyon Copper Company.[104]

The Canyon Copper Company under its general manager, Harry H. Smith, expanded operations between 1902 and 1907 by sinking new shafts and erecting new buildings on Horseshoe Mesa to supplement corrals, miners' quarters, and blacksmith shop built earlier by Berry and his partners. The new firm shipped over one thousand tons of 30 percent copper ore when fluctuating prices dropped below fifteen cents per pound, and lower-grade ore when prices rose higher. They sent altogether perhaps one hundred thousand dollars worth of rock to El Paso, but expenses began to exceed revenues within a few years and when copper dropped to twelve and one-half cents in 1907, the mines closed for good.[105]

Despite the bustle of mining activity at Grandview Point, Pete Berry diversified his interests to take advantage of growing numbers of Grand Canyon vacationers. In 1892, he replaced the earlier temporary structure with a formidable log building, and continued to improve it until by 1897 he had completed the Grandview Hotel, a rambling but respectable two-story lodge of native ponderosa pine logs. Pete and Martha decorated the rustic interior with Navajo blankets, Hopi crafts, and simple homemade furnishings.[106]

The Berrys boasted that the Grandview was the "only first-class hotel at the Grand Canyon." The "first-class" label might be debated, but it certainly was the best decorated and roomiest hotel from 1897 until the Santa Fe's El Tovar Hotel opened in 1905. Rimside facilities during these years consisted of simple canvas tents, tent-cabins, and nondescript frame hotels run by Bill Bass at Bass Camp, James Thurber and J.H. Tolfree at Hance Ranch, James Thurber then Martin Buggeln at the Bright Angel Hotel,

and Ralph Cameron at Cameron's Hotel and Camps. Considering the competition, the Berrys' boast may well have meant something to contemporary vacationers.

Mining at Horseshoe Mesa and tourism at the Grandview Hotel and Hance Ranch, coupled with regular stage service from Flagstaff, the fastest growing regional community, made the southeastern rim the center of Grand Canyon activity during the 1890s. Flagstaff's *Coconino Sun* newspaper reported in 1896 that fifty-one visitors rode down the Grandview Trail in one ten-day period.[107] These visitors and others who came to the Berrys' establishment in escalating numbers enjoyed fair accommodations and spectacular views for two dollars per day, meals prepared by a European chef, surrey tours along the rim for a dollar, and saddle trips along the Hance, Tanner, and Grandview Trails for about three dollars. Discovery of Grand Canyon Caverns beneath the western rim of Horseshoe Mesa in 1896, plus the genuine interest early visitors expressed for sharing the

Grandview Trail and Horseshoe Mesa with picturesque miners, enhanced vacationers' visits.[108]

Activity at the southeastern rim was rapidly eclipsed after 1901 when the railroad arrived, but Pete and Martha Berry, like the Bass family far to the west, were not ones to give up their livelihood without a struggle. Pete reacted to the transportation revolution by opening a free stage line from the railroad depot to the Grandview Hotel. After the Canyon Copper Company bought them out in 1902, the couple put up a three-story frame building on their adjacent 160-acre homestead and opened it as the Summit Hotel. The Berrys and Harry Smith decided to combine their efforts and run the two hotels, only thirty yards apart, as the new Grandview Hotel from 1903 to 1907, with Smith as manager, Martha as head cook and housekeeper, and Pete as chief muleskinner and guide.[109] Advertising brochures during these years boasted a post office, complete canyon library, oversized fireplaces, steam heat in every room, good beds, excellent cuisine, baths, and

Left: Guide and tourist on the Grandview Trail near the top of the Coconino Sandstone, ca. 1905. GRCA 15830

Right: Grandview Hotel with nearby tents and guests, 1899.
Sharlot Hall Museum BU-H 7040P

Nearing retirement at Ralph Berry's homestead: Martha, Pete, unknown woman (likely Ralph's wife), and Ralph. GRCA 6935

pure spring water, as well as scenic trails and unlimited views of the canyon, forest, and distant Painted Desert.[110] Continuing competitive pressure exerted by the Santa Fe and Fred Harvey companies along with declining copper prices forced all Grandview ventures to close in 1907. The Berrys remained, however, to serve the few visitors who happened by on the old stage road and others who took Fred Harvey rides along the rim. In 1911, they and the copper company reopened the hotel but soon ran into more financial difficulties. The Berrys attempted to subdivide their homestead and offered a free lot to anyone who would build a home and cistern in apparent efforts to create a town competitive to Grand Canyon Village, but there were no takers. With pressure from creditors and offers from the Santa Fe for the Grandview properties ranging from twenty-five to thirty thousand dollars, they had no choice but to sell. They would not succumb, however, to the company that had run them out of business.[111]

In 1913, Berry sold his homestead and Summit Hotel to millionaire newspaperman William Randolph Hearst for forty-eight thousand dollars. Berry at the same time brokered the sale of Canyon Copper Company properties, including two patented millsites on the rim, the Grandview Hotel, and Horseshoe Mesa mining claims, to Hearst for an additional

twenty-five thousand dollars. Both hotels closed in 1913, but Pete and Martha remained as Hearst's caretakers and as occasional tourist hosts through 1917.[112]

In 1919, Pete and Martha Berry moved about five miles southeast of Hearst's rimside properties to the fifty-acre homestead of Pete's son, Ralph. When Ralph died of influenza in the same year, they remained at his ranch entertaining family and earning a little money from trapping and trade in Navajo rugs. Martha died in 1931 and was buried at Grand Canyon Cemetery. Pete joined her in death and resting place the following year.[113]

The Berrys lived long enough to gain enormous satisfaction from Hearst's purchase of the Grandview properties. The Santa Fe and Fred Harvey companies, as well as the forest service and later park service, did not know what to make of the influential millionaire who enjoyed taunting them with rumors of luxury hotels and other grand developments on his two hundred acres of prime real estate. Hearst tore down the original Grandview Hotel in 1929 and later donated some of its logs to Mary Colter's Desert View Watchtower project, but hung on to the properties and continued to suggest imminent projects of his own. Despite these provocations, which federal managers considered threats, he never used the land for other than cattle grazing and occasional visits.[114]

Hearst's game continued for more than two decades until the park service employed an obscure law in 1939 to condemn the properties and force a sale. Indignant, Hearst sent a battery of attorneys into the ensuing legal battle and recruited local media and Coconino County officials to his side. Newspapers called it a park

PIONEER VERSUS PARK SERVICE TRAILS

The location of early trails into Grand Canyon followed geologic faults and erosional contours with grades that allowed animals and people to descend without sliding to their deaths. American Indians after millennia of accessing inner-canyon resources wore so many paths that the canyon's most diligent hiker, Harvey Butchart, in four decades of weekend explorations, discovered more than a hundred and surely did not find them all. Explorers, geologists, pioneers, and cattlemen improved some of these—perhaps two dozen—to reach grass, water, and mineral deposits on inner-canyon benches and favorable crossings of the Colorado River. Where Indian footpaths might be eight inches wide or less with hand holds and ladders for hair-raising descents, the later developers with pick, shovel, and sometimes black powder sought a continuous grade that allowed livestock to reach bottom. Prospectors-turned-tourism-operators sometimes improved these paths to two-foot widths to lessen fears of a few paying visitors.

The National Park Service arrived just as spiraling tourist numbers coincided with advanced trail-building technology. Park superintendents with trained engineers considered limited construction funds, visitation demography, state-of-the-art building techniques, and increased concerns for visitor safety before settling on an overall strategy to abandon most pioneer paths to concentrate on refurbishing the canyon's central travel corridor. An important task, and one that contrasts pioneer and modern trails, entailed reconstruction of the Bright Angel Trail.

When the park service finally acquired the trail in May 1928, they found a path that had already evolved during the pioneer period from a Havasupai route to the initial efforts of Pete Berry and his partners. Buckey O'Neill had spent a little time and money clearing, reducing gradients, and rerouting the trail, including the trailhead, about 1897, and Ralph Cameron had invested as much as thirteen thousand dollars between 1898 and 1903 to upgrade the path and extend it to the Colorado River. Cameron's trail by 1903 was in fair shape for adventuresome tourists riding imperturbable Missouri mules, but hardly resembled today's comparative boulevard.

The pioneer trail as improved by 1903 left the rim more or less as it does today from Kolb Studio, but quickly plummeted down the slope immediately east of today's first tunnel in switchbacks with 40 percent grades. It continued this way to a point below the later second tunnel, where it swung west of the fault drainage and intersected with Dan Hogan's Battleship Trail before returning east to the top of the Redwall. Here it descended Jacobs Ladder, a narrow ledge blasted from the sheer cliff face with reinforcement on the downslope and sunken log tread. It was a heart-pounding descent for well-dressed, inexperienced eastern tourists who had to dismount to lead their animals gingerly down to the cliff base where they could remount and follow the boulder-strewn drainage to Indian Garden. In about 1908, Cameron bored today's second tunnel and rerouted the trail through it to reduce overall grades.

The trail to the river as completed by Niles Cameron and others in 1899 veered east on the Tonto Trail then descended the west slope of what was then called Salt Creek, crossing the drainage and following its east side until bisecting today's trail through the Vishnu schist. It then nosedived in an infamous set of tight switchbacks known as the Devils Corkscrew to reach Pipe Creek just south of the mining adit seen along today's trail—Cameron's Magician copper claim and Alder millsite. (This old alignment from Indian Garden to Pipe Creek is today revealed by extant poles of the 1935 transcanyon telephone system.) Early visitors simply continued within the creekbed to the river, passing along the way another Cameron-controlled feature, the Wizard copper claim and Willow millsite, evidenced today by another mine shaft on the left. Once at the river, one could do little more than row across in a shallow-draft rowboat to gain Bright Angel Creek more than a mile upstream, camp out at the mouth of Pipe Creek, or about-face for the return trip.

With acquisition of the Bright Angel Trail, park superintendent Minor Tillotson and park engineer C.M. Carrel first considered its role, if it were to have one, within the scheme of a central corridor trail system. The 6.8-mile-long Yaki (South Kaibab) Trail had been completed in 1925 specifically to obviate the Bright Angel. That seventy-thousand-dollar, four-foot-wide, state-of-the-art freeway had been chiseled out of whole rock where no trail had gone before, and offered panoramic views as it led directly to the brand new Kaibab suspension bridge and recently reconstructed North Kaibab Trail. Some argued for the sufficiency of these trails and abandonment of the dilapidated Bright Angel, but counter-arguments concerning its strategic location, popularity, and potential as a south side alternate won out. Tillotson and Carrel scheduled total reconstruction in three separate projects.

The first 1.82-mile segment which completely bypassed the Tonto Trail-Salt Creek alignment got underway in November 1929. Trail crews used tons of powder, compressed-air jack-hammers, as well as picks and shovels to manufacture a new trail through Tapeats Narrows along Garden Creek to the top of the Vishnu Schist, then blasted down and across Salt Creek perpendicular to the old trail to a lower point above Pipe Creek, then down a new Devils Corkscrew at maximum 16 percent grades to the creekbed. Construction costs totalled nineteen thousand dollars.

The second project ran from October 1930 through May 1931 as crews at Indian Garden and the Kolb Studio worked toward each other to reconstruct the upper trail. Allocated thirty thousand dollars for this segment, Carrel chose a completely new alignment in order to reduce grades to an average 13 percent (17 percent maximum), retaining only the path of Jacobs Ladder which required extensive blasting to bring the ledge out to the standard width of four feet. Crews "shot through" the upper tunnel, built earlier by Cameron to access Mallerys Grotto, and routed the trail through it in a wide arc to gain the easiest grade possible above the Coconino Sandstone. Carrel added downslope, dry-rubble retaining walls and water breaks for safety before running out of money.

Civilian Conservation Corps recruits did their part toward upgrading the trail by obliterating the old upper one and one-half miles of switchbacks—which, nonetheless, can still be discerned from the Trailview pullout along West Rim Drive—and building the trail shelters still seen today at Three-Mile Resthouse, 1935; Mile-and-a-Half Resthouse, 1936; the river, 1936; and Indian Garden, 1937. Then in February 1938, a park crew completed reconstruction along Pipe Creek from the base of the new corkscrew. This seemingly simplistic segment required blasting a new trail above flood stage in sheer granite cliffs some 75 percent of its distance to the river, cost twenty thousand dollars and took four and one-half months to complete.

The Bright Angel when finished in 1938 ended at the western terminus of the Colorado River Trail, a strategic two-mile connector path dynamited from solid granite between 1933 and 1936 by Company 818 of the Civilian Conservation Corps. These young men, who were stationed at Phantom Ranch during winters to work on the trail and at the North Rim in summers, expended forty thousand pounds of powder, ten thousand special jack bits, five air compressors, ten jackhammers, and tens of thousands of hours to join the Bright Angel and South Kaibab Trails near river level. Today's "silver bridge," built in the mid-1960s to carry the transcanyon water pipeline from Roaring Springs to Grand Canyon Village, added the last bit of travel flexibility, cutting a half mile or so from the journey between Phantom Ranch and Indian Garden. In 1981, all four trails comprising Grand Canyon's central corridor were designated a National Recreation Trail within the National Trails System, and have recently been nominated to the National Register of Historic Places.

Note: See map on page 98.

Photo (previous page): GCRA 277

service land grab; county supervisors called it Nazism and "Russian tactics of the lowest denominator"; federal courts called it legal and set the sale price at eighty-five thousand dollars in 1941.[115]

In 1959, the park service removed the dilapidated Summit Hotel and other Hearst buildings at the rim, but left mining structures on Horseshoe Mesa to crumble on their own.[116] Today's visitors will find nothing of a pioneer nature at Grandview Point, but can hike Pete Berry's historic Grandview Trail and poke around scattered mining debris on the mesa and at its base along the path to Page Spring. Upper portions of the trail display extensive log rip-rap retaining walls and cobblestone tread, examples of some of the finest and most imaginative trail construction undertaken at Grand Canyon during the pioneer period.

SOUTHCENTRAL

As John Hance and the families of Bill Bass, Pete Berry, James Thurber, and J. H. Tolfree developed mining claims and modest tourist facilities beside Grand Canyon's southwestern and southeastern rims, men seeking similar opportunities arrived at its central corridor. Prospectors probed the Tonto Platform for minerals, convenient transport routes between rim and river, and crossings to the north side. They discovered few deposits worth exploiting, but found, improved, and extended a Havasupai footpath which would become the primary tourist trail to the inner canyon. By the turn of the century, high-grade copper deposits in a direct line south from this central location toward Williams led to a railroad, which guaranteed that nearly all future development at the

South Rim would take place at today's Grand Canyon Village.

Settlement history at the southcentral rim unfolds within this outline of European-American events, but the first individuals known to live in the vicinity were the family of Vesna "Big Jim."[117] Within Havasupai lifestyles, extended families often spent summers away from the tribe's Havasu Canyon village, preferring the solitude of minor canyons with perennial springs. For generations, perhaps centuries, Big Jim's family held traditional rights to the acres surrounding abundant springs at Indian Garden, due north of today's village and three thousand vertical feet below the rim. They slept in wickiups beside the springs, set wildfires to condition the soil, irrigated a small plot of peach trees and vegetables, and filled stacked-stone bins in nearby cliffs with emergency food supplies.[118]

Big Jim was born at these springs in the 1850s. As an old man he recounted that about 1863, when he was a child, his family travelled to Prescott to confirm rumors that whites had moved into the region.[119] To reach the nascent town, they climbed out from Indian Garden, as they had each autumn, along a centuries-old footpath up natural breaks in the Redwall Limestone and Coconino Sandstone caused by the one of the region's prominent geologic features, the Bright Angel Fault. The first prospectors to follow this path in the late 1880s would note decayed log ladders at several troublesome spots as well as Indian pictographs, still seen today along the trail and just beneath the

The Berrys' three-story Summit Hotel beside the original Grandview Hotel, ca. 1905. Seaver Center 7720C P-4129 (85-86)

Big Jim, the person longest associated with Grand Canyon's pioneer era.

GRCA 5543

*Louis Boucher's Dripping Springs Camp
after the turn of the century.* GRCA 7735

rim at Mallerys Grotto.[120]

For nine decades following his first exposure to whites, Big Jim interacted extensively with many individuals of the new culture as they approached then settled at the South Rim. His life story is sketchy, however, written in brief asides of prospectors, tourism operators, and park administrators, often in the context of helping early settlers find their way within the region he knew so well or as a later tourist curiosity. He continued the traditional lifestyle for most of his life, an independent shadow amid growing numbers of tourists, moving between his summer home at Indian Garden and winter homes on the rim, including a cabin at Supai Camp and another near Rowe Well. He was also known to farm a little at Pasture Wash near Bass Camp.[121]

Big Jim's mobility was not at all unusual, since early white settlers and Havasupais mingled freely. Admittedly, most pioneers took whatever land they wished and stereotyped tribal members as a cheap labor force or tourist attraction, but they accepted individuals' regional habitation rights and thought highly of many, especially Big Jim.[122] By the 1920s, he had become a headman among his people and a local celebrity among residents at Grand Canyon Village. A tall man of stately bearing—park superintendent Minor Tillotson described him as "a picturesque character"—he often came to town wearing a frock coat, top hat, and official decoration given him by a canyon tourist, King Albert of Belgium. Big Jim remained near the southcentral rim into the late 1940s, while relatives including grandson William Little Jim continued to live at Supai Camp at least until the 1950s.[123]

Louis D. Boucher, a native of Sherbrooke, Quebec, Canada, was one of the first European Americans to enter Big Jim's domain, arriving between 1889 and 1891. Boucher no doubt prospected all along the Coconino Plateau and Tonto Platform, but by 1891 chose to make his home far beneath the canyon edge at Dripping Springs, about nine miles west of the Bright Angel Fault. With help from another prospector, Edward Murphy, he built the Silver Bell Trail (today's Dripping Springs Trail) from the rim to this perennial water source where he set up a small tent camp and corral. Within a few years, he built the Boucher Trail to the river through Long Canyon (renamed Boucher Canyon) and established a second camp about a mile from the river, where he located a copper mine, built several stone cabins and outbuildings, and planted a small garden and orchard.[124]

Boucher's contemporaries knew him by his given name, but later writers labeled him the Hermit, apparently because the inoffensive bachelor chose to live alone and remained aloof of power struggles waged by friends at Grand Canyon Village. A retiring nature and eccentric appearance—as a white-hatted, white-bearded man riding Calamity Jane, his white mule sporting a silver bell necklace—may have contributed to the epithet. Actually, during his twenty-year residence, Boucher frequently interacted with other early residents and entertained guests at his isolated inner-canyon homes. He also worked with Pete Berry and John Hance as a hired hand and tourist guide and with Niles Cameron as part-time manager of Ralph Cameron's Indian Garden Camp.[125]

During the 1890s, Boucher worked several claims along his trail system while occasionally leading tourists to his camps. After 1901, when the railroad brought visitors in greater numbers, and encouraged by the success of friends Pete Berry and Ralph Cameron, he began to promote his camps, trails, and guide services in a limited way.[126] Although he earned little, if anything, from mining, Boucher managed to meet expenses through the 1900s with his small tourism business and wage work.

Louis Boucher abruptly left the canyon after 1909. In that year, he negotiated with the Santa Fe and Fred Harvey Company to sell his trails and camps. The Santa Fe had expressed interest in buying his rights in order to circumvent Ralph Cameron's control of the Bright Angel Trail, but the deal fell through because Boucher proved too difficult a negotiator or the trail and camps did not fit the company's needs. In either event, the railroad purchased only the upper portion of his trail and he soon moved on to

Mohrland, Utah, occasionally returning to visit Pete Berry at the Grandview Hotel.[127]

While Boucher explored the region immediately west of the Bright Angel Fault, he undoubtedly bumped into another prospector, Daniel Lorain Hogan. Born in Syracuse, New York, on 9 August 1866, Hogan ended up in Flagstaff in May 1890 and spent his first Arizona autumn prospecting along the Bright Angel Fault. With companions Jeffrey Sykes and Charles McLane, he transported supplies from Flagstaff to the head of Big Jim's trail by following the Grandview stage road and old Moqui Trail as far as Rain Tank, then tracing cattle tracks north to the rim. The men unloaded a frame-and-canvas boat and lugged it as far as Indian Garden where they built a stacked-stone cabin with canvas roof to serve as a winter home. The craft never made it to the river, but the men swam across near the mouth of Pipe Creek to prospect lower Bright Angel Creek. Hogan returned in 1891 with several friends to complete the first known rim-to-rim-to-rim backpacking trip through the central corridor.[128]

During his first excursion in winter 1890-91, local Havasupais, perhaps Big Jim himself, led Hogan to some telltale green mineral stains within an obscure side canyon, 1,100 vertical feet below the rim at Maricopa Point. Although he

Ralph Cameron's Indian Garden Camp, 1905. NAU.PH.568.5704

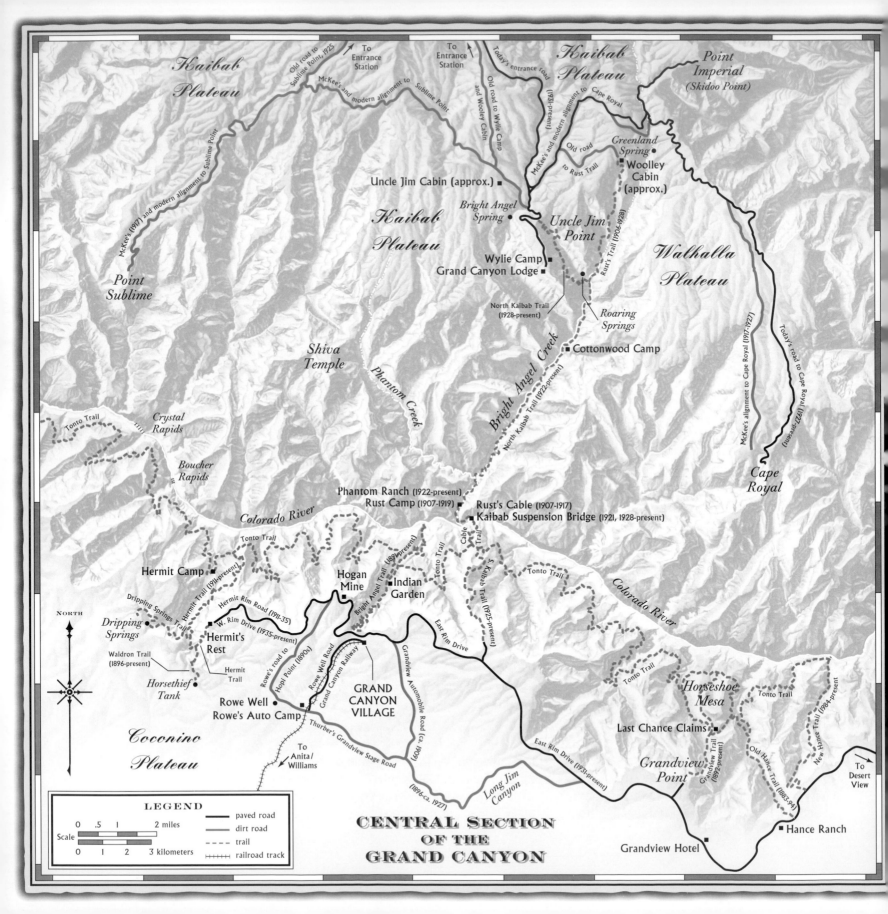

Kaibab Plateau

Old road to Sublime Point, 1925

To Entrance Station

To Entrance Station

McKee's and modern alignment to Sublime Point

Old road to Wylie Camp and Wooley Cabin

Today's entrance road (1931–present)

Kaibab Plateau

Point Imperial (Skidoo Point)

McKee's and modern alignment to Cape Royal

Old road to Rust Trail

McKee's (1917) and modern alignment to Sublime Point

Point Sublime

Kaibab Plateau

Uncle Jim Cabin (approx.) ▪

Greenland Spring ●

Woolley Cabin (approx.) ▪

Bright Angel Spring ●

Uncle Jim Point

Rust's Trail (1906–1928)

Walhalla Plateau

Wylie Camp ▪

Grand Canyon Lodge ▪

●

Shiva Temple

Phantom Creek

North Kaibab Trail (1928–present)

Roaring Springs

Bright Angel Creek

▪ Cottonwood Camp

Crystal Rapids

Tonto Trail

North Kaibab Trail (1922–present)

McKee's alignment to Cape Royal (1917–1927)

Today's road to Cape Royal (1927–present)

Boucher Rapids

Cape Royal

Colorado River

Phantom Ranch (1922–present)
Rust Camp (1907–1919) ▪

Rust's Cable (1907–1917)
▪ Kaibab Suspension Bridge (1921, 1928–present)

Tonto Trail

Cable Trail

Tonto Trail

Hermit Camp ▪

Hermit Trail (1911–present)

Hogan Mine

▪ *Indian Garden*

Bright Angel Trail (1891–present)

Tonto Trail

S. Kaibab Trail (1925–present)

Tonto Trail

Colorado River

Dripping Springs Trail

Hermit Rim Road (1911–35)

Dripping Springs ●

▪ W. Rim Drive (1935–present)

Waldron Trail (1896–present)

Hermit's Rest ▪

Hermit Trail

East Rim Drive

Tonto Trail

Horsethief Tank ●

Rowe's road to Hopi Point (1890s)

Rowe Well Road

Grand Canyon Railway

Horseshoe Mesa

Tonto Trail

NORTH

Rowe Well
Rowe's Auto Camp ●

GRAND CANYON VILLAGE

Grandview Automobile Road (ca. 1909)

East Rim Drive (1931–present)

Grandview Trail (1892–present)

Last Chance Claims ▪

Old Hance Trail (1883–94)

New Hance Trail (1984–present)

Coconino Plateau

To Anita / Williams

Thurber's Grandview Stage Road

Long Jim Canyon

Grandview Point

To Desert View

(1896–ca. 1927)

CENTRAL SECTION OF THE GRAND CANYON

Grandview Hotel

▪ Hance Ranch

continued to prospect westward within Hermit Basin, Hogan returned to this spot in 1893 with partner Henry Ward to file the Orphan copper claim and thereafter focused on development of his Orphan Mine.

Like most early miners and tourism operators, Hogan spent the better part of a year in Flagstaff where he worked in construction and for a brief period as deputy sheriff. When things got slow in the big city, he returned to the canyon to extract a little copper ore and make improvements to his claim. In 1895 or 1896, Hogan, Ward, and another prospector named Charlie Carruthers located a millsite associated with the Orphan Mine a few miles west of Rowe Well along the old trail to Supai. Here they built Horsethief Tank to store water for stock and milling operations, and several years later built the Waldron Trail from the tank down to Hermit Basin which connected with Boucher's Silver Bell Trail to Dripping Springs.[129]

The Orphan claim comprised 20.64 acres of scenic property less than two miles west of today's village. Four acres abutted the canyon edge while the remainder plummeted to the mine's principal shaft in the cliff face.[130] Hogan constructed two trails to access his diggings, the safer of the two using the upper one and one-half miles of the Bright Angel Trail before skirting Maricopa Point another three and one-half miles to the mine site. Named the Battleship Trail for a nearby geologic formation, this path was renovated by later mining interests in 1951 and 1952 but has since been abandoned.[131] Hogan's second "trail" consisted of a rope along with peg holes and toe holds chiseled into the side of the cliff from his mine shaft to the rim above. Though shorter than the Battleship Trail by a long shot, few other than Hogan chose this

harrowing route which he dubbed "the slide" and others called the Hummingbird Trail.[132]

After serving in Cuba with Theodore Roosevelt's Rough Riders, Hogan returned to Flagstaff and in March 1906, patented the Orphan Lode Mining Claim with his financial backer, Charlie Babbitt. Other partners came and left but as struggles for ownership unfolded at Grand Canyon Village and at Grandview, Hogan remained slightly to one side and stubbornly clung to his claim. In 1936, he opened a tourist facility on his few rim acres that evolved under several lessees, among them Will Rogers Jr., to include twenty cabins, a trading post, curio shop, and saloon. This private complex, long coveted by the park service since it represented unregulated development so close to the village, operated as the Grand Canyon Trading Post (Hogan's original venture) and later as the Kachina Lodge and Rogers' Place.[133]

Federal restrictions and rationing during the war years limited tourism and ended Hogan's enterprise, but in 1947, he managed to sell the property for fifty thousand dollars to Madeleine Jacobs, who reopened the tourist facility as the Grand Canyon Inn. In 1951, Jacobs learned that the dark ore which Hogan had kicked aside for decades as a nuisance contained some of the richest uranium in the Southwest. In 1953, she sold the mineral rights to Western Gold and Uranium Inc. which extracted as much as seven thousand tons of U_3O_8 ore per month into the 1960s. The company purchased the entire property in 1959, reorganized as Western Equities, and in 1962 sold it to the federal government.

Hogan's direct route to the rim along "the slide," also known as the Hummingbird Trail, 1913.
NAU.PH.568.3056A

Above: As late as the 1940s, one could buy four acres of rimside real estate and 16 acres of the canyon itself (with a mine thrown in) for $25,000 or less. Grand Canyon Inn, 1954. GRCA 2703

Center: Plat map of property. GRCA

Below: Dan Hogan's sign photographed in 1931. GRCA 15

Mining operations continued until 1969, however, and Western's mineral rights did not expire until 1987.[134] Today, 1950s structural ruins at Dan Hogan's Orphan claim suffer from benign neglect and are targeted for demolition. They cannot be accessed since the park service has fenced the low-level radioactive area, but can be viewed from the path leading to the Powell Memorial off West Rim Drive.

Dan Hogan, who owned the Orphan for almost sixty years, saw his nearly worthless copper claim produce millions in uranium under subsequent owners. Despite working in an unventilated radioactive mine shaft for decades he lived to the age of ninety, dying of pneumonia at the veteran's hospital in Sawtelle, California, on 12 May 1957.[135]

As Louis Boucher and Dan Hogan built trails and filed claims a few miles west of today's village site, a former buffalo hunter by the name of Sanford H. Rowe arrived from the Great Plains region with an eye to developing a tourist business in the same vicinity. Rowe wanted to open a trail to the canyon, but first needed to find or develop a water source, the challenge faced by every South Rim pioneer. In the company of an English tourist named Harry Hankley, Rowe rode to the Grandview area in June 1890 to consult with the Hull brothers and John Hance, who told him of a cattle tank near the head of Big Jim's trail. Big Jim happened into Hance's ranch about the same time and guided Rowe to the head of his trail, to several springs within Hermit Basin, and to a soggy piece of ground along the old Moqui Trail

three miles south of the rim. At the latter site, Rowe found water a few feet beneath the earth and developed what is still known today as Rowe Well.[136]

As one of very few sources of "living water" along the South Rim, Rowe's well was a priceless asset. He had used his homestead right elsewhere, however, so he had to find a way to possess the site. He settled on the standard ploy of filing for a five-acre millsite, but also had to locate a credible mineral claim somewhere nearby to justify the mill. Rowe was not an experienced prospector and had no interest in mining, but managed to relocate an abandoned claim a few miles to the south and stockpiled sufficient copper ore near the well to appease authorities. Later, he caught on to the simplicity of early land acquisition and expanded his holdings by claiming then patenting the five-acre Highland Mary millsite (1914), Highland Mary lode (1916), and two nearby twenty-acre parcels named the Lucky Strike and Little Mamie (1917).[137]

With ample property and a dependable water source for a tourist camp, Rowe purchased Bill Bass's livery and intermittent stage line which had run from Williams to Bass Camp. In 1892, he began to drive tourists to his wellside camp where he had built a few simple cabins and likely pitched a few tents. By April of that year, Rowe offered his guests guided horseback trips to the rim at Rowes Point where he built another overnight shelter. He also worked out a deal with Pete Berry and Ralph Cameron that allowed him to guide guests down the Bright Angel Trail, completed as far as Indian Garden the prior year, in exchange for water from Rowe Well. Sanford Rowe thus became the first tourism operator at the southcentral rim and the first person to use

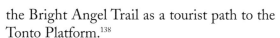

the Bright Angel Trail as a tourist path to the Tonto Platform.[138]

Rowe's business did well through the 1890s, but probably suffered for a decade or more after 1901 when the railway bypassed his camp in its run to the canyon edge. Bill Bass managed to secure a flag stop a few miles south along the tracks in 1902, but Rowe could only glimpse tourists' eager faces pressed against window glass as daily trains chugged past his property toward accommodations at the rim. Despite rerouting the terminal segment of the Ash Fork Road in the 1890s so that it passed through Rowe Well, and the evolution of an informal road beside the railway tracks from Williams after the turn of the century, few were willing to pay fifteen to twenty dollars for a hellish all-day stage ride when the railway charged only four dollars for a comfortable three-hour trip. Rowe's operation faced oblivion, but …

On 6 January 1902, the first automobile to Grand Canyon pulled up to Pete Berry's hotel just three months after the first locomotive arrived, and although the problem-plagued jaunt seemed anything but auspicious, it in fact presaged Sanford Rowe's salvation and the railway's ultimate eclipse. Ironically, the Santa Fe sponsored the automotive adventure when it con-

vinced the editor of the *Los Angeles Herald*, Winfield Hogaboom, to make the promotional ride in company with Santa Fe photographer Oliver Lippincott (who owned the vehicle), retired newspaperman Tom Chapman, and local guide Al Doyle. When the steam-powered auto—a 2,200-pound, eight-horsepower, Toledo Locomobile—left Flagstaff along the stage road towing a trailer crammed with gasoline, water, and assorted supplies, its crew expected only a three-and-one-half-to four-hour trip. After two and one-half days of mud baths and assorted breakdowns, however, the party ended up thirty miles short of their goal without gasoline, water, and food. The escapade ended ignominiously when Pete Berry and a span of mules towed the vehicle and occupants the final distance to Grandview.[139]

The automobile era had arrived, but motorists did not follow in noticeable numbers until after 1910 when they breathed new life into Sanford Rowe's business. With three of the four South Rim access roads (such as they were) converging near his property, Rowe gave up his Bright Angel Trail and Hopi Point activities, by then congested with rimside concessioners anyway, to develop an automobile camp on the southeast corner of his Little Mamie claim.

Left: Rowe Well Auto Camp in 1931. The site today is marked by the ramada on the west side of Rowe Well Road.
NAU PH R91

Center: Sanford Rowe's original camp, three miles south of the rim. The larger structure later served as the Rowe Well U.S.F.S. ranger cabin. Rowe built a trail then road (left) that leads to Hopi Point and today serves as a fire road.
Huntington Library

Right: Ed Hamilton and friend Bill Donelson at Rowe Well, 1930s.
NAU.PH.90.9.137

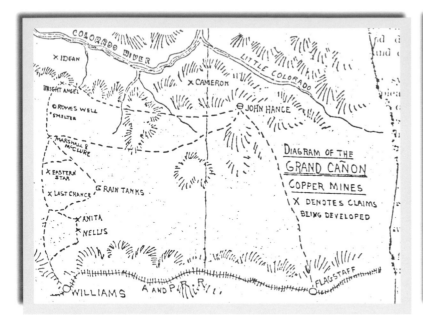

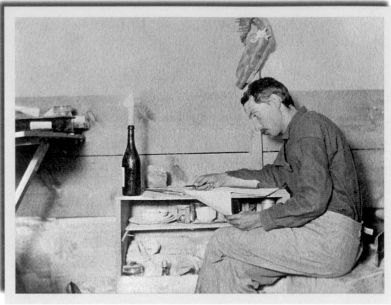

Maude J. Hamilton and her husband, Edward, joined with Rowe to pipe well water down the hill to this spot along the road and build a garage, filling station, general store, and campsites to take advantage of the growing number of motorists. Although it remained a tourist camp three miles from visitors' ultimate destination, the three partners managed to make a living charging only a dollar per day for cabins and nothing for auto campsites, lights, water, and wood.[140]

The Hamiltons continued to operate the automobile camp into the 1930s, expanding services to include a bowling alley, coffee shop, saloon, dance hall, and motel. The new facilities proved a favored "watering hole" for village residents more than tourists, however, and deteriorated by the 1950s. The National Park Service acquired the properties in 1956 and demolished the last of the buildings in 1961.[141] Today, one can still follow Rowe Well Road south from West Rim Drive toward Forest

Road 328, passing the picnic ramada which marks the Hamilton store and garage sites.

About 1924, Sanford Rowe left the business to his partners and moved to Coconino Basin east of Grand Canyon National Park where he established Rowe Ranch. Here the aging pioneer businessman opened a filling station and store along Fred Harvey's Navahopi Road to Cameron, then sold the property to J.C. Schweikart shortly before his death in 1929.[142] Today's motorist can glimpse the buildings at Rowe Ranch from Arizona Highway 64, about four miles east of the park boundary and one-half mile south of the highway.

In 1896, James Wilbur Thurber joined the cast of independent prospectors and tourism operators milling about the central rim. Thurber, like Rowe, cared little about mining but seemed determined to gain the lion's share of South Rim tourism. In the prior year with J.H. Tolfree he had purchased John Hance's ranch and tourist operation near Grandview and taken over the stage line from Flagstaff. Not content to compete with Pete Berry's Grandview Hotel, Thurber extended the stage road west a dozen miles through Long Jim and Shoski Canyons to the area of Rowe Well, then north to the canyon edge. In 1895 or 1896, he hired Andy Lester and Bill Motz to build a cabin at the site of today's Bright Angel Lodge, the first known structure of any type erected at Grand Canyon Village.[143] In the latter year, Thurber opened the Bright Angel Hotel and tent campground at this remote site, the first tourist facility to be built along the southcentral rim.[144]

• • •

James Thurber and Sanford Rowe might have spent their declining years peacefully entertaining a few guests amidst the ponderosas and along the juniper-studded central rim if not for the arrival of the affable, ambitious William Owen "Buckey" O'Neill. O'Neill, born on 2 February 1860 in St. Louis, Missouri, earned a law degree by the age of nineteen, but rather than accept an offer to practice law in Washington, D.C., he migrated to southern Arizona in 1879 where he wandered from town to town looking for something resembling a career.

Newspapers seemed promising in the freewheeling atmosphere of territorial Arizona, so Buckey went to work as a typesetter and later editor for the *Phoenix Herald*, became the first editor of the *Phoenix Gazette*, and served a brief stint as reporter for John Clum's *Tombstone Epitaph* before settling in Prescott in 1883.

In Prescott, the territorial capital and Yavapai County seat, Buckey started his own paper, the *Hoof and Horn*. Running a newspaper would keep most men occupied, but O'Neill found time to practice law, write freelance frontier yarns, work on and off as district court recorder, and serve as probate judge, county sheriff, superintendent of schools, and tax assessor, all before his thirtieth birthday. In 1894 and 1896, he became a standard bearer for the Populist Party as candidate for territorial delegate to the United States Congress, but like most of the party's national candidates, lost both elections. While working his many jobs and dabbling in local, state, and federal politics, he decided to amble north to do a little prospecting.[145]

Grand Canyon had seen few the likes of Buckey O'Neill. All who ventured to the largely undeveloped region in the 1890s were imaginative and optimistic, of course. All worked hard to make any kind of living from the grand crevasse. But none shared the unshakable confidence and promotional abilities of the thirty-one-year-old O'Neill. Juggling election campaigns and odd jobs between 1891 and 1897, Buckey found time to prospect along the central trail corridor, stake a few mining claims, buy others, and occupy two log cabins: one beside Thurber's Bright Angel Hotel which he used as an office; the other, a bunkhouse just a few yards back among the ponderosa pines.[146] Up to this point, O'Neill differed little from others who had staked claims and settled for simple structures, but when he came upon a long belt of copper deposits running

south from Rowe Well toward Williams, his imagination leapt to the future. Why not build a railroad to connect the Atlantic and Pacific line at Williams to his new found copper claims, then continue it another twenty miles to tourism facilities at the rim?[147]

O'Neill was not the first to envision or attempt to build a railroad to the South Rim. Federal laws dating to the 1860s and Arizona territorial laws of 1887 and 1889 offered numerous incentives like lucrative rights-of-way, ample depot acreage, and generous tax breaks. Since 1886, businessmen in Flagstaff and Williams had offered encouragement and money to anyone who would lay track, formed corporations to do so themselves, and gone so far as to run surveys from both towns.[148] The United States Congress proved more than willing to help, introducing bills nearly on an annual basis to grant rights-of-way over federal lands to the South Rim.[149] All schemes had failed, however, due to the cost of laying track and operating a railway calculated against potential returns. Capitalists simply had not yet grasped Grand Canyon's economic promise.

Opinions changed in the years 1894-97 as Buckey O'Neill lobbied tirelessly in Flagstaff and Williams for local money and back East for the really big dollars required. He first convinced the New York investment firm of Lombard, Goode and Company to form the Tusayan Development Company and buy up claims proliferating along the mineral belt between Williams and Rowe Well. Residents of northern Arizona had known of the deposits since the 1860s and had formed the Francis and Grand Canyon mining districts to establish local mining regulations. Not until early 1897, however, when Buckey began working his recent discoveries, did others start to excavate the rich copper ore. By July 1897, the Tusayan company had purchased four of the most promising camps and continued to buy more, lending credence to the mining boom.[150]

As O'Neill and Lowry Goode created the economic reason to build a railroad, namely, ore shipment, they also worked to attract investment from the Santa Fe Pacific Railroad Company. Santa Fe managers refused to back Lombard, Goode and Company, a firm they considered unstable, but the two men convinced a number of local businessmen to put up about two hundred thousand dollars to finance the Santa Fe and Grand Canyon Railroad Company. Formed in July 1897 with "General" Buckey O'Neill and other locals as directors, the new corporation completed rolling-stock agreements with the Santa Fe, hired local surveyor William Lockridge to run a survey from Williams to the rim, and began laying track in June 1899. They reached the Tusayan copper mines at Anita and trains began to roll in March 1900, but could not continue to the rim because of financial problems. The Anita mines proved moderately profitable for a few high-grade miners but could not produce the revenues needed to fund a railroad, despite completion of a Williams smelter that promised to funnel all South Rim ore shipments along the new railway.

Local investors along with Lombard, Goode and Company lost their shirts in the ensuing financial reorganization. Not surprisingly, the Santa Fe Pacific stepped in to purchase the nearly completed railroad, formed its subsidiary Grand Canyon Railway, and finished laying track to the rim in September 1901.[151]

A railroad had finally arrived at the South Rim after fifteen years of unfulfilled dreams, but the man who more than any other made it happen did not live to see a single mile of track. True to his political interests and restless spirit, Buckey O'Neill took office as mayor of Prescott in January 1898, then immediately stepped down to join the First Volunteer Cavalry, the Rough Riders, and left Arizona to fight with Teddy (Theodore) Roosevelt and Dan Hogan in the Spanish-American War. As his corporation back home negotiated shared-use details of the new railroad with the Santa Fe Pacific, thirty-eight-year-old Captain Buckey O'Neill fell with a bullet through his neck in a charge up Kettle Hill on 1 July 1898.[152]

• • •

With the formation of the Santa Fe and Grand Canyon Railroad Company in mid-1897, and as rails haltingly inched their way northward between 1899 and 1901, the entire complexion of South Rim development began to change. Although isolated geographically, Grand Canyon residents remained sharply attuned to national events and well understood what railroads had meant for Yellowstone, Yosemite, Mount Rainier, and other scenic

destinations in the West. They surmised that the Santa Fe Pacific held financial reserves akin to the Northern Pacific, Southern Pacific, and Union Pacific Railroads which were developing and promoting western parks, and believed it held the same vision. A railroad would mean efficient and low cost transport of mineral ores, making marginal copper and asbestos claims more valuable, perhaps even profitable. More importantly, it would bring tourists in big numbers.

No one understood the implications better than Pete Berry and Bill Bass, whose mining claims and tourist operations lay, respectively, thirteen miles east and twenty-five miles west of the point where the railroad would touch the rim. Berry might hope that the line would continue through the Grandview area as the federal right-of-way allowed, but neither wasted time before running stages to Anita where the track ended in early 1900, and later to Coconino Siding where construction again halted temporarily. Tracks never continued to the Berrys' Grandview Hotel, however, and despite their free stage service, Pete and Martha watched their business wither over the following decade. The railway simply worked as a vacuum to suck the life out of far flung South Rim enterprises and to draw cross-country travelers directly north to the depot adjacent to the Bright Angel Hotel.

Although managers of the Santa Fe Pacific probably knew they would end up with the railroad long before acquisition in 1901, they did not immediately try to

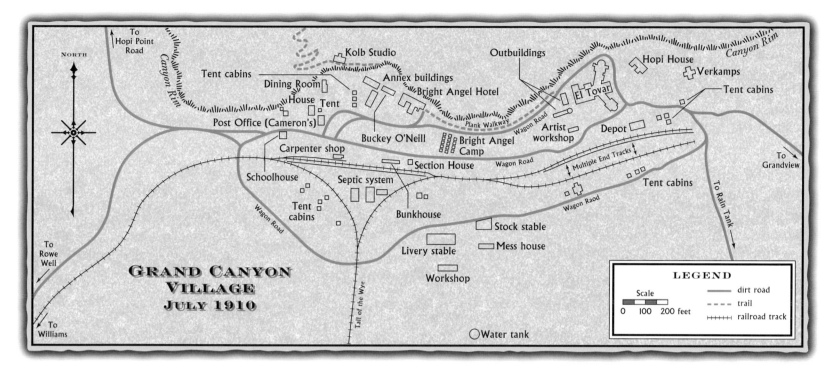

GRAND CANYON VILLAGE JULY 1910

LEGEND

Scale

0   100   200 feet

dirt road
trail
railroad track

monopolize tourist developments at the rim. This gave Bass and Berry an initial opportunity to adjust and also promised to benefit James Thurber as the tracks made a beeline for his hotel. Thurber, perhaps because the railway had doomed his stage business from Flagstaff or because he did not like the way competition was shaping up, sold out to Martin and Emma Buggeln in June 1901, however, just as rails approached the rim. Buggeln continued to run the Thurber stage to a temporary railway terminus at Coconino Siding (between Anita and the village) until September, after which all stage businesses to the southcentral rim became obsolete.[153]

The railroad's arrival also promised to benefit a man who had come to Grand Canyon as a prospector in the late 1880s

but played a secondary role in its development until he saw ample rewards on the horizon. Ralph Henry Cameron, born in 1863 in Southport, Maine, moved to Flagstaff in 1883. Like Bill Bass who arrived in the same year, by the same means, also looking for a life, Cameron proved an intelligent and energetic man. During the 1880s he worked at the Flagstaff sawmill, as a railroad clerk, as manager and later owner of a merchandise store, and as agent for the Haywood Cattle Company. In these same years he ran a few cattle of his own and six thousand sheep on shares while building a reputation for dependability. Like Buckey O'Neill, Cameron gained the approbation of working-class people. Coconino County supervisors appointed him their first county sheriff in 1891, a job he held

for several terms through the 1890s, and his popularity would ultimately lead to elective positions as county supervisor, territorial delegate to the United States Congress, and United States senator.[154]

Although significant events awaited him after the turn of the century, Ralph Cameron began his relationship with Grand Canyon like most everyone else, as a hopeful prospector. In 1890, he filed on the Last Chance copper claim on Horseshoe Mesa with his brother Niles, who had arrived from Southport in 1886, good friend Pete Berry, Ed Gale, and others. The partners developed that lucrative claim under Berry's management while a third Cameron brother, Burton, arrived from Maine and joined Niles and Ralph in their canyon forays. The brothers used trails down Hance Creek and along

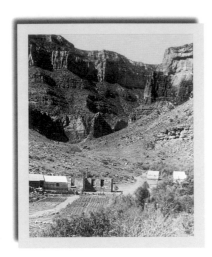

Ralph Cameron's Indian Garden Camp soon after the turn of the century. Dan Hogan's roofless stone building is flanked by tourism facilities and irrigated garden. This photograph looks south up the Bright Angel Fault toward the developing Grand Canyon Village.

NAU.PH.568-3355

the Tonto Platform to range west with other prospectors like John Hance, John Marshall, William Ashurst, Curtis McClure, Robert Ferguson, and Millard Love. In March 1890, Ashurst and Marshall filed a water claim at Indian Garden, which they called Grand Canyon Springs, and informed the county that they planned to build a trail from that point up the Bright Angel Fault to the South Rim, but turned their claim and trail rights over to Cameron and Berry later in the year.[155]

As at their Grandview properties, Cameron delegated trail construction to the harder working Berry, who, with Niles Cameron, Ferguson, McClure, and Love, began work with pick and shovel in late December 1890. They followed portions of Big Jim's footpath along the Bright Angel Fault to complete a passable trail down to Indian Garden within two months, and in January 1891, Berry recorded the Bright Angel Toll Road with Yavapai County. Although filed in Berry's name alone, each of the men involved, including Ralph Cameron who had hired Love to do his work for him, agreed on equal ownership.[156]

Through the 1890s, just about everyone who had anything to do with Grand Canyon regularly used the Bright Angel Toll Road, sometimes called the Cameron Trail but most often referred to as the Bright Angel Trail. Cattleman George T. Campbell, William Ashurst, and others used it to drive livestock down to pasturage; dozens of prospectors found it convenient as a central passage to the inner canyon; Sanford Rowe led his guests along it and beyond Indian Garden to Plateau Point; and James Thurber's guests likely hiked and rode the trail as well. Berry and others maintained it infrequently as it was just one of several travel routes, and the partnership did not

charge for its use even though they had every right to do so. The trail took on a whole new importance by early 1898, however, when all realized that a railway would approach within a hundred yards of the trailhead.[157]

In 1898, Buckey O'Neill as an agent of Lombard, Goode and Company hired men to improve the Bright Angel Trail, apparently as part of the company's overall plan to develop tourism and mineral deposits near their envisioned town of "Lombard." Buckey was perhaps unaware that Berry had registered the toll trail or may have thought the partners had abandoned it, but in either event, made substantial improvements. Had O'Neill lived longer and the Lombard company remained afloat they might have had something to say about ownership. As it happened, Berry retained control and hired Curtis McClure, John R. Holford, D.W. Barter, and Niles Cameron to extend the trail to the Colorado River in winter 1898-99, ostensibly to access minerals on the north side of the river but more likely to secure the route with more mining claims and prepare for longer tourist excursions to the river.[158]

As the century elapsed and while the railroad remained a dozen miles short of the rim, Ralph Cameron pounced on the opportunity to gain a large slice of the approaching tourism bonanza. When Pete Berry's ten-year trail franchise expired in January 1901, Coconino County readily extended it the allowable five years, recognizing that hardly a dime had been earned since its construction. The partners then willingly transferred the franchise to Cameron who spent several thousand dollars refurbishing the trail to tourist standards. Cameron also bought out various mining claims at Indian Garden, erected a few tents, and opened his inner-canyon tourist facility named Indian Garden Camp. By early 1903, he had acquired the relocated Red Horse stage station, added a second story, set up a dozen adjacent tents, and opened Cameron's Hotel and Camps within a stone's throw of Martin Buggeln's Bright Angel Hotel.[159]

One might guess that Buggeln and Cameron, though competitors on adjacent properties, would work out agreements to serve the tourism boom approaching the southcentral rim. The anticipated rush by rail promised more than any one operator could handle and other small businessmen like Pete Berry and J.H. Tolfree who competed in the Grandview area seemed to get along peaceably enough. What developed, however, was not a case of cooperative concessioners but a bitter fight lacking only gunplay in the streets of the developing village. Battles that would not subside for nearly three decades erupted from a variety of circumstances, not the least of which entailed questionable concepts of free enterprise within public lands undergoing increasing levels of federal protection. When the dust finally cleared, the pioneer period at Grand Canyon's South Rim had passed.

AFTER THE RAILROAD

Despite persistent efforts of United States senator Benjamin Harrison of Indiana, who introduced legislation in 1882, 1883, and 1886 to set aside Grand Canyon as a "public park," Arizona's major scenic attraction remained an unregulated segment of the public domain until 1893.[160] In that year, Harrison as president of the United States set aside Grand Canyon Forest Reserve, with management in 1897 delegated to the Department of Interior's General Land Office, an agency more concerned with disposing of public lands than preserving them. In 1905, however, care of the nation's forest reserves transferred to the Department of Agriculture's United States Forest Service, headed by its conservationist chief forester, Gifford Pinchot. The reserve became Grand Canyon National Forest in 1907, but not until 1908, when President Theodore Roosevelt proclaimed the most scenic portion (958 square miles) to be Grand Canyon National Monument, did the canyon receive its first real measure of protection.[161]

South Rim pioneers followed these escalating regulatory trends with keen interest and through the years used whatever means the government allowed to secure their piece of the natural wonder. Many simply built structures on a desired piece of land and did nothing to gain real possession, an illegal but tolerated practice known as "squatting." A few, like John Hance and Pete Berry, filed homesteads and many more filed mineral, millsite, and water-right claims. All knew that national monument status would remove the canyon from private entry, but those who understood federal policy believed that prior rights would be respected.[162] Thus, in the first years of the twentieth century, old-timers who glimpsed the economic future staked a flurry of claims, leaving questions of legitimacy for later resolution. By 1908, ownership patterns beside the South Rim and astride roads and trails resembled a patchwork quilt. These private inholdings would irritate federal managers for another eighty years, but in the loosely regulated

Bright Angel Hotel ca. 1910 with the cabin attributed to Buckey O'Neill on the right. The frame hotel would be torn down and replaced in the 1930s by today's Bright Angel Lodge, but O'Neill's cabin remained as a guest lodge. Note the locomotive smoke in the background. NAU.PH.568.11338

GRAND CANYON'S ARCHITECT

Grand Canyon is graced with the buildings of several significant architects including Francis Wilson's railway depot, Gilbert Underwood's North Rim lodge, and Charles Whittlesey's El Tovar Hotel, but none approach the body of work produced by Mary Elizabeth Jane Colter (1869-1958), architect and/or decorator of eight historic South Rim structures and the sole remaining inner-canyon resort.

Colter attended the California School of Design and simultaneously worked as an apprentice during the 1880s when there were few men and almost no women licensed within the architectural profession. Upon graduation in 1890, she returned east to teach until the Fred Harvey Company offered her work in the Southwest in 1902, a relationship which lasted forty-six years. Colter began as an interior designer, but soon moved up to designing structures, building models, and drawing elevations and floor plans which passed to Santa Fe architects who created working drawings from her efforts. Though she probably never received a license, Colter was in every sense an architect, and a conscientious one who spent more time at project sites than her male contemporaries, sometimes supervising the laying of individual stones.

All who knew Colter described a determined person who used diplomacy to get what she wanted from management yet often harangued co-workers and workmen; a perfectionist in pursuit of her own southwestern vision. The Spanish Mission Revival style emerging during the years of her training sparked that vision, but she redirected her insight toward an "indigenous" or "pueblo revival" style of natural constructions, often mimicking American Indian ruins and design motifs. All of her buildings and interiors at Grand Canyon reflect a restrained though sometimes eccentric use of rustic materials: the Hopi House, her first architectural assignment, 1905; El Tovar, interior only, 1905; the Lookout, 1914; Hermits Rest, 1914; Phantom Ranch, 1922; the Watchtower, 1932; Bright Angel Lodge, designed in 1916 but built in 1935; the Fred Harvey Men's Dormitory, 1936; and a new Women's Dormitory for the Harvey Girls, 1937, later renamed Colter Hall.

Colter submitted designs for a lodge to be built at Indian Garden in 1916, but the Camerons still controlled the site in that year and the project was never revisited after the park service took possession. Instead, they accepted her design for an inner-canyon complex near the mouth of Bright Angel Creek which the Harvey company labeled Roosevelt's Chalet but Colter renamed Phantom Ranch. Today, look for the four cabins of mostly native stone and the north half of the central dining lodge to imagine her original effort, which cost the railroad twenty thousand dollars to build. Fred Harvey and the Civilian Conservation Corps completed most of the remainder of today's ranch by the mid-1930s.

Recommended Reading:
Virginia L. Grattan, *Mary Colter: Builder Upon the Red Earth* (Grand Canyon Natural History Association, 1992)

Above: Mary Colter, ca. 1910. GRCA 16950
Below: Lobby of El Tovar Hotel, ca. 1906.
University of Arizona

first decade of this century ignited quarrels primarily among private interests.[163]

Ralph Cameron, not content with gaining toll rights to the Bright Angel Trail from Pete Berry, used the favored method of filing multiple mining claims to secure not only the property he would need to run his tourist operations, but most of the fabric comprising the ownership quilt. He and brother Niles, who went so far as to suggest a bogus homestead in their mother's name, tied up small parcels at Indian Garden, along the Bright Angel Trail, and on the rim until scarcely a square mile between Grandview Point and Hermit Basin lacked a Cameron claim.[164] Some say he eventually controlled thirteen thousand acres in this manner, a high estimate, perhaps, considering the twenty-acre size restriction, but an accurate indication of his mania to control the canyon's southern edge.[165]

When the Grand Canyon Railway approached the Bright Angel Hotel in 1901, Santa Fe managers had every reason to believe that they would dictate future development. One can imagine their confidence as employees of the Santa Fe Pacific, a corporation with money, political connections, and the precedent of western railroad development on its side. They likely did not know Ralph Cameron's intentions, perhaps had not even heard of the man, but in either case would not think twice of rolling over him or anyone else who stood in the way of their own plans for corporate gain.[166]

Railroad managers may have first detected Cameron's presence in late 1901 when they surveyed a twenty-acre depot site and stumbled upon his nearby mining claims. By some oversight, or in deference to James Thurber, or perhaps because he wanted to leave room for the rails to end near his trail, Cameron had not

Bright Angel trailhead, 1910. Niles Cameron with hand extended, on the right; Ellsworth Kolb standing at the end of the building. Pete Berry, Ralph Cameron, Lannes Ferrall, and Coconino County operated the toll trail from 1891 to 1928. NAU.PH.568.3.19.67

claimed the land surrounding the Bright Angel Hotel. The railroad promptly surveyed this site and built a small frame depot below the hotel's doorstep. Because Thurber had not bothered to claim the land when he built his hotel in 1896, the Buggelns, who had only recently purchased Thurber's improvements, became Santa Fe land tenants. Martin Buggeln readily secured an operating agreement, however, since the railroad had not yet built its own tourist facilities.[167]

Ralph Cameron's subsequent hostility toward the Santa Fe Pacific and the Buggelns appears to have originated from a deal Cameron had arranged with Buckey O'Neill's defunct Santa Fe and Grand Canyon Railroad Company, wherein the tracks would end at a Cameron tourist hotel near the Bright Angel trailhead—an agreement he felt had been abrogated when the recently formed Grand Canyon

Grand Canyon Hotel

MARTIN BUGGELN, Proprietor.   AMERICAN PLAN   WILLIAMS, ARIZ.
Livery in Connection

Money, Jewelry and Valuables must be deposited in the Office Safe, otherwise the Proprietors will not be responsible for any loss.

September 24 1904 — Continued

NAME	RESIDENCE	Time	Rooms

The Buggeln family, like the Farlees and a few other canyon tourism operators, provided accommodations and a livery at one of the A & P Railroad towns. Most, like Buggeln, also ran stage lines to move customers from town to the South Rim and back. The Buggelns purchased the Grand Canyon Hotel at Williams before 1901.

NAU.PH.R12 #3

Railway chose to make other arrangements with the Buggelns.[168]

Cameron was not about to be left staring at each train's caboose while passengers alighted at the Bright Angel Hotel. In April 1902, he filed his Cape Horn and Golden Eagle mining claims which secured the Bright Angel trailhead and deliberately overlapped the depot site, effectually challenging its legitimacy.[169] With his own hotel placed as close to the depot as possible, but carefully to one side of the surveyed boundary, Cameron pressed his competition in 1903 by erecting a gate at the Bright Angel trailhead then notifying Buggeln that henceforth all mounted users would pay a one dollar toll.[170]

Several lawsuits immediately followed. The Santa Fe naturally contested Cameron's recent claims which encroached on their prior and legitimate survey, and Martin Buggeln, backed by railroad resources, filed suit against Cameron's tolls. The court decided in 1906 that Cameron could keep his claims to the extent that they did not overlap the depot site; thus, he failed to dislodge the railroad but kept his adjoining property and facilities.[171] Jurors in the latter suit, the Territory of Arizona vs. Ralph H. Cameron, determined that Pete Berry had not the right to transfer the toll franchise to Cameron in 1901, but the decision confirmed Berry's right to collect tolls and he simply continued to allow his friend to run the show. Buggeln and

the Santa Fe followed with an injunction and another lawsuit to strip the franchise from Berry, but the Arizona Supreme Court upheld the lower court's decision in late 1904.[172]

These early bouts ended largely in Ralph Cameron's favor, but he did not appreciate being placed on the defensive in any contest. He soon evidenced his regional popularity as well as willingness to use political influence in a personal struggle when residents of Coconino County elected him to their Board of Supervisors in 1904. Taking office as board chairman in 1905, Cameron immediately announced that the Grand Canyon Railway had never paid county taxes and belonged on the tax rolls. As the Board of Supervisors also sat as a territorial Board of Equalization, with Ralph Cameron acting as chairman and brother Burton serving helpfully as county tax assessor, the railroad found itself assessed forty-five hundred dollars per track mile which amounted to about three hundred thousand dollars per year.[173] The Santa Fe naturally challenged the ruling and easily won its case in 1909, since legislators eager to promote development at the turn of the century had always afforded generous tax exemptions to any railroad concern and its successors. Cameron, who would eventually promote a few railroads himself, likely understood that he would lose this sideshow but no doubt enjoyed the cost, inconvenience, and five-year legal distraction visited on railroad management.

As the parties continued to wrestle for control of the Bright Angel Trail, Cameron proved time and again that he and the county could more than match railroad attorneys. When trail ownership passed to Coconino County in January 1906 upon expiration of Berry's five-year extension, Cameron, still serving on the

Board of Supervisors, tried but failed to secure the franchise for himself. He succeeded, however, in having it awarded to Lannes L. Ferrall who was allowed to keep all tolls in exchange for trail maintenance. Since Ferrall happened to be a close Cameron friend and manager of his rimside hotel, railroad managers fumed over the decision. They mounted a flank attack by applying for a federal permit to operate the trail. But when the county warned the federal government to steer clear of the issue, then ordered its sheriff to protect the trail from interlopers, the United States Forest Service—managers of the reserve yet unsure of the legitimacy of Cameron's mining claims—chose not to enter the debate.[174]

Foiled in its attempted end run, the Santa Fe filed suit against the county, claiming that it did not have the authority to operate a toll trail or to transfer its franchise. The corporation might have won this argument except that while the case languished in the courts, Cameron, in probably his most flagrant use of politics as a personal tool, convinced the Arizona territorial legislature to pass the "Cameron bill," an act that gave the county exactly the needed authority! Federally appointed Territorial Governor Joseph H. Kibbey quickly vetoed the bill on advice of the Department of the Interior, but the popularly elected territorial legislature unanimously overrode his veto. Securely in control of the trail by 1907, Coconino County again infuriated the railroad by using its new authority to transfer the franchise from Ferrall to Cameron for 10 percent of collected tolls, despite the railroad's counter-offer to give 70 percent to the county as well as provide liability insurance. The Arizona Supreme Court heard testimony on this issue for the nineteenth time in January

1909, when it finally ruled that Coconino County owned the Bright Angel Trail.[175] Ralph Cameron, staunchly supported by county and territorial everymen, had won his seven-year battle against big business, but until this year, the federal government had hardly entered the fray.

• • •

Early legal and political warfare to control the south-central rim inevitably spilled over into day-to-day tourist operations within the emerging South Rim village. Nervous residents toted sidearms and Cameron's people distributed leaflets charging that

… the main object of the [Santa Fe] is to ruin Cameron. They are in the habit of circulating false statements intended to injure Cameron and his business [because] tourists are constantly abandoning the Bright Angel hotel for Cameron's … You will find that Cameron's rooms and even his tents are neater and cozier than the Bright Angel hotel can show you … When you can get as good and better from a private individual—are you going to patronize a greedy, grasping corporation?[176]

Westerners often carried guns, and subtlety was not a strong suit of competing businesses one hundred years ago, but visitors must have realized that this was not all western wear and frontier rhetoric. Cameron's employees stood on the depot platform encouraging disembarking passengers to hike down Bright Angel Wash a little ways to Cameron's hotel rather than step up to an inferior establishment, and carried luggage at no charge. Competition proved intense.

Interior of a Santa Fe Pullman coach, 1901. It is not hard to understand why tourists preferred a three-hour ride to the canyon in this type of conveyance for four dollars over a one- or two-day stage ride costing fifteen to twenty dollars.

Kansas State Historical Society

Left: Cameron's Hotel and Camps, with the canyon's first schoolhouse beside the railroad tracks, ca. 1910. The hotel's bottom floor was reassembled from a stage station along the Grandview road about 1900. Cameron built the second floor by 1903. The entire building remained intact as a post office (first floor) and postal employee residence (second floor) from 1910 until sold to the Fred Harvey Company about 1932 when the top floor was removed. Today it is one of the Bright Angel Lodge cabins.
NAU.PH.568.5629

Right: Tent-cabins of Bright Angel Camp on the east side of Bright Angel Hotel. Martin Buggeln managed the hotel and camp until 1906 when he sold out to the railway. Tent-cabins remained until the 1930s when today's wood cabins were built in conjunction with the new Bright Angel Lodge.
NAU.PH.568.5666

The Buggelns in partnership with the Santa Fe had the early edge in supplying tourist services. Contrary to Cameron's advertisement, in 1901 the Bright Angel Hotel consisted of the log-and-frame main building's eight guest rooms and large reception room enlivened with Navajo rugs, a large fireplace, rocking chairs, and piano for songfests, along with a frame annex of six rooms, each with two beds, a stove, dressing table, and Navajo carpets. Services included a restaurant with edible, if not gourmet, food, a curio shop, rental stock, surreys, an adjacent livery, and guided trips down the Bright Angel Trail. From 1901 to 1903, the Buggelns charged two to three dollars for a room, three dollars for a horse, and five dollars for a guide while paying the railroad 40 percent of profits in 1902 and 60 percent in 1903.[177] To earn their percentage, the railroad delivered a plentiful number of customers each day, provided supplies and water free of charge, added rooms to the hotel, and erected several rows of tidy tent-cabins that the Buggelns also managed as Bright Angel Camp.

Despite gearing up for the rush, however, demand for services immediately surpassed what the railroad and Buggelns could offer.[178]

Ralph Cameron met some of the surplus demand when he completed Cameron's Hotel and Camps soon after the rails arrived. He offered similar services at slightly lower rates, charging a dollar and a half to three dollars for a room, only a dollar for a horse, and four dollars for a guide. He also served simple meals and offered buggy rides along the rim and guided trips down the Bright Angel Trail. Nearly two thousand tourists per year registered at his rim-top establishment in 1904 through 1906, while others patronized his tent camp at Indian Garden. Tolls collected from mounted trail users (pedestrians traveled free) amounted to three thousand dollars in the 1907 travel season alone.[179]

While the Buggelns and Cameron operated the earliest hotels, tent camps, and liveries following the railroad's appearance, others who would have more lasting relationships with

*A few of the earliest non-miner
residents at Grand Canyon Village,
1902. Left to right: Ellsworth Kolb, an
unnamed clerk employed by the Bright
Angel Hotel, and hotel trail guide
Jim Lane.* GRCA 9090

*Ralph Cameron, son, and wife,
Ida Spaulding, on the Bright Angel
Trail, 1907.* NAU.PH.568.7081

*Mr. and Mrs. Ted Straight, Ralph
Cameron employees, ca. 1903.* GRCA 9091

Left: Kolb Studio, soon after completion in 1904. The Kolbs built their studio on one of Ralph Cameron's rimside mining claims—a convenient point from which to collect tolls for Cameron and photograph mule parties. Emery Kolb lived here from 1904 until his death in 1976.

NAU.PH.568.1197

Center: Veteran Canyon residents Blanche Kolb and young Edith on David Rust's cable across the Colorado River, ca. 1910.

NAU.PH.568-325

Right: Hubert Lauzon (center) and Emery Kolb portaging at River Mile 246 during their 1911-12 motion picture expedition down the Colorado River.

NAU.PH.568.3356

Grand Canyon arrived to get in on the tourism boom. John G. Verkamp appeared about the time tracklayers reached the rim to open a small curio shop in a tent near the Bright Angel Hotel. Verkamp had trouble selling the Indian arts and crafts he had obtained from various sources, including the Babbitt brothers, perhaps because railroad crowds had not yet arrived. He sold out to Martin Buggeln within a few weeks, but returned in 1905. The store he opened in 1906 still stands and operates just east of the Hopi House under management of John G.'s descendants. By 1910, the Babbitts themselves came up from Flagstaff to open a general store, automotive camp, and grocery.[180] Their family store also dates to the earlier period, though the original building located on the east side of the village disappeared long ago and the second building, which later housed the

town library, burned to the ground in a 1994 electrical fire.

The first train had barely chugged into the depot when a young man from Pennsylvania, Ellsworth Kolb, walked the ties from Williams toward the rim in late 1901. Kolb chopped wood and worked as a porter at Bright Angel Camp at first, but when brother Emery arrived the following year, the two men bought out a Williams photography studio and in 1903 carried the equipment north to shoot the tourists. Evidencing primitive as well as arid conditions in these years, the Kolbs opened their studio in a floorless tent beside Cameron's hotel, used a shallow mine shaft as a darkroom, and developed prints with murky water obtained from cattle ponds as far away as Rain Tank. In 1904, they upgraded to a small frame studio on Cameron's mining claim at the Bright Angel

94

NRGC 8678

trailhead which, with additions in 1915 and 1925, still stands as one of the oldest buildings within Grand Canyon National Park. In 1906, they completed a wood frame photo-finishing cabin near the springs at Indian Garden, but for years thereafter Emery still had to jog the nine-mile round trip from rimside studio to inner-canyon cabin—a knee-jerking three-thousand-foot descent and equally heart-pounding ascent—as many as three times each day for the luxury of clean water.[181]

In 1905, Emery married Blanche Bender, and in 1908 daughter Edith was born, probably the first European-American child delivered and for some years the only child to live at Grand Canyon Village where she grew up through the remainder of the pioneer period. Together, Blanche and Edith shared many of the brothers' adventures between and beside both rims, Edith as an infant travelling in her mother's arms or fastened securely within a burro pack. Blanche worked for the Kolb business as retail clerk and bookkeeper, remaining on the job until her death in 1960.[182]

The brothers made history when they recorded the first motion picture of a river trip—their own in winter 1911-12—through Grand Canyon, and earned money for years thereafter showing the film on national lecture tours and at their studio. They also became excellent geographers, having photographed most every rock by 1910, and willingly worked as guides, consultants, and rescuers to river parties and hikers. Ellsworth abruptly left the partnership in 1913 because of a business dispute and moved to Los Angeles, but returned occasionally until his death in 1960. Emery continued to work and live in his studio/home until his death in 1976 at the age of ninety-five, leaving tens of thousands of photographs and several hundred pieces of camera equipment for today's history students.[183] His seventy-three-year residence at the very edge of the abyss is the longest of any person at Grand Canyon Village.

Santa Fe managers had always envisioned better tourist services than small concessioners like the Buggelns, Kolbs, Verkamps, Babbitts, and Cameron could hope to offer. They acted

Left and center: Rustic architecture and American Indian motifs were the norm among early Grand Canyon concessions. Above pictures show the interior (along with plat map) of Verkamps Curios, completed in 1905 and situated east of the Grand Canyon Railway depot grounds. NAU.PH.568.3353; GRCA

Right: Edith Kolb, one of the few children to grow up at Grand Canyon Village during the pioneer era, and the first to cross the wooden suspension bridge that replaced the Rust cable in 1921. NAU.PH.568.157A

AND WHO WERE THE HARVEY GIRLS?

As the Atcheson, Topeka and Santa Fe Railroad Company laid track from Kansas into Colorado, New Mexico, and west across the thirty-fifth parallel, an English immigrant with a taste for fine cuisine, knowledge of railroads, and awareness that the two did not often coincide tagged along. Frederick Henry Harvey (1835-1901) struck a deal with the Santa Fe in 1876—on a handshake alone—to provide fine dining and service to its passengers. By the late 1880s, track-side Harvey Houses elbowed depots every hundred miles or so along the entire Santa Fe line and were soon joined by a dozen fine hotels, most within northern Arizona and New Mexico. Since Harvey insisted on the finest service and foods—oysters on the half shell, sea turtle, sage-fed grouse graced many menus—and charged only seventy-five cents per meal, Harvey Houses ran at a perennial loss. Nevertheless, the Santa Fe built and gladly subsidized the hotels and restaurants within which Harvey operated since Harvey's reputation and that of his waitresses sold railway tickets by the tens of thousands.

Harvey's waitresses became known as the Harvey Girls. Often driven to work by economic need, they responded in droves to Harvey's eastern advertisements for women aged eighteen to thirty, of fine character, good education, clear speech, attractiveness, and neatness. They underwent rigorous training and for the length of their six, nine, or twelve-month contracts lived under strict rules of propriety while working ten-hour days, six and seven days per week. In return, they enjoyed above-average salaries ranging up to fifty dollars per month with free room and board, laundry, and rail passes, as well as job security, geographical mobility, and great pride in their employment.

The first Harvey Girls began work in 1883 and others, more than one hundred thousand all told, continued to fill the ranks until faster trains requiring fewer stops, automobiles, and airplanes severely curtailed the tradition by the 1950s. Many worked at Grand Canyon's El Tovar Hotel and later Bright Angel Lodge, and in the earliest years it was their elegant presence in crisp uniforms as much as railroad pressure that drove pioneer tourist operations to the brink of bankruptcy. Although the single young women shared abysmal living conditions with other village residents during their first two decades, by the 1920s the assignment had become more appealing and recruits often remained for years. Because they worked in an isolated community at the end of the track, Harvey rules concerning fraternization were relaxed and the young women made their own fun riding the trails and staging dances with local cowboys, mule wranglers, stage guides, railway workers, and fellow Harvey employees.

The Harvey Girls helped fill the feminine vacuum in the old West with first-class human beings, who worked not only as premier waitresses but remained when their contracts expired to assume roles as ranchers, homesteaders, teachers, hotel keepers, shop owners, doctors, and frontier wives. These pleasant, educated, hard working, and necessarily confident ladies attracted northern Arizona's men like iron shavings to a magnet, so many folks living in the region today can fondly remember that their mothers and grandmothers were once Grand Canyon Harvey Girls.

Recommended Reading:
Lesley Poling-Kempes, *The Harvey Girls: Women Who Opened the West* (New York: Paragon House, 1989).

Above: A Harvey Girl at work behind a lunch counter. Fred Harvey Collection, GRCA 16153B

on their vision in 1902 when they laid plans for a first-class one-hundred-room hotel on station grounds east of the Bright Angel Hotel. The facility's early working name, Bright Angel Tavern, did not reflect the elegance intended, so in late 1904, they renamed the nearly finished structure El Tovar Hotel for Coronado's lieutenant.[184] Architect Charles Whittlesey's two-hundred-and-fifty-thousand-dollar masterpiece opened in January 1905 with advanced utilities such as steam heat, hot and cold running water, indoor plumbing, septic sewage system, electric lights, and a fire suppression system as well as spacious accommodations that included a large dining room, lounge, art galleries, and recreation rooms.[185]

El Tovar dwarfed and sharply contrasted nearby meager hotels which offered little more than bed, meals, outhouse, and horse, and fulfilled the concessioner's plan to attract affluent visitors. The Santa Fe furthered this strategy by recruiting their long-time service partner, the Fred Harvey Company, to operate the hotel and future railroad concessions. With Harvey's reputation for reasonably priced fine foods, and incomparable service provided by the nationally renowned Harvey Girls, superior accommodations had arrived at Grand Canyon.[186]

El Tovar doubled the number of guest rooms at the South Rim and raised tourist facilities to new heights. On a national level, the elegant four-story building with its stone and log materials reflected transition from ornate victorian country lodges toward a naturalistic rustic style which by the 1920s would gain ascendance in all western national parks.[187] On a local level, it set an informal zoning standard which might persuade builders away from the pioneer vernacular—at best, log and wood

Louis Akin's vision of El Tovar Hotel and Hopi House, painted in 1906.
GRCA 5429B

frame buildings of no particular form—toward more visually pleasing structures. Grand Canyon National Park would embrace the style fully in the 1920s, but in the early 1900s the railroad set the trend and complemented El Tovar between 1905 and 1908 with Mary Colter's adjacent Hopi House as well as rustic utility buildings that still stand along today's Village Loop Drive.[188]

Physical improvements introduced by the railroad are highlighted through contrast to the remainder of the village in the 1900s. Essentially, no official zoning existed during the pioneer period because no government other than a distant and indifferent county seat at Flagstaff might effectively influence growth. Also, both full- and part-time residents knew that their possession of land through squatters rights and mining claims could be disallowed at any

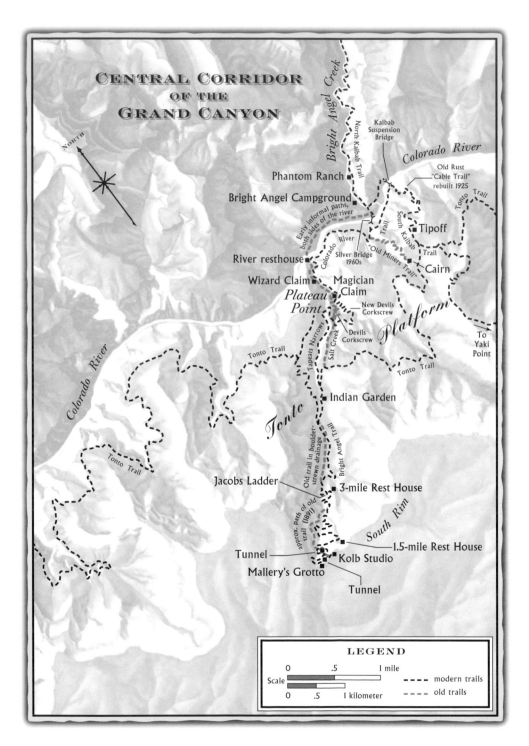

CENTRAL CORRIDOR OF THE GRAND CANYON

moment, thus, few chose to invest in substantial buildings or to care for the landscape. The railroad with its two-hundred-foot-wide right-of-way along the track and twenty-acre depot site had the land, confidence, and money to build for the future, but even its improvements focused on commercial facilities. Initially, they gave little thought to the needs of employees who numbered 22 in 1901, 50 in 1902, and as many as 350 by 1920. Since most worked on a summer seasonal basis for low wages and were nearly as transient as the guests they served, one could hardly expect them to create, of their own volition, a pleasing little cottage town.[189]

The early village in fact resembled a western mining camp. Several roads led to the community from Ash Fork, Williams, and Flagstaff, but all had been built by pioneers to only passable standards and since 1901 had deteriorated from diminished use. Once these wagon ruts reached the village they vanished amid lacework paths approaching scattered facilities. Even as late as 1918, village planner and landscape architect, Frank A. Waugh, wrote that

The present town is without form. The miscellaneous buildings are scattered at random over the land. There are no streets. Two county roads have wandered aimlessly into the territory, where they seem to have lost their way.[190]

As trains steamed slowly up Bright Angel Wash each morning and left in early afternoon, passengers began and ended their vacations by staring through Pullman windows at filth and disorganization permeating the village along the tracks. Workers lived in tents, tent-cabins, wood frame shacks, and even boxcars strung out along the right-of-way. Door yards brimmed with discarded crates and other wooden debris for cook stoves. More than a dozen open trash heaps lay scattered about the village. An assortment of unpleasant scents exacerbated the distasteful visual experience. Crude incinerators spewed fumes into the atmosphere, further choking all who walked on dusty roads and paths and obscuring pristine views when breezes drifted northward. Outhouses dotted the landscape and functioned poorly in thin limestone soil. Liveries, one each adjoining the three hotels, contributed their perfume. Even residents, who lived in a community with little domestic water, must have steered clear of visitors out of common courtesy.

Cattle, mules, horses, and Indian ponies grazed freely throughout the village up to the canyon's very edge, lending not only their associated scents, flies, and flops to the potpourri but their disturbing presence to eastern visitors not accustomed to large animals at close quarters. Gentlemen and ladies in expensive footwear, who wisely kept one wary eye to the ground, bumped into the creatures wherever they walked. As Forest Supervisor W.R. Mattoon observed in 1909

Persons who are city bred, and particularly women, are frightened by the sight of animals with horns at close range, and this feeling is obviously intensified at the brink of a canyon a mile in depth.[191]

Adding to dismal residential conditions resulting from no zoning, no sanitation, plentiful livestock, and little water was the absence of schools, churches, cemetery, affordable groceries, community centers, and any other service intended for residents rather than the vacationing public. The single exception was the post office, a community gossip center that Martin Buggeln opened in 1902 within the Bright Angel Hotel and that continued after 1910 within Ralph Cameron's abandoned hotel.[192]

As the Santa Fe introduced modern facilities and at least a small measure of order to the village by 1908, it found a friend in the United States Forest Service. The railroad's interest in the developing alliance could hardly be clearer. It had bought out the Buggelns in 1906 and had resisted the Kolbs' attempts to make a living since 1903.[193] It brought in nearly all the South Rim's fresh water in tank cars and refused to give or even sell water to anyone it cared to exclude. Railroad managers of course hated Ralph Cameron, who had bested them over the Bright Angel Trail and insolently competed just a few dozen yards west of their Bright Angel Hotel, but they also considered anyone who assisted or even peaceably coexisted with their archenemy to be nearly as bad. The railroad aimed to be the major concessioner at the South Rim and to control others whom it might graciously allow to operate. Federal power could help achieve that goal.

Such arrogance and avarice are easy enough to understand of a "greedy, grasping corporation," but United States Forest Service motivations for supporting a would-be monopolist were a bit more subtle. Since Gifford Pinchot had joined the Department of Agriculture's Division of Forestry in 1898, the agency's overall mission had evolved into one of sustained use of the nation's forests, principally through lumbering, grazing, and mining. When Teddy Roosevelt proclaimed Grand Canyon National Monument, yet retained the forest service as its manager, he reversed the agency's mission in this instance from extractive use to "recreation" and "preservation." These terms hardly had entered the agency's vocabulary by 1908, thus, a management framework within which to implement the new mandate did not exist. Worse, forest service

Private campsite near the South Rim, ca. 1900. Prior to automotive camping in the middle 1920s, most visitors stayed in concessioner accommodations. However, nothing prevented families, prospectors, and others from setting up camp anywhere they chose, which caused some problems of visitor congestion for monument rangers. This family appears settled in for an extended visit.
Huntington Library

Hull Cabin ranger station, 1905. The U.S. Forest Service acquired Philip and William Hull's property after their deaths and closed off Hull Tank to tourist use, severely limiting water availability in the Grandview/Hance Ranch area. During their management tenure, 1905-19, rangers stationed here patrolled southeast and southcentral portions of the monument. GRCA 15792

supervisors well understood that they did not have the money to do much more than prevent trees from burning, and had little indication that Congress would soon loosen the purse strings. An ally—or as they viewed it, a benevolent backer with a plan, deep pockets, and a willingness to work over the long term for the enjoyment of the most visitors—would be heartily appreciated.[194]

That is not to say that forest service employees disliked all prospectors-and-miners-turned-small-businessmen. Rangers had gotten along well enough with these early pioneers, even respected them for opening up the area for their agency's former canyon mission: beneficial extractive use. Pete Berry, though a bitter forest service opponent in later years, admitted that in the early days, forest rangers stopped at the Grandview Hotel to chat and learn more about the canyon. They invariably dropped by at meal time and perhaps indulged Berry's frontier hospitality a bit too often, but were friendly

nonetheless.[195] They commended his hotel and services, lamented the fact that railroad competition had caused the "ill prosperity of the place," and thought of him as a friend. Rangers also liked Louis Boucher and described him as a "man of notable courtesy." They had few problems initially with Bill Bass.[196] Good relations were vital in this sparsely settled region where rangers focused on fire suppression and scattered settlers reported fires, helped fight them, and stored tools that otherwise would have to be packed in from scattered forest service stations at Rowe Well, Anita, and Hull Tank.

Minor problems with pioneer residents began with the permit system for resource use that was implemented just before the turn of the century. Although forest supervisors routinely, and usually without bias, issued permits to everyone throughout their 1905-19 management tenure, just the thought of external controls irked some old-timers who felt they had a prior right to regional resources. The most severe rift,

however, emerged from rampant land fraud committed by nearly all of the canyon's first settlers. Before 1908, rangers cared little about the validity of mining claims and never investigated them since it was not their job to do so. Within a month of Roosevelt's proclamation, however, they began to prowl the monument checking up on claims, and called in General Land Office inspectors when they found irregularities. Men and families who had built their livelihoods on the land in question resented this intrusion. Rangers concluded that the "country was all plastered up with fraudulent mining claims so a person that wants to get anywhere or do anything cannot get any ground."[197]

Left: Forest service ranger George Reed checking up on mining claims at Grandview Point with John Page of the Canyon Copper Company, 1913. Reed was a long-time Grand Canyon ranger who also homesteaded at what is now the town of Tusayan. GRCA 16024

Right: Niles Cameron, canyon prospector, miner, manager at Indian Garden Camp. Niles was a more constant canyon resident than his ambitious brother, intimately involved in South Rim affairs during 1888–1918. NAU.PH.568.8282

By 1910, most residents at the South Rim, other than those associated with the Santa Fe and Fred Harvey Company, held a real dislike for the United States Forest Service and the feeling had become mutual.[198] Aside from the agency's need to implement land-use and facility controls in the face of their new mandate and spiraling visitation numbers, disaffection arose from simple polarization between people drawn to Ralph Cameron's orbit and those who opposed him. The forest service could no longer remain neutral as it had in the 1906 Bright Angel Trail dispute. For example, Niles Cameron complained to his brother in 1909 that rangers, working to improve visitor services, planned to erect a rest house and stables on one of Cameron's Grandview claims, and that if the county sheriff did not chase them off, he would do it with a "No. 12" shotgun.[199] Lannes Ferrall at Cameron's hotel was certain that the forest service served only the railroad and

Harvey company, and reminded his boss that *... every move the Forestry Department makes here in connection with the Harvey outfit involves something that is against our interest ... the Corporation are the only ones that ever get any consideration in the way of concessions on this end.*[200]

In February 1909, mining officials inspected Cameron's claims at forest service request and not surprisingly found most to be farcical. The Department of the Interior consequently rejected nearly all, citing examples of "salting" to make claims appear mineral bearing, erecting a crude arastra at a supposed millsite to crunch a nearby pile of mineral-barren rocks, and leading water to another millsite without bothering to build a mill.[201] Interior declared the faulty claims to be public land within the national monument, and although Cameron would ignore the ruling and retain these claims for another fourteen years, the rift had opened wider.[202] A more important issue arose in May 1909, however, when the Santa Fe realized it would never possess the Bright Angel Trail and laid plans to build a new road, trail, and inner-canyon resort on the Tonto Platform west of the village. They intended to treat Cameron's hotel and toll trail as if they did not exist. Cameron exploded when he learned the news so closely on the heels of Interior's unfavorable mining claim decision.

Cameron's anger actually erupted from the forest service's participation in helping to plan and promote the new facilities. District Forester Arthur C. Ringland and Forest Examiner W.R. Mattoon accompanied the railroad's chief engineer and landscape architect George E. Kessler as they surveyed the monument's first scenic rim drive from the village to a point overlooking Hermit Basin.[203] Working together, the railroad and forest service chose a route almost eight miles long that would offer numerous scenic vistas while preserving the natural setting. Landscape engineering had come to Grand Canyon, and the forest service was enthusiastic about the project since it fit their plans to improve monument roads and trails in an unobtrusive manner. They were ecstatic that the railroad would front the considerable funds required for construction, with the understanding that the federal agency almost certainly would not be able to reimburse them (and never did).

Cameron likely went from angry red to livid purple when he learned that the forest service planned to issue a permit that not only would allow the construction, but also would encourage the railroad to operate the Bright Angel Trail as a free-use trail.[204] Although the agency carefully worded its permission to respect valid interests of county and individuals, its authors knew of Interior's recent decision on Cameron's claims along the Bright Angel Trail and the document appeared a blatant invitation to challenge his control. When Cameron fired a letter to Gifford Pinchot protesting the permit, the forest service delayed long enough to review his objections and check on some of his mining claims along the proposed route. By early 1911, however, they had issued the permit and railroad managers readily accepted the invitation to bypass Cameron, though they did not confront him over the Bright Angel Trail.[205]

Despite Cameron's interference—letters to influential people, injunctions, notices of trespass, and at least one lawsuit—the Santa Fe between 1911 and 1913 built its Hermit Rim Road, Hermit Trail, and Hermit Camp, all along the route trampling over bogus mining claims.[206] Cameron was nothing if not persistent, however, and as an inducement to give up his

fight and future claims in this particular area, the railroad paid him forty thousand dollars in late 1912.[207]

Quality, expense, and landscape considerations of the Santa Fe's Hermit project illustrate why a financially pressed, inexperienced government agency would ally itself with a "grasping" corporation. Hermit Rim Road, though not built for automobiles, proved of higher quality than any highway in northern Arizona in the year of its construction. The water-bound macadam surface, a precursor to later asphaltic surfaces, alone cost forty-five hundred dollars per mile.[208] Hermit Trail easily exceeded the workmanship of all other inner-canyon paths. The L.J. Smith Construction Company built the four-foot-wide path to the Tonto Platform with cobblestone pavement and cement corrugation for dependable traction and added artistically crafted masonry rest stops.[209] The road and trail followed natural paths through rimside

The early forest service was more comfortable managing lumber operations than the national monument. The Saginaw Lumber Company organized in 1894 and built a mill at Williams. Temporary railroads operated just south of the national park boundary during the 1920s. Lumbermen hauled logs on "logging wheels" to a scattered network of hastily laid tracks, then loaded flat cars using hoists. Locomotives pulled the cargo back to the Grand Canyon Railway near Anita for transport to the mill. The park service disallowed commercial timber cutting within the park. NAU.PH.140

*Hermit Camp below Pima Point, 1910s.
A relatively elegant inner-canyon
alternative to Cameron's Indian Garden
Camp, Bill Bass's Shinumo Camp, and
David Rust's camp near the mouth of
Bright Angel Creek.* University of Arizona

junipers and along inner-canyon cliffs, their vol-
canic-cinder and crushed-limestone surfaces
blending harmoniously with geologic formations.

Hermit Camp resembled in form early facilities of Bass, Thurber, Tolfree, and Cameron
with its wood frame dining hall, adjacent tent-
cabins, and stable, but exceeded the quality of
these pioneer establishments. Cabin furnishings
at least were first class, and a Fred Harvey chef
may have helped divert visitors' minds from the
limitations of inner-canyon camps. The railroad
improved the facility a few years later with
telephones, a blacksmith shop, restrooms, and
showers. About 1925, it installed a cable tram
from Pima Point to the camp 3,600 vertical feet
below, which, at 6,300 feet in length, was touted
as the longest single-span cable tram in the
United States.[210] The cable system also represented the only rim-to-inner-canyon tourism
tramway ever built within Grand Canyon.[211]
Hermit Camp improvements ultimately cost
the Santa Fe seventy-two thousand dollars, but
despite its serviceable condition and popularity,
would be closed in 1930 and razed in 1936 after
the National Park Service redirected tourism
along a renovated central corridor from Grand
Canyon Village to Bright Angel Point.

The Santa Fe and Fred Harvey Company
continued to curry United States Forest Service
favor after 1910 by furthering the agency's desire
to upgrade South Rim commercial facilities. The
railroad assigned architect Mary Colter to design
a rustic rest stop at the end of Hermit Rim Road,
and in 1914 spent thirteen thousand dollars to
build the pueblo-revival structure which they
called Hermits Rest. In the same year, they
opened yet another Colter-designed tourist facility named the Lookout.[212] They also upgraded
service and residential facilities with a dormitory

for Fred Harvey managers in 1913, the Fred
Harvey Garage about 1914, and several railroad
executives' homes in 1914.[213]

As the cooperative relationship evolved
between the United States Forest Service and
corporate concessioners, Ralph Cameron's
enterprises took a sharp turn for the worse. The
railroad had banned his solicitors from the
depot and station grounds as early as 1905, but
coincident with its plans to bypass his hotel,
camps, and trail with the Hermit project, it
moved the depot site itself about one-quarter
mile east to the base of El Tovar. They did this
to upgrade the terminal facility and more closely
approach their hotel, but also to get as far from
Cameron's operation as possible. In 1909, they
assigned another of their architects, Francis
Wilson, to design the new depot in a style
harmonious to El Tovar. When Wilson's rustic
structure, today one of only three log depots
still standing in the United States, opened in
1910, the railroad abandoned its original wood
frame structure and left Cameron a bit higher
and drier.[214]

Cameron's Hotel and Camps closed in 1910
because of the railroad's actions and resultant
lack of business, but also because its proprietor
no longer held an intimate interest in its operation.[215] Cameron and wife, Ida May Spaulding,
had never been full-time residents, preferring
like many to live in Flagstaff and occasionally
commute to look after canyon interests. After
assuming office as Arizona delegate to the
United States Congress in 1909, Ralph spent
even less time at the national monument,
entrusting operations to brother Niles, Clarence
Spaulding, Lannes and Louisa Ferrall, and a
dozen or so other employees who kept him well
informed and received their directions by

telegram and letter.[216] Close communications,
however, proved insufficient to keep the rimside
hotel and tent camp afloat.

Cameron's election to the United States
Congress, like his elections to county sheriff
and supervisor in earlier years, illustrated his
continuing popularity among regional residents
and elevated his political and personal influence
to territorial and federal levels. Despite closing
facilities at the rim, he stubbornly clung to the
trail franchise, tent camp at Indian Garden, and
fraudulent mining claims while trying hard to

*The open, dusty, horse-drawn buggy
was the vehicle for scenic rim drives
from 1890 to 1915. This photograph
captures the standard conveyance along
Hermit Rim Road in late 1909.*
GRCA 9605

use his political position to milk maximum profits from these properties. In 1908, he influenced legislation to allow a scenic railway along the South Rim, but the plan failed, probably due to Gifford Pinchot's opposition. As delegate in 1909 and again in 1912, while others introduced bills to promote the monument to national park status, Cameron introduced legislation to again allow a rimside railway, the valuable path of which would no doubt cross some of his many mining claims. These efforts, too, died in congressional committees.[217] His attempts to stop the Hermit project from 1909 to 1912 also proved a failure.

Once again a full-time Arizona resident in 1912, Ralph Cameron had turned bitter from too many failures to reap a bona fide fortune and, if possible, became even more opportunistic. He wrote Pete Berry that the forest service, Santa Fe, and Harvey company had "caused us so much unnecessary trouble and expense that I feel like getting even to some extent, and if I live I certainly will."[218] Cameron lived more than enough years to ensure that the forest service and park service would feel his revenge.

In 1912, he announced sale of thirty-five of his claims beside the Bright Angel Trail to a syndicate that planned to build a reservoir and hydroelectric plant within Garden Creek's narrows below Indian Garden. This reported five-million-dollar deal to industrialize the inner canyon no doubt horrified the forest service and Harvey company, but never materialized, so Cameron formed his own company in 1913 to extract nonexistent platinum from

some of these claims.[219] This venture like the others went nowhere, but garish development schemes for their central tourism corridor made foresters sweat, and prompted the Santa Fe to purchase still more of his claims in 1916.

As pressure increased after 1910 for national park status, Ralph Cameron's supposed developmental plans reflected personal greed more than a symbolic stand for the rights of small businessmen. Most of his fellow pioneers, though many remained ornery into the 1920s and 1930s, had given up their tourist enterprises and none expected more than a modest retirement from sale of their old mining properties. Even Cameron's chief allies, the people of Coconino County, had awakened to the advantages of a national park in their back yards and exhibited little interest and dwindling enthusiasm for his hollow proposals.

Cameron did not see or did not care about what was happening at Grand Canyon Village and allowed his facilities to fall apart in the face of mounting tourist usage. While running unsuccessfully for the United States Senate in 1912 and Arizona governor in 1914, he pursued business opportunities elsewhere in Arizona. His agents continued to collect tolls along the Bright Angel Trail, twenty thousand dollars in 1915 alone, yet spent little to maintain the monument's most popular tourism path and even less to keep up Indian Garden Camp. Niles Cameron, his brother's constant supporter and manager of the camp, died in 1918, by which year the property had become an eyesore

with trash littering the ground beside a seriously polluted Garden Creek.[220]

The United States Forest Service began another round of legal battles in 1913 to invalidate Ralph Cameron's mining claims, but it fell to the National Park Service after 1919 to witness the final release of his stranglehold on the south-central rim. In 1920, the United States Supreme Court invalidated nearly all of these claims and labeled him a trespasser within the one-year-old national park. Seemingly on the ropes in his twenty-year-long prize fight with big business and bigger government, Cameron rebounded by riding President Warren Harding's Republican coattails to the United States Senate, and from this lofty political perch thumbed his nose at the nation's highest court. Not until 1923 did United States Attorney General Harlan F. Stone evict Cameron's employees from Indian Garden Camp, ending his economic interests.[221]

Ralph Cameron would make no more money from Grand Canyon, but his influence on the park's development during his 1921-27 senatorial term remained strong. Transferring his animosity from the United States Forest Service to the National Park Service, he succeeded in 1922 in temporarily removing operating funds for Grand Canyon National Park from the Department of the Interior budget.[222] Of greater significance, he continued to fight against the federal government's acquisition of the Bright Angel Trail, the only toll trail remaining within the entire national park system by the 1920s. Despite efforts of

Arizona Congressman Carl Hayden to arrange the trail's transfer to the park, Cameron helped defeat a 1924 referendum which would have accomplished the sale. The defeat prompted an exasperated park service to build the seventy-thousand-dollar South Kaibab Trail in 1925, the second trail built solely to bypass Cameron's personal interests, and not until 1928 would the Bright Angel pass to the federal government.[223]

Cameron lost his bid for reelection in 1926 and faded from regional history, but remained a tourism promoter and fighter for individuals' rights, mostly his own, for the remainder of his long life. While still in the Senate, he used personal knowledge of federal reservoir sites along the Colorado River to advantage, enlisting wife, children, and friends to stake mining claims at potential building sites for Boulder Dam.[224] Shortly before his death in 1953 at the age of eighty-nine, he promoted a radium springs tourist ranch in Yuma, Arizona, and was still railing against federal control of western lands. Burton Cameron, a solid Flagstaff citizen and the least controversial of the three siblings, died in Phoenix in 1959.[225]

• • •

Ralph Cameron's story is essential to this history because it envelops the struggle among early entrepreneurs, big business, and the federal government to control Grand Canyon's South Rim. It was easy in an era awakening to progressive conservation, and easier still today in a loftier atmosphere of natural preservation, to label Cameron an exploitative villain, but such issues were not then, nor are they now, so clear cut. In his earliest defense of rugged individualism and the common person's right to public lands, he enjoyed the support of most canyon

residents as well as the county and territorial populace.[226] Similar issues are still argued in our western forests and grazing lands where lumbermen swat at federally supported spotted owls and cattlemen fight preservationists to keep their public pasturage. Interests and arguments in today's struggles echo those of seventy-five years ago, though alliances have shifted at times, and few engaged are actual villains.

Cameron met a bitter end because greed outlasted his concern for personal rights and he did not sense shifting moods and needs, but it would be incorrect to assume that he stood alone. Well into the 1920s, Cameron supporters and nonaligned individualists remained thorns in the sides of United States Forest Service and National Park Service officials, resisting and

Ranger Perry Brown collecting entrance fees, 1931. The park began issuing automobile permits in 1926 costing fifty cents. Ironically, this caused problems with Arizona state road commissioners who considered the fee to be a toll. The road commission by law could not build or maintain toll roads, and the NPS had some trouble explaining how their fees at the end of the state's south approach road differed from those of Ralph Cameron at the Bright Angel Trail! GRCA 30

Motor vehicles began to replace buggies by 1915, and in the 1920s, sophisticated touring cars driven by chauffeurs in livery were the norm. William Guy Bass, Fred Harvey driver, is pictured at Hermits Rest before 1926.

Arizona Historical Society

often defying early regulations. They diminished in number and eventually became silent, not because they learned to accept federal mandates and managers, but because the South Rim had become a maelstrom of tourists on wheels, far beyond the financial resources of small businessmen and primitive infrastructure to control or accommodate. In the end, popularity and necessity, driven relentlessly by the automobile, closed the pioneer period at the southcentral rim.

United States Forest Service managers saw it coming, but could do little to implement effective controls. They planned, and planned again—in 1909, 1910, 1916, 1917, and 1918—to bring order to South Rim chaos, but failed for several reasons. The agency was ill experienced with tourism and would not identify "visitation" as a beneficial use of public lands until after their canyon tenure had passed.[227] Its administrators might have kept a respectable

distance behind demand had plans for village growth been implemented, but legislators then as now allocated funds to meet federal mandates in a miserly way, and national monuments received abysmal funding prior to the 1920s, often amounting to only hundreds of dollars annually. Forest service managers also suffered because they, too, were pioneers, meeting the first resistance of feisty entrepreneurs who knew well their way around federal laws, as well as arrogant railroad magnates who valued the government as an ally but not as a controlling force.

While the forest service struggled with Ralph Cameron and Grand Canyon's rising popularity, Congress in 1916 created the National Park Service within the Department of the Interior. Interior Secretary Franklin K. Lane found just the right man to run the new agency, Stephen Mather, a wealthy business executive with time on his hands and a sincere interest in the western parks. Lane immediately teamed Mather with Horace Albright, a young Californian who would succeed his boss as director in 1929 and influence park service policy until his death in the 1980s. The two men forged the mold for their new agency, Mather with his vision, money, and public relations skills, Albright through his deft political and administrative abilities. Together they made a formidable management team.[228]

A consummate executive, Mather immediately identified goals for the national parks. He believed that in order for them to prosper, they would have to be embraced by the public who might then prod legislators for necessary operational funds. To engage the public, Mather developed intimate partnerships with managers of the nation's largest railroads who had already invested millions to develop quality accommodations but, in Mather's mind, had not invested enough in residential and other support services. By offering tycoons long-term concession monopolies and delineating spheres of influence —that is, which railroads got to develop which parks—he cemented relationships that would last into the 1960s.[229]

As an avid motorist, Mather also foresaw the importance, if not the ultimate impact, of automobile travel to the national parks, and deplored the condition of park roads built for wagons at the dawn of the automotive age. He and Albright went to work on legislation that would make special appropriations available by 1924 for regional approaches as well as inner-park roads. In the same year, he secured the aid of the federal Bureau of Public Roads to build quality automotive highways within the parks according to park service landscape engineering specifications, a relationship which continues today through the same agency, renamed the Federal Highway Administration.[230]

The National Park Service's early goals coincided with the act of 26 February 1919 creating Grand Canyon National Park. In August 1919, the park's first acting superintendent, William H. Peters, arrived with four rangers and an entrance checker to assume management from the United States Forest Service. Peters found gratifying structural improvements made by the Santa Fe, Fred Harvey Company, Verkamps, Kolbs, and Babbitts, but also livestock still grazing freely among tourists, water and sewage problems, no suitable administrative offices, poor roads, deplorable housing, antiquated medical and telephone services, and recalcitrant pioneers still clinging to their inholdings. Little had changed

to facilitate visitors and park employees since El Tovar Hotel opened its doors in 1905.[231]

Peters' response in the first year of little funding and few personnel reflected Mather's and Albright's priority objectives to reconstruct administrative facilities, roads, and trails. Peters reiterated Mather's opinion of roads approaching the park, labeling them "a disgrace to the State of Arizona and Coconino County." It actually saddened him that perhaps 60 percent of motorists traveling the National Old Trails Highway did not turn north for the canyon, despite the park's inability to comfortably accommodate more visitors. He could do nothing about roads outside park boundaries in 1919 and 1920 however, and instead set men to work rebuilding the primitive thirty-two-mile dirt road from El Tovar to Desert View and repaving Hermit Rim Road, which had disintegrated within months of allowing automobiles upon its six-year-old macadam surface.[232]

The park's first "permanent" superintendent, Dewitt L. Raeburn, arrived in 1920, and by mid-1921 reported an improved central trail corridor with completion of a 420-foot suspension bridge spanning the Colorado River. He also supervised construction of several remote fire towers connected to village headquarters via telephone, effected road and trail maintenance, and built a few administrative buildings. Reinforced park

Henry Fountain Ashurst's congressional legislation to create Grand Canyon National Park, introduced in 1917 and ultimately succeeding two years later.

GRCA 13705

The park service adopted the forest service permit policy to control Grand Canyon land and concession uses, including hotels, camps, and transportation. This unusual 1921 permit allowed Uncle Jim Owens to graze sixty-four head of buffalo on the Walhalla Plateau near Bright Angel Point for the nominal fee of one dollar. GRCA 5309

forces now consisted of ten rangers, five clerks, and a maintenance crew of as many as forty part-time employees who hastened progress. Aside from physical improvements, Raeburn tightened controls against hunting and had some success keeping cattle out of the village area, measures which sightseers appreciated but cattlemen resented. The year also witnessed arrival of the park's first doctor, G.C. Rice of the Public Health Service. Meanwhile, annual South Rim visitation jumped to 66,000, nearly 15,000 of whom arrived in more than 5,000 automobiles. South Rim concessioners doubled local automotive traffic by carrying 42,000 passengers in 5,400 bus trips along the rim from Hermits Rest to Desert View.[233]

The park's next superintendent, Walter W. Crosby, continued South Rim improvements between 1922 and 1924, working with appropriations totalling one hundred thousand dollars in 1922 and seventy-five thousand dollars in 1923, considerably more money than the forest service ever saw, but far less than required for Crosby's ambitious plans. He directed park funds to road, trail, and building maintenance, then expanded camping facilities as motorists began to opt for a night's rest under the stars rather than a hotel ceiling. As South Rim visitation in 1923 approached 100,000, 35,000

arriving by automobile, some of those out under the stars had no choice as the only hotel additions since 1905 had been a few tent-cabins at Bright Angel Camp. Under these cramped conditions, park administrators imposed no restrictions on at-large camping at the rim or village and commiserated with visitors forced to sleep in their vehicles.[234]

As visitation escalated during the early 1920s and appropriations failed to keep pace with needed improvements, the importance of Stephen Mather's efforts to ally the federal agency with concession arms of regional railroads became ever more apparent. The park service had signed a twenty-year contract with Fred Harvey in 1920 for South Rim concession services in return for restrictive zoning and architectural controls. The Harvey company and Santa Fe responded by maintaining facilities to high standards and improving employee quarters and services to some extent. In 1922, they added the inner-canyon Phantom Ranch, a Colter-designed tourist facility near the mouth of Bright Angel Creek.[235] While the park service struggled for funds to maintain and improve park infrastructure through the 1920s and into the 1930s, the Santa Fe invested more than one million dollars from 1925 to 1930 and allocated another three and one-half million for 1930-35.[236]

Before spending the big dollars, the railroad went to work on its first master plan for Grand Canyon Village. In 1922, they hired the Chicago architectural firm Graham, Anderson, Probst and White to organize the village and outline its growth, while the park service contributed its landscape engineering department, Superintendent Crosby, and park engineer Minor Tillotson to the effort.[237] The architectural firm's chief designer, Pierce Anderson, borrowed heavily from Frank Waugh's 1918 forest service plan to suggest rustic architecture for future constructions and to establish village zoning. The completed 1924 plan called for a visitation zone between Hermit Rim Road and the rim for most tourist facilities, an industrial zone flanking and mostly south of the railroad tracks, a civic plaza south of the tracks along the southeast segment of today's Village Loop Drive, and residential areas west and east of a new south entrance road.[238] Visitors today may still discern the ghost of this plan within today's village, although many new constructions and fifty times the automotive traffic certainly obscure the architects' original intent.

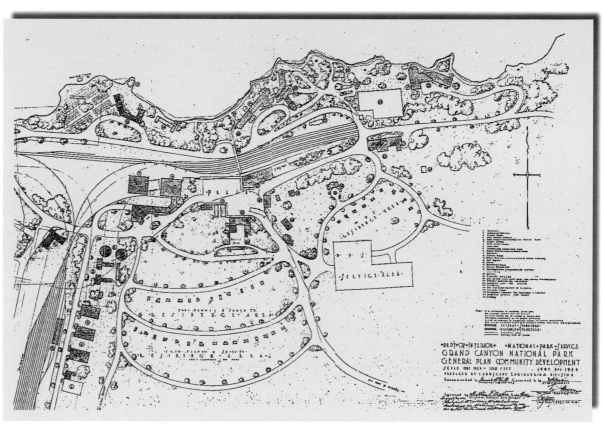

Architect's concept of how Grand Canyon Village should be zoned, from the 1924 NPS/Santa Fe master plan. This layout originated in the progressive City Beautiful movement at the turn of the century, and strongly resembles earlier U.S. Forest Service plans proposed by landscape architect Frank Waugh. Implementation of this plan from 1924 to 1939, along with stricter controls and the elimination of small concessioners, ended the pioneer period at Grand Canyon's South Rim.

Abandoned mines and hotel sites littered with rusted machinery and collapsed clapboard buildings evidenced the end of the pioneer period at Grand Canyon's southwest and southeast rims. Directly the opposite marked the era's eclipse at the chasm's southcentral edge. With a workable master plan, millions of dollars budgeted by the Santa Fe and Fred Harvey companies, special road and trail appropriations, and the symbolic demise of Ralph Cameron, the end is more aptly identified with the onset of feverish growth between 1925 and 1928. Much remained to be built, including all types of tourist facilities, new roads and trails, sanitation and water systems, administrative and community buildings, residences, and medical facilities, but the master plan accounted for these needs and all would be built within a logical scheme under superintendents John R. Eakin (1924-27) and Minor R. Tillotson (1927-38). Among early residents on hand to witness the overall South Rim transformation, one wonders most what Big Jim, the only man to see it all happen, might say of this half-century-long evolution from wilderness to national playground.

CHAPTER FOUR
North Rim

THE PIONEER PERIOD AT GRAND CANYON'S SOUTH RIM INEXORABLY FADED BETWEEN 1908 AND THE LATE 1920s through concerted efforts of the United States Forest Service and National Park Service to order the chaos of tourist visitation. Meanwhile, the North Rim, separated by the immense gulf and relatively undisturbed by visitation of any type, developed at its own slower pace, an afterthought of south-side federal administrators with more pressing concerns. The entire northern region, in fact, evolved differently from its southern counterpart, such that even today's visitor along the Arizona Strip cannot help but feel in another physical and cultural domain.

Charles Jesse "Buffalo" Jones, an early resident at Grand Canyon.
Kansas State Historical Society QL.5 BU.1

Opposite: Rust Camp
NAU.PH.568.4689

Railroads made the fundamental difference. The south side had two: one along the thirty-fifth parallel that brought settlers, developers, and tourists from around the world; the other, from Williams, to the canyon's very edge. The north side had none: no regional lines ever approached nearer than the Union Pacific's San Pedro, Los Angeles and Salt Lake Railroad through far western Utah, Nevada, and California; and the Denver and Rio Grande Railroad across central Utah. Both of these left nearly two hundred miles of high plateaus and

otherwise rugged terrain to intervene between depots and the northern rim. Regional boosters tried repeatedly to attract a railway, and the United States Congress considered three bills, in 1914, 1916, and 1921, to help the cause, but the closest rails would ever approach were spur lines to Marysvale, Utah, after the turn of the century and to Cedar City, Utah, in 1923.[1] Travel from these railheads to Grand Canyon as late as the 1920s required a full day or more on some of the nation's worst interstate roads.

Jacob Hamblin guides a North Rim party that includes John Wesley Powell and Thomas Moran, 1873. Hamblin's service as Mormon and guide encompassed the late 1850s through the early 1880s. By the latter years, Mormon cattlemen and others had settled the Arizona Strip. NAU.PH.268-77

REGIONAL DISCOVERY

A region which most in the nineteenth century would consider a wasteland, separate from the rest of the nation and empty of European Americans, actually attracted the first white settlers and cultural determinants: members of the Church of Jesus Christ of Latter-day Saints. The Saints, better known as Mormons, had spent much of their time since the church's founding in 1830 on the move, driven ever westward from New York by frequent conflicts with non-Mormon neighbors. After a mob murdered their leader, Joseph Smith, in a Carthage, Illinois, jail cell in 1844, most church members left their Mississippi River enclave of Nauvoo, Illinois, following Smith's successor, Brigham Young. As tens of thousands of other Americans during this decade left the Midwest for Oregon and California farmlands, Young and his followers joined the migration across the Great Plains toward their own dreams of open space. They travelled in measured stages, ultimately scaling the Rocky Mountains and descending to the Great Basin in July 1847, where they rested within the desolate terrain east of the Great Salt Lake. All understood at once that whatever green pastures lay in their future would have to be of their own making.[2]

Young and other Mormon leaders never planned to settle a single Salt Lake city, but rather to carve a Mormon state they called Deseret from a vast region nominally controlled by the Mexican government.[3] Salt Lake happened to be where they stopped first, and they made the city that quickly emerged their capital, but residents barely had a crop in the ground before Young sent scouts in all directions to find additional colonization sites. The patriarch expected these men to understand the principles of his wasteland settlement strategy, that is, his plan to create oases in the desert. Towns, once established, would become way stations to farther destinations, while their pioneer residents in subsequent years would expand laterally from the line of march to fill in habitable gaps. In this manner, the church would control a religious, political, and economic empire of its own design.

In pursuit of his vision, Young's standards for judging a settlement site "promising" within the high desert region were necessarily low and always secondary to the overall goal. A bit of flat ground with a nearby spring or stream sufficed, and if church explorers found a resource of value, like iron, coal, or copper, settlement surely followed. The church needed zealots to accomplish its plan and found them in men like Parley Pratt, John D. Lee, and Jacob Hamblin who led generations of obedient Mormons southward to create the envisioned state. It proved a hard vision for families "called" to make the desert bloom, but they succeeded despite the difficulties.[4] By 1877, the year of Young's death, more than 350 Mormon towns dotted the American West; by the turn of the century, the number topped one thousand. Half as many more failed in the making.

In December 1849, Mormon explorer and colonizer Parley P. Pratt sparked the movement to southwestern Utah. Tracing the eastern edge of the Great Basin along the Wasatch Range,

Pratt picked up the trail blazed by Francisco Atanasio Dominguez and Jedediah Smith, then followed it down Ash Creek to the Virgin River and Santa Clara Creek, the later site of St. George. His report of rich iron deposits along the way prompted church apostle George A. Smith to build the town of Parowan in January 1851.[5] From this "mother community of southern Utah," settlers who streamed in from the north were as quickly dispatched southward along the Old Spanish Trail to found Cedar City (1851), New Harmony (1852), and Santa Clara (1854). Colonization in the 1850s and early 1860s spawned intervening towns passed today along Interstate 15 like Kanarraville (1861), Pintura (1858), Toquerville (1858), Harrisburg (1859), and St. George (1861).[6] In the same years, nearly a dozen small settlements representing lateral expansion stretched up the Virgin River as far as today's Zion National Park. With the onset of the American Civil War in 1861, Brigham Young sent hundreds from central Utah to reinforce these southwestern towns and named the region Dixie for its promise to grow cotton.

As colonists streamed south and a bit west on the Old Spanish Trail— known by the 1850s as the Mormon Outlet Trail—others formed a second line of march within narrow valleys to the east. John D. Lee, a man best known for his role in the Mountain Meadows Massacre but who also deserves recognition as Mormon scout and colonizer, led the way. Lee had come west with Brigham Young and followed Pratt to the lower Virgin River country between 1850 and 1852, driving the first wagons along the route of today's Interstate 15 and building a road of sorts as he came.[7] He helped establish Parowan and later New Harmony, but also explored the Markagunt Plateau from Parowan east to

Panguitch, thence south beside the Sevier and East Fork Virgin Rivers of Long Valley. Colonists followed Lee's exploration to found another string of settlements parallel to those in Dixie. Early towns which survive along this route, today's U.S. Highway 89, include Alton (1865), Glendale (1864), Mt. Carmel (1864), and Kanab (1864, 1870).[8]

While others led the way southwest from St. George to settle Littlefield, Arizona; Las Vegas, Nevada; and San Bernardino, California, to secure a supply line to the Pacific Ocean, the best-remembered of Mormon scouts pioneered a southeastern path of colonization into northern Arizona.[9] Jacob Hamblin, known as the "buckskin apostle" for his mode of dress and many years in the wilderness, was born in Salem, Ohio, in 1819, and like Lee converted to the Mormon faith as its members moved west from New York. He was among twenty or so men Brigham Young called in 1854 to serve as missionaries to the Indians and helped found Santa Clara in that year, but Young sent him far east from Dixie in 1858 to begin his work among the Hopi Indians and twenty-year career as regional explorer.

Hamblin's route in 1858 took him across the Arizona Strip where he located the later settlement sites of Pipe Spring and Lees Ferry. He generally duplicated the trek of the Dominguez-Escalante Expedition to the Crossing of the Fathers and south to the mesa-top pueblos where he, like the earlier Spanish priests, found the Hopi resistant to foreign religions. Fortunately, he enjoyed a little better luck with Southern Paiutes who had camped with him at Pipe Spring and proffered a guide named Naraguts, without whose help Hamblin would surely have become as lost as the Catholic missionaries.

John Doyle Lee—Mormon explorer, road builder, and town founder not long before his execution in 1877.
NAPHS 666-32

Emma Batchelor Lee, ca. 1890, after her marriage to Franklin French. Emma in later years was respectfully called Doctor French by her Winslow neighbors for her successful, though informal, practice of medicine. NAPHS 666-33

Despite the Hopis' antipathy toward outsiders, they tolerated and perhaps liked the fearless, soft-spoken man; enough, at least, to allow his annual return.[10]

Hamblin's early missions to the Hopi and Navajo ultimately refined an east-west trail which would become the Mormon wagon road of emigration from Utah into Arizona. During his 1860 trip, another Paiute guide whom Hamblin called Enoch pointed out springs at the base of the Vermilion Cliffs which would serve as important camp sites along the trail. Hamblin brought a small boat along on this journey, intending to locate a regular river crossing, and managed to get as far as the springs later called Jacobs Pools before abandoning the boat and wagon that carried it in deep sand.[11] He pushed on to the Paria River mouth and tried but failed, like the Spanish priests eighty-four years earlier, to cross the Colorado River in a makeshift raft. In March 1864, however, Hamblin became the first to raft the river at "Pahreah Crossing," thereafter eliminating the far more difficult and lengthy trail segment to the Crossing of the Fathers. By 1876, Hamblin, other scouts, and colonizers had worn a trail directly south from the crossing just west of the Echo Cliffs to mission, ranch, and town sites at Moenave, Moenkopi, Tuba City, and along the Little Colorado River.[12]

When problems with Navajo residents began to surface in the early 1860s, Brigham Young instructed Hamblin to develop an alternate Colorado River crossing and wagon route west of Grand Canyon. Hamblin responded in 1862 with an exploratory trip that encircled the gorge in a counterclockwise direction, beginning with a temporary crossing west of the Grand Wash Cliffs. His party likely travelled up Grapevine Wash near today's Meadview, picked up the old Moqui Trail west of Peach Springs, and followed it eastward to the Hualapai and Havasupai Indians then on to the Hopi pueblos. Here he regained his familiar trail north to the Crossing of the Fathers and west along his 1858-60 path to Dixie.

In 1863, Hamblin relocated the western crossing to a point nearer the Grand Wash Cliffs, a site where another Mormon pioneer, Harrison Pearce, established a regular ferry service in 1876. Pearce ran "Pierces" Ferry (the name is misspelled on many modern maps) only from 1877 to 1882, but the site and others downstream served as alternate, less frequently used crossings during the heaviest years of Mormon emigration.[13] Although a roundabout path to the direct line of Mormon emigration through the Little Colorado River settlements, it offered a well-watered east-west journey upon the Beale wagon road as well as connections to the lower Colorado River and central Arizona.

While Hamblin explored the major routes into the heart of Arizona, a few others tentatively settled favorable sites within the Arizona Strip west of the Kaibab-Paiute Plateau. In 1862, William B. Maxwell established a cattle ranch at Short Creek, a site nudging the south side of an indistinct Arizona-Utah border that refugee polygamist families later renamed Colorado City. By the following year, Dr. James Whitmore located a ranch at Pipe Spring and Moccasin within today's Kaibab Indian Reservation. In 1864, others continuing the hesitant eastward march developed still another isolated ranch at the later site of Kanab.[14]

Settlement would have proceeded rapidly from these first efforts had not Brigham Young's apprehension concerning Indian relations proved correct. Despite a relatively benevolent attitude toward American Indians, whom their religion held to be descendants of a lost tribe of Israel, Mormon settlers to the Sevier Valley, Dixie, and the western strip hunted game, appropriated water sources, and grazed livestock which upset Ute and Paiute subsistence lifestyles. Competition for natural resources led to the Black Hawk War between settlers and Utes of the Sevier Valley to the north. Paiutes joined in the hostilities along the strip and allied themselves at times with Navajos, whose raiding patterns by the 1860s had shifted north and west as far as Cedar City as a result of United States Cavalry operations in northeastern Arizona. Between 1865 and 1870, the Mormon territorial militia fought exasperating guerrilla battles with these tribes on multiple fronts, but proved largely ineffective against the stealthy horsemen. Far more livestock than humans lost their lives in these skirmishes, but isolated settlers abandoned their ranches and retreated to Dixie until Jacob Hamblin achieved peace with the Navajos in late 1870.[15]

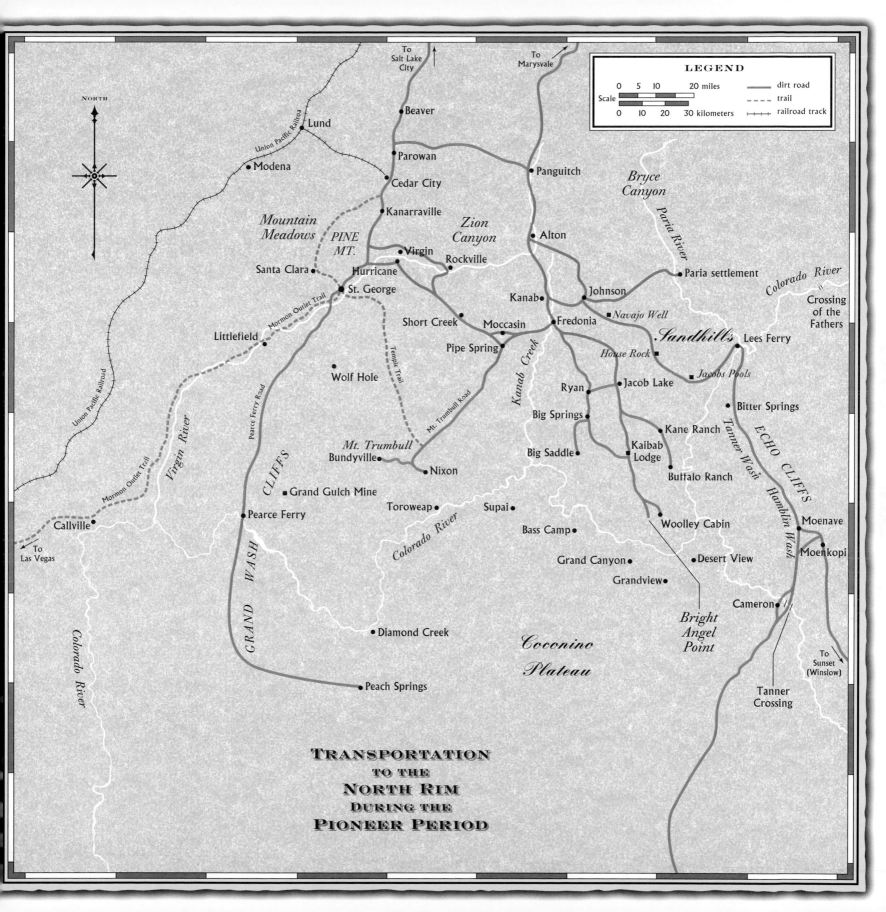

North

To Salt Lake City

To Marysvale

LEGEND

Scale
0   5   10   20 miles
0   10   20   30 kilometers

dirt road
trail
railroad track

Union Pacific Railroad

Lund

Beaver

Modena

Parowan

Panguitch

Bryce Canyon

Cedar City

Paria River

Kanarraville

Zion Canyon

Alton

Mountain Meadows

PINE MT.

Virgin

Rockville

Paria settlement

Colorado River

Santa Clara

Hurricane

Kanab

Johnson

Crossing of the Fathers

St. George

Mormon Outlet Trail

Short Creek

Moccasin

Fredonia

Navajo Well

Sandhills

Lees Ferry

Littlefield

Pipe Spring

House Rock

Pearce Ferry Road

Kanab Creek

Jacobs Pools

Wolf Hole

Ryan

Jacob Lake

Bitter Springs

Temple Trail

Mt. Trumbull Road

Big Springs

Kane Ranch

Tanner Wash

ECHO CLIFFS

Virgin River

Mormon Outlet Trail

Big Saddle

Kaibab Lodge

Mt. Trumbull

Bundyville

Nixon

Buffalo Ranch

Hamblin Wash

CLIFFS

Grand Gulch Mine

Woolley Cabin

Moenave

Callville

Pearce Ferry

Toroweap

Supai

Moenkopi

To Las Vegas

GRAND WASH

Colorado River

Bass Camp

Desert View

Grand Canyon

Cameron

Grandview

Bright Angel Point

Coconino Plateau

To Sunset (Winslow)

Diamond Creek

Colorado River

Peach Springs

Tanner Crossing

TRANSPORTATION
TO THE
NORTH RIM
DURING THE
PIONEER PERIOD

Charles Spencer's gold processing plant at Lees Ferry, 1911. Spencer used the technique known as hydraulic mining to wash ore from nearby cliffs with hoses powered by steam engines.
NAU.PH.568.5576

An uninterrupted period of Mormon colonization followed the Indian wars. Ranchers moved back to Short Creek and Pipe Spring then settled at many other perennial water sites uncovered by Hamblin and far-ranging militiamen. St. George masons constructed a fort at Kanab in 1869, and Brigham Young personally accompanied Levi Stewart's colonization party which platted a nearby townsite in September 1870. John D. Lee, restlessly a few steps ahead of federal marshals who wanted him for the Mountain Meadows Massacre as well as his nineteen marriages, left New Harmony to settle at a little place named Skutumpah northeast of Kanab where he and Stewart erected a sawmill. Lee sold out to Stewart's son, John, who moved the mill to Big Springs beside the Kaibab Plateau's western slope, while Lee moved to

Pahreah Crossing on the advice of both Hamblin and Young.[16]

Mormon militiamen had built a small stone cabin called Fort Meeks at the base of the Paria cliffs in 1869, and patrolled the area to prevent Navajos from crossing or to bushwhack those who did, but no one had settled here until Lee arrived with wives Emma Batchelor and Rachel Woolsey in December 1871. Prior to his arrival, the site had been known alternately as Lonely Dell and Pahreah Crossing, the latter name lingering awhile since the mobile Mormon had good reason not to advertise his name. Near the mouth of the Paria River, Lee, wives, and children developed a small farm, which assumed the name Lonely Dell, and also ran cattle to the west beneath the Vermilion Cliffs within House Rock Valley. In May 1872, Rachel and her children moved to Jacobs Pools, about twenty miles west along the emigrant wagon road, in order to better manage the dispersed cattle herd. As Kanab workers improved the road between 1871 and 1873 anticipating southward migration, Lee traded the pools to Jacob Hamblin in exchange for a more remote site at Moenave Spring, still along the developing wagon road, but sixty miles south of the crossing and high up in the Echo Cliffs. Rachel moved to Moenave in late summer 1873 and Lee occasionally fled to her home when rumors of approaching lawmen caught his ear.[17]

John and Emma Lee employed an assortment of rickety rowboats and flat-bottomed scows in the first year or two of ferry operations, reluctantly responding to spine-chilling pistol shots that signalled the rare traveller's intent to cross. In 1873, as Brigham Young developed plans for a concerted push to the Little Colorado River, the church sent men from St. George to build a real boat christened the *Colorado*, which they launched and the Lees quickly lost downstream in the same year. A succession of crafts ferried Mormon explorers between 1873 and 1875 and a flood of colonizing parties thereafter as the church expanded southeasterly up the Little Colorado River, south to the Salt River, and on into Mexico. Lee himself left in 1874 when the law caught up with him, and a firing squad ended his life in 1877 for his role at Mountain Meadows. Emma stayed on until 1879 when the church purchased the site. In succeeding years, the ferry functioned under Warren M. Johnson's several families, 1875-96; James S. Emett family, 1896-1909; Grand Canyon Cattle Company, from 1909 until sale to Coconino County in 1910; and finally Warren Johnson's sons, Jerry and Frank, who worked for the county until 1928 when a fatal accident combined with the near completion of nearby Navajo Bridge ended the ferry's life.[18]

As the only reasonably safe crossing of the Colorado River within hundreds of miles up and down stream, a natural north-south regional travel route, and pleasant stop for early river trips, Lees Ferry witnessed some of the Southwest's most interesting history. Every manner of person approached its banks, including regional Indians; Spanish priests; Mormon explorers, missionaries, militia, settlers, and polygamous fugitives; outlaws and cattlemen (often the same fellows); sheepmen; English lords; prospectors and miners; river runners; and early regional tourists. They came by shoe leather, horse, mule, wagon, raft, skiff, dory, motorboat, steamboat, and automobile. Its most persistent users, however, were young couples who, between 1877 and 1928, travelled months in wagons—later, days in automobiles—from all

The Charles Spencer *docked at Lees Ferry, 1912. The only steam-powered vessel to float the upper Colorado River, it was constructed at the ferry site and intended to haul coal from Warm Creek to fuel Spencer's hydraulic gold-mining operations. The craft was abandoned after a few runs, when the mining enterprise failed, and sank near this site not many years later. Left to right: Pete Hanna, captain; unidentified man; "Rip Van Winkle" Schneider; "Smitty" Smith; Lees Ferryman Jerry Johnson; Bert Leach; and Al Byers.*
Museum of Northern Arizona MS 106-1-8

parts of Arizona to St. George, Utah, to have marriages sealed in the Mormon temple. It certainly was a difficult path to travel, especially at the cliffside approach to the ferry known as Lee's Backbone, but a rewarding interlude in otherwise mundane pioneer lives.

The emigrant road, today called the Honeymoon Trail by most, followed the route first explored by Jacob Hamblin and can still be seen, though not driven, by today's motorist. Travelling north from Cameron on U.S. Highway 89, glance eastward to the Echo Cliffs. Horse-drawn wagons from the Little Colorado settlements of Sunset and Joseph City made their way north along the cliffs

Lees Ferry in 1921. Several crossing sites were used during more than a half century of operation. The lower site near the Paria rapids was preferred as it avoided rugged south side terrain termed "Lee's Backbone," but could only be used at low river flows. The upper ferry site pictured here was used more often, and after 1898, continuously as a better dugway was finished in that year. See Will Rusho's and Gregory Crampton's Lee's Ferry: Desert River Crossing, *second edition (Salt Lake City: Cricket Productions, 1992) for a complete history of the ferry and immediate region.* GRCA 5456

within an almost always dry Hamblin Wash.[19] Pioneer parties continued north beside the Echo Cliffs within Tanner Wash to Lees Ferry, while today's motorists travelling U.S. Highway 89A cross the Colorado River at Navajo Bridge, five miles downstream. Once across the river, wagons turned and followed the base of the east-west Vermilion Cliffs to Jacobs Pools, House Rock Spring, and Kanab. They crossed and re-crossed today's road before turning northwest up House Rock Valley, while drivers today continue on U.S. Highway 89A over the Kaibab Plateau past Jacob Lake. Once west of Fredonia, the old wagon path parallels Arizona Highway 389, as early travelers leaving Kanab for the final haul to St. George stopped for dependable water at Moccasin and Pipe Spring.[20]

• • •

Grand Canyon diverted the flow of Mormon expansion like a boulder at midstream, but not all wagon trains kept moving around the obstacle for southern destinations. While no one other than far-ranging cowboys and footloose prospectors had yet approached the South Rim by the 1870s, a few men and families ventured south from Kanab and east from Dixie to see what the rugged land might offer. No town would ever be located along the rim itself and tourist developments would lag thirty years behind those at Grandview, Bass Camp, and Grand Canyon Village, but people did wander above and below the northern edge between 1870 and 1906 to find what they could of economic advantage. Most of these owed what little topographical knowledge they possessed to the second coming of Major John Wesley Powell and subsequent federal mapmakers.

From the moment in 1869 when Mormons plucked Powell and the remnants of his ragged crew from the Colorado River, he was certain of two things: that he would have to return to recollect scientific data lost on the first trip, and that he might have a better time doing so if he located supply points along the river with the aid of regional residents. The national populace, and more importantly the United States Congress, had been hugely impressed by his first romantic exploration of the great unknown, so Powell on the next go-round found himself in charge of an official Powell Survey (1870-74). Armed with status, dollars, and fond sentiments for his Mormon deliverers, he returned to the West to spend much of 1870 scouting the Colorado River within Grand and Glen Canyons.[21]

Powell first met with Brigham Young, who gave the second expedition his blessing and introduced the major to Jacob Hamblin, the most topographically informed white man in the Grand Canyon region by 1870. Hamblin and a Kaibabits chief named Chuarruunpeak guided Powell to Uinkaret and Shivwits Paiute Indians near the mountain Powell would soon name Mt. Trumbull, only twenty miles north of the rim. With Hamblin's interpretive help, Powell learned that the three men who left his first expedition had been killed by angry Shivwits who believed they had raped a Paiute woman. More important to his current assignment, the bands promised that his next expedition could travel their lands without harm. Aiming to please yet not entirely willing to help, they showed him a difficult path to the river when far easier trails were available, another instance of tribal reluctance to share information with white men unless it led to their departure.[22]

Hamblin and Powell left the western strip for the promising supply point at Pahreah Crossing, but first Chuarruunpeak led the party along the North Rim to scout for other descents to the river. They camped at Big Springs, the site John Stewart would settle in the following year (likely on Hamblin's advice), then proceeded south up Nail Canyon through country even Hamblin had not explored. Chuarruunpeak led them across the Kaibab Plateau to Point Sublime, then to the Walhalla Plateau and Point Imperial where they obtained a near view toward the Little Colorado confluence and far view beyond Navajo Mountain more than a hundred miles upriver into Glen Canyon.

The scene on a smog-free summer day must have been worth the journey, and the topographical glimpse of upstream terrain might later benefit Powell's party, but this first European-American tour of the North Rim did not reveal paths to the Inner Gorge. Reminiscent of Hopi guides who led Spaniards to a fine view of no practical value, Chuarruunpeak failed to point out several intervening routes to the river long used by Paiute bands and later developed by prospectors, cattlemen, and surveyors.[23] Among the amenable tributaries somehow "overlooked" are those now penetrated by the extensive Thunder River, Deer Creek, and Tapeats Creek trail system; the North Bass Trail down White and Shinumo Creeks; and two variations of the North Kaibab Trail along Bright Angel Creek and Roaring Springs Canyon. The men returned to Big Springs, presumably along the same or a similar path, but again uncovered no practical descents to the river. As a result, Powell gained information of value to his later topographical parties on the Kaibab Plateau, but failed to find much of use for his upcoming river trip.

OUR FIRST CAMP.

Hamblin did assist Powell's immediate plans by allowing him to accompany his mission to the Hopi and Navajo in autumn 1870. Powell's role in this peace initiative to end the Mormon-Navajo wars was entirely unofficial, but he did have an interest in scouting the trail to the Paria, learning more about the Crossing of the Fathers, and securing safe passage from the Navajos who could easily intercept his river party.[24] Hamblin's arguments at Fort Defiance proved successful and Powell learned what he needed to know about the two crossings which would serve as supply points. By the end of the year he returned east to prepare for the following spring's expedition.

Powell's second descent of the Colorado River proved entirely unlike his first. Foremost, it was not an "exploration" since he had completed that task two years before and knew that the river would not turn to falls or a trap door

Members of the 1871-72 Powell expedition in camp on 4 May 1871 near Green River, Wyoming. Left to right: Almon Thompson, second in command to Powell; Andy Hattan, cook; Stephen Jones and John Steward, "scientists"; Walter Powell, photographer's assistant; Frank Richardson; Frederick Dellenbaugh; and Francis Bishop. O.E. Beaman is the photographer. Not pictured are Jack Hillers, and two who joined the party at Kanab—James Fennimore, a photographer who briefly replaced Beaman, and William Johnson.
GRCA 17236

Professor Almon H. Thompson, field leader of the 1871-72 Powell Survey and discoverer of the last-named mountain range and river in the continental United States. GRCA 9101

to Hades. It might still be dreaded for its nasty hydraulic waves, hazardous boulders, and grueling portages, but no longer posed a feared mystery, as Powell evidenced by casually reciting poetry while perched on a chair in the lead boat. Also, the nominal leader had little to do with the trip other than top-level management. Powell's brother-in-law, Almon H. Thompson, commanded much of the river running and most of the field studies while the major regularly left to busy himself in politics and visit his pregnant wife back east. The men ran into fewer mishaps, none disastrous, and while they suffered from hunger and harsh conditions, Hamblin, his sons, and others supplied them en route at Gunnison Crossing, the Crossing of the Fathers, and Lees Ferry.[25] They lost no men, boats, or critical supplies to the river or to Indians.

While not as adventurous as the first river trip, the overall 1871-73 expedition proved far more productive in terms of regional exploration. After floating from Green River, Wyoming, to Pahreah Crossing in May through October 1871, the men, without Powell, who had left at the Crossing of the Fathers, stashed their boats and waited for supplies at the as yet unsettled Lonely Dell. They dawdled awhile here and at House Rock Spring before continuing up Hamblin's trail to Kanab where they pitched a number of base camps within a few miles of town and at Pipe Spring. Thompson remained in charge of topographic mapping during the 1871-72 winter season, discovering in the meanwhile the Escalante River and Henry Mountains, the last mapped river and mountain range in the continental United States. The party established a nine-mile-long base line south of Kanab, and while doing so, fixed the exact location of the thirty-seventh parallel (Arizona-Utah boundary). With an astronomically accurate base line, Thompson's men roamed far and wide across the Arizona Strip and southern Utah triangulating then mapping regional topography.[26]

In December 1871, Powell's survey unintentionally set off a minor gold rush that incidentally revealed the region to the outside world. While searching for a supply route to the mouth of Kanab Creek, two packers, George Riley and John Bonnemort, who had served the expedition since the Crossing of the Fathers, panned a little flour gold from the sandbars of the Colorado River. John Stewart reported the find at Pipe Spring, where the news started on its way to Salt Lake City in January 1872 via the Deseret Telegraph which had only recently connected the Arizona Strip with the Mormon capital. By March, hundreds of "gentiles" flooded the area, many of whom must have startled John D. Lee as they were among the first to use his services at Pahreah Crossing. Transient prospectors irritated the strip's Mormon settlers and inflamed local Paiute bands, such that when the river trip resumed from Lees Ferry in August 1872, Powell ended it prematurely at Kanab Creek, not at all certain that the Paiute promise of safe passage remained in effect. Meanwhile, Kanab Canyon resembled a busy two-lane highway for a year or less as prospectors who descended as quickly emerged, "swearing vengeance on the originator of the story."[27]

• • •

The Powell Survey's field work ended in January 1873, but government scientists and mapmakers in succeeding years continued to uncover and delineate North Rim topography for Arizona Strip pioneers. In 1880, geologist Clarence E. Dutton used Thompson's map to cover some of the same ground as the Kanab Creek gold panners when he followed a prospector's trail from the North Rim above Tapeats Amphitheater to the Esplanade below. He descended a break in the Redwall Limestone along a portion of today's Thunder River Trail to Surprise Valley, named by Powell Survey photographer E.O. Beaman and George Riley in December 1871, and continued down Deer Creek to the Colorado River.[28] Dutton's 1880 season at the North Rim was soon revealed in his 1882 publication, *Tertiary History of the Grand Cañon District*, a scientific as well as romantic regional description illustrated by famed western artist Thomas Moran and talented artist, later geologist, William Henry Holmes. Dutton also produced a set of atlas maps which further described the region north of the Colorado River.

Dr. Charles D. Walcott was another scientist in the employ of the United States Geological Survey who followed an old trail from the North Rim to the river to unravel mysteries of the Inner Gorge. Powell and Walcott, with a few local laborers, improved an Indian trail from Saddle Mountain down Nankoweap Creek to the Colorado above its confluence with the Little Colorado. Powell recalled the tilted strata in this vicinity from his river trips and exploration to Point Imperial with Jacob Hamblin and assigned Walcott the task of making geologic sense of it all. Walcott, who would later succeed Powell as director of the geological survey, spent the winter of 1882-83 doing just that.[29] His trail would later be used as the northern segment of the Horsethief Trail, and with modern variations it remains a remote

backcountry trail within the national park.

The next detailed mapping of both North and South Rims awaited another United States Geological Survey topographical mapmaker, a Dutch emigrant, François Emile Matthes. In 1902, Matthes arrived at the South Rim a seasoned surveyor of rugged western lands, but his current assignment seemed daunting. In his own words, having

… successfully wrestled with and conquered in turn three tall mountain ranges in the West, the writer next found himself commissioned with the survey of a hole in the ground. Not a mere depression of moderate extent, but a horrible, ragged rent, a chasm two hundred miles long … in fact, the Grand Canyon itself.[30]

Jack Hillers on the Kaibab Plateau, 1872. Hillers replaced E.O. Beaman and James Fennimore as photographer of the Powell Survey of 1871-73 and recorded some of the first glass-plate images of Grand Canyon. Photographic equipment for nineteenth-century expeditions often weighed half a ton, requiring several mules for transport. GRCA 17259

LOST GOLD ON THE ARIZONA STRIP

Every region should have a story of buried treasure, and here is a reliable one for the Arizona Strip. In March 1886, while Mormon settlers went about their business and government map makers further unveiled Grand Canyon's North Rim, a family who had given up on pushing cattle in southern Arizona deserts sold their ranch and headed for Oregon. Sam and Charlotte Clevinger with fourteen-year-old daughter Jessie rolled north by covered wagon along the Mormon emigrant road in company of two itinerant helpers: part-time cowboy and more frequent gambler Frank Wilson and a recently discharged United States Cavalry buffalo soldier named John Johnson.

Two months later, cowboy Elmore Adams rode to the Buckskin Mountain and made a grisly discovery: a man and woman who had been murdered with an axe and buried near the trail in a shallow grave, since excavated by coyotes. Yavapai County Sheriff William Mulvenon and deputies John Francis and E.F. Odell travelled north 370 miles from Prescott to investigate, and diligent sleuthing revealed that the murdered couple were the Clevingers. No trace remained of the family's wagon, forty head of cattle, Wilson, Johnson, or Jessie. Also no trace of the murders' motive—seventeen thousand dollars in gold coin, proceeds of the cattle ranch which friends knew for certain they had brought along.

While a region-wide alert went out for the missing persons, Mulvenon and Francis followed clues given them by the Johnsons at Lees Ferry and a shopkeeper at Kanab. They remained hot on the trail up the Mormon freight road to Marysvale, Provo, and Salt Lake City, then into Idaho where they caught up with Wilson and Jessie at Oakley in the northern part of the state. The local sheriff in Duckwater, Nevada, nabbed Johnson, and Mulvenon picked him up on the long return trek for Prescott. Interrogations at the county seat revealed that the two men had joined in the murders and it took a jury only forty minutes to decide both would swing, but Wilson lost a hand of high-low poker to his accomplice and took the fall, earning a rope for himself but a commuted life sentence in Yuma Territorial Prison for Johnson.

The secret of the gold coin rested with Jessie. The murderers knew it existed but had been unable to beat its location out of the young woman. Once free of Wilson's grasp, she confided that each night she helped her mother carry it part way into the darkness, then returned to camp while her mother chose the exact hiding place. The night before the murders, she had helped carry the wooden box containing baking soda cans filled with gold at least five hundred yards from the trail and neither had carried tools for burial. Jessie had reason to believe her mother had simply dropped it in a shallow hole and covered it with brush.

Men learned of the story and went looking for the treasure but never found it. More than a hundred years later, tins of gold coin perhaps exposed through erosion lie waiting along the emigrant road to the Buckskin. One or two old-timers know where the last campsite lies. But they're not talking.

Above: Gold coins. Index Stock, © Leslie Harris

The task of producing accurate topographic maps had its own challenges, but living conditions within what might still be described in 1902 as wilderness proved equally hard. With rodman, camp cook, teamster, and pack animals, Matthes crossed the canyon upon Bill Bass's trails and spent a considerable portion of two summer seasons struggling with the trees and terrain of the Kaibab Plateau, seasons he described as "nomadic rambling which it is difficult for city folks to realize." While travelers to the South Rim in 1902 enjoyed railways, wagon roads, and hotels, Matthes found only animal paths, week-long saddle treks to and from Kanab for supplies, and the great outdoors.[31] Developmental differences between the separate worlds of North and South Rims were never more evident than in the few years following the turn of the century, but Matthes' men, informed by their explorations and frequently in contact with the inquisitive townsfolk of Kanab, would indirectly help narrow the gap.

Despite trying problems of plotting Grand Canyon from top to bottom with nothing more than experience and a plane table, Matthes produced two accurate and beautiful maps of unequalled value to those wishing to exploit the near region or simply to travel within its depths and along its rims. Published in 1906, the Bright Angel and Vishnu quadrangles found their way into knapsacks and saddlebags of all knowing travelers for decades thereafter.[32]

ARIZONA STRIP SETTLEMENT

As government scientists reduced Grand Canyon and the Arizona Strip to lines on a map during the years 1871-1906, early residents of Kanab, St. George, and smaller communities went about the business of settling a region. Left in the backwaters of Mormon expansion, they developed area resources in ways similar to south side settlers, yet limited by physical and cultural factors. Physical constraints stemmed from the absence of nearby railroads but also from chronically poor wagon roads, the result of being far removed in distance and concern from political purse strings at Phoenix and Salt Lake City and a long way from transcontinental highways. Isolation, the condition desired by early church leaders, slowed regional development throughout the pioneer period.[33]

Cultural limitations derived from settlement by members of the Mormon faith, who lived under secular as well as religious guidance of church leaders. Brigham Young's ideas for development can be characterized as cooperative, insular, and purposeful. Whether communities operated within the United Order of Zion—a communal lifestyle introduced by Joseph Smith and reinforced by Young in the Southwest—or under looser forms of mutual assistance for large projects such as irrigation works, Mormon secular tenets emphasized cooperation, which dampened the entrepreneurial spirit so rampant at the canyon's South Rim. The people also valued self-sufficiency, always necessary in a harsh land but desired as well to limit contact with potentially destructive influences of the non-Mormon world. Self-sufficiency encouraged residents to look askance at speculative or frivolous enterprises and to pursue mainstay occupations like farming, ranching, and home manufacture.

Homesteading success along the Arizona Strip relied on locating near dependable water sources: alongside a creek, spring, limestone sink hole, or dammed intermittent stream. Dry farming succeeded in most years during the 1906-20 wet period, but failed consistently when normal precipitation returned to the region. A drive today along the road to Tuweap Valley reveals snug cabins like this one fallen to ruins since the 1920s when nearly all homesteads failed and properties reverted to cattlemen. Arizona Historical Society

This recipe for living remains important to residents even today, but was far more critical in the final decades of the nineteenth century as Mormons struggled with pioneer conditions and often fought federal and state authorities over the polygamy issue. After the church grudgingly outlawed plural marriage in 1890 in order to achieve Utah's statehood by 1896, and its members entered mainstream American political life at the turn of the century, developments took a slightly different turn. Economies, however, remained traditional and continued to lag behind the better-travelled and more densely populated South Rim region.

Church philosophy is nowhere better illustrated than in the relative paucity of mining claims filed at the canyon's northern edge during the pioneer period. Leaders had nothing against mining as an occupation and encouraged development of useful mineral deposits like abundant iron ore near Parowan, but discouraged members from seeking gold, silver, or unproductive bodies of any mineral. Residents early revealed this general rule by refusing to participate in the 1871 gold discovery at the mouth of Kanab Creek, their disdain for gentiles who did, and the very few claims ever recorded at unpromising sites, whether on the rim or within the canyon. The several asbestos and copper claims north of the river belonged to non-Mormons operating from the south side like Bill Bass within Hakatai and Shinumo Canyons; John Hance, who developed asbestos claims high above the river near the mouth of

Red Canyon; and William Ashurst, who worked a few claims along Bright Angel Creek. All of these men transported what little ore they extracted by way of south side trails to the railroad.[34]

Despite local residents' aversion to speculative ventures, mining did figure into early North Rim history in a small way. Prospectors organized the Bentley District in 1873 and developed its chief mineral producer, the silver-copper Grand Gulch Mine, along with other claims near the Grand Wash Cliffs. The Warm Springs District on the west slope of the Kaibab Plateau, twenty miles north of the rim, enjoyed some success after 1890 with the discovery of extensive deposits west of Jacob Lake ranging up to 40 percent (average 7 percent) copper. The ore attracted a short-lived community known as Coconino City, renamed Ryan about 1900 when its mining properties changed hands. Ryan witnessed some impressive waterworks, power and leaching plants, furnaces, electric lights, and even a short utility railway within Warm Springs Canyon. Although a few high graders continued to work the district into the 1940s after larger operations shut down about 1907, the Warm Springs District delivered less ore than the best of south side ventures.[35]

Generally scant mineral deposits, poor transportation, and contempt for get-rich-quick ventures coupled with an early indifference to tourism accounted for a nearly total lack of mining claims north of the river within the narrower bounds of what would become Grand Canyon

National Park. This area's evolution to game preserve in 1906, national monument in 1908, and national park in 1919 ensured that when regional residents did awaken to tourism possibilities, the fraudulent mechanism so effectively employed on the South Rim could no longer be used to tie up desirable parcels. For these reasons, and perhaps because Mormon settlers were less inclined to file bogus claims, the United States Forest Service and National Park Service would entirely avoid regulatory struggles which erupted over private inholdings along the South Rim.[36]

Early settlers engaged in lumbering in the Mt. Trumbull and Kaibab Plateau areas, but did so for specific purposes rather than to create an industry.[37] For example, the church operated mills through the 1870s at Mt. Trumbull to supply lumber for the St. George temple, but sold them soon after completing the beautiful structure in 1877. Residents often imported steam-powered portable mills to favorable sites with water, hired local crews to cut and mill abundant ponderosa pine until fulfilling the purpose or depleting the timber, then sold the equipment to other residents or moved it to take on other building contracts. In this way, small lumber mills made their way back and forth all along the line of Mormon emigration from Salt Lake to Mexico. Two mills' sketchy biographies help illustrate this pattern.

Among the first lumber mills on the Arizona Strip was the one Brigham Young shipped south in 1870 to Levi Stewart and John D. Lee at Scutumpah.

Levi and John Stewart moved the equipment to their ranch at Big Springs, and between the two locations during 1870 and 1871, produced most of the lumber to build Kanab. This same sawmill moved again during the 1870s to Castle Spring, but disappeared by 1878. Speculatively, it reappeared at Jacob Lake in the early 1880s in the hands of Hiram Shumway before he sold it to long-time lumberman John Franklin Brown in 1901. Brown operated the mill until summer 1911 when it died, as all pioneer mills died, in an accidental fire. By 1913, however, Brown installed a similar mill acquired from another part-time lumberman in LeFevre Canyon a few miles north of Jacob Lake, where he kept the sawdust flying through the second decade of the century.[38]

John "Grandpa" Brown, who worked off-seasons as a Kanab attorney, county sheriff, and high-grade miner at Ryan, passed his mill and carpentry skills on to his son, Joseph. Joe and Anna Fawcett Brown spent the early years of their married life, 1918-32, moving the lumber mill all over the Kaibab Plateau where they employed as many as twenty-five Kanab and Fredonia men from early spring to late summer. For a brief period about 1920, they moved to Bryce where lumbermen often filed for home-steads on promising parcels, cut off the useable timber, then moved on before "proving up." The Browns brought the mill back to the plateau in the early 1920s with an assignment to rebuild the old fire tower near Bright Angel Point. Their largest and last projects from the late 1920s through the early 1930s found them cutting lumber to build guest cabins at Bright Angel Point and to rebuild Grand Canyon Lodge. When the Browns settled down to work for the Utah Parks Company at the North Rim after

completing the lodge, they sold their sawmill to a man in Cedar City, Utah. If it did not go up in smoke, the mill may still be churning out boards somewhere along the Arizona Strip.[39]

• • •

Subsistence agriculture through irrigation was the typical mainstay occupation of south-western Mormon communities, but, like mining and lumbering, it played a relatively minor role in early Arizona Strip history. Within the standard scheme of colonization, settlers brought wagons to a stop along a watercourse, planted a crop, then went to work building diversion dams and ditches, all within hours of arrival. These simple irrigation works of the nineteenth century, like the American Indian systems they emulated, could not stand up to floods triggered by

Dams built by Mormons in the 1870s and 1890s resembled this log-and-earthen structure at Kanab, Utah, pictured here in the 1880s or 1890s. Collapse of a Kanab Creek dam (perhaps this one) in 1886 scoured clean the silted creek bed, which encouraged founding of the irrigation colony called Stewart that same year (renamed Fredonia in 1888). Such structures would have to be rebuilt almost on an annual basis. NAU.PH.438-1

Cattle grazing near Jacobs Pools below the Vermilion Cliffs, 1919. The last cattle drive from House Rock Valley took place in 1934 when Ron Mace and Cecil Cram drove a herd to the railhead at Cedar City, Utah. In the following year the Taylor Grazing Act reduced the size of herds, and trucks took over where men on horseback left off. NAU.PH.150

spring snowmelt and summer monsoon rains, thus settlers invariably spent most summer daylight hours replacing waterworks with ever larger structures that also washed away. The recurrent pattern of plant, build, flood, replant, and rebuild in heartbreaking repetition held true from drainages of the Virgin and Sevier Rivers of southern Utah to the Little Colorado, Salt, and San Pedro Rivers of Arizona, and accounted for the abandonment of many communities.[40]

Most farmers on the Arizona Strip were spared the misery of constant flood repairs only because few drainages amenable to irrigation flow south from the Vermilion Cliffs or east and west from the flanks of the Kaibab Plateau. Many took lessons from Southern

Paiute families who had traditionally irrigated a few acres adjacent to springs and limestone sinks.[41] Mormons simply usurped Indian watering holes and expanded agricultural capacity by running a pipe or flume from water source to field. Those who did not or could not adapt, such as the Lees and Johnsons at Lonely Dell along the lower Paria River and farmers along Kanab Creek, suffered the typical effects of annual floods.

Dry farming ventures aided by amendments to the homestead laws in 1906, 1909, and 1912, along with above-average rainfall from 1906 to 1920, account for most of the very few communities ever to sprout within Arizona north of Grand Canyon.[42] President Woodrow Wilson's withdrawal of half a million acres from the Dixie National Forest surrounding Mt. Trumbull and the Parashaunt area in 1916 also encouraged homesteading and small towns within the region. The smallest of the communities, Cross Creek and Cane Beds, cropped up after the turn of the century at the sites of prior cattle ranches along Jacob Hamblin's wagon road from St. George. Situated just below the Utah-Arizona line and separated from the Arizona state capital by Grand Canyon and hundreds of miles of bad roads, these two farming and ranching communities became relatively safe havens for those who persisted in polygamy.[43]

Bundyville was another small community that owed its brief communal life to dry-land farming as well as ranching. Its founders—members of the Abraham Bundy family with a liberal sprinkling of Iversons, Alldredges, and Vanleuvens—arrived west of Mt. Trumbull in 1916 after an odyssey that took them from Utah to Arizona to Mexico. Pancho Villa's antics south of the border convinced them to return whence they came, and recent homestead amendments encouraged the families to stake their futures west of the early lumbering sites of Nixon and Tuweep. Known officially as Mt. Trumbull, the community of at most several hundred residents thrived in the 1930s and persisted through the middle decades of this century before succumbing to the 1934 Taylor Grazing Act and declining opportunities for its young people. At one time it boasted a post office, school, and church ward, all of which

closed in 1954, 1968, and 1970 respectively. Today, some descendants still own the patented homesteads of their pioneer families, but most populate St. George, Fredonia, and Kanab where residents say good naturedly, "you can't toss a rock around here without hitting a Bundy."[44]

Agriculture also accounts for the founding of Stewart, the unassuming village along U.S. Highway 89A only a few miles south of Kanab and a mile or two below the Arizona-Utah state line. Seven shareholders from Kanab originally developed the site in 1886 with plans to irrigate fields from nearby Kanab Creek. They built the small town, renamed Fredonia in 1888, along the lines of a typical Mormon agricultural community with stake president Dee Woolley and ward bishop Robinson surveying the townsite while settlers drew lots for ten-acre town parcels and nearby fields. Twenty-one families comprised the initial company taking up residence, and although polygamists from across the state line found its location attractive, population twenty years later had grown to only twenty-seven families. Despite its lumber mill, United States Forest Service headquarters, and strategic location along roads to Pipe Spring National Monument and Grand Canyon's North Rim, Fredonia remains a quiet town of several hundred, many of whom descend from original area residents.[45]

. . .

To these early settlers of the Arizona Strip it was far more important to occupy an area where they could live their faith

free from external influences than to pursue any particular economic livelihood. A town lot with accompanying garden and a few dairy cattle, or an isolated ranch with more of the same, nearly sufficed. Coupled with a sophisticated network of wealth distribution through the church, simple barter, and informal sharing, few residents fared worse than their neighbors. Still, they needed cash to purchase manufactured goods, and rarely produced sufficient dollars from mining, lumbering, or agricultural endeavors. The solution lay in the rich bunch grasses which blanketed most of northern Arizona during the nineteenth century. Grazing cattle, horses, sheep, and goats became the primary cash industry and largest employer for most of the earliest settlers who, if they needed a few dollars or a temporary job, could always work for one of several large cattle companies, tend goats or sheep on shares, or graze a few head of their own.

Federal regulation of public domain grazing lands did not come about until the 1934 Taylor Grazing Act, thus ranching across much of the Arizona Strip during the pioneer period remained a first-come, first-served free-for-all. Independent Mormon ranchers preceded all others, centering their operations at the best springs of the western strip by the middle 1860s. These men seldom made legal claims to the valuable water sources on which they depended, but acknowledged prior rights of those who arrived first. Informal claimants in turn allowed others to use the water when quantity permitted. This practice, generous at first

Salt cabin at Greenland Lake, built by Kaibab Plateau cattlemen about 1895. Cabins like this dotting the Kaibab Plateau and larger Arizona Strip were used freely by anyone who happened into the area—including early forest service and park service rangers. GRCA 5331

glance, contributed to the decline of grazing lands well before the turn of the century as nonresident cattlemen, sheepmen, and goat herders arriving seasonally from California, Nevada, and Utah had access to water and over-stocked the range. Nonetheless, ranching remained the princi-pal regional economy until overtaken by tourism in the 1930s, and is still important today.

Following the Mormon-Indian wars in 1870, Brigham Young and other church investors formed the Canaan Cooperative Stock Company with one of its several ranches located at Pipe Spring to expand the church's cattle herd eastward from St. George.[46] From 1870 to 1872, Young supervised construction of "Winsor Castle," the principal attraction at today's Pipe Spring National Monument, which served as a regional fort and living quarters for early fore-man Anson P. Winsor. After several reorganiza-tions, and with increasing federal pressure on the church to divest itself of secular properties, the Canaan company sold part of its holdings to a sympathetic non-Mormon, Benjamin (B.F.) Saunders, in 1883. Saunders consolidated the range on the western strip by buying out the interests of small outfits then filing fraudulent mining claims on water sources to keep others from trespassing. He sold most of his western properties to Preston Nutter in 1893 when he moved his operations to House Rock Valley. Nutter further monopolized the western strip by taking advantage of an 1897 law that allowed him to select thirty-two forty-acre parcels sur-rounding additional water sources in exchange

for forest land he owned in California. Nutter retained this control until his death in 1936.[47]

Ranching east of the Kaibab Plateau in House Rock Valley began with John D. Lee's small herd west of Pahreah Crossing at several springs along the Vermilion Cliffs. The Emetts and Johnsons also ran a few cattle in this relatively flat area which enclosed some 1,750 square miles from Lees Ferry west to the Kaibab Plateau and Marble Canyon north to the valley's head. Another church-organized cattle company, the OUO (named for the United Order of Orderville, Utah), gained control of most of the valley's waterholes by the late 1870s along with another outfit of uncertain origins that ran cattle under the VT brand.[48] By the late 1890s, B.F. Saunders bought these outfits and filed more bogus mining claims at the best springs along the Vermilion Cliffs. In 1907, Saunders sold his holdings and Bar Z brand to the Grand Canyon Cattle Company (GCCC), a corporation which afterwards controlled most of House Rock Valley until selling out to small ranchers in 1924.[49]

Whatever the size of the outfit, ranchers on both ends of the Arizona Strip used the central Kaibab Plateau for summer range, beginning with Levi and John Stewart's few head of cattle at Big Springs in 1871. The Stewarts were the first to claim water rights and graze cattle at DeMotte Park, always known by locals during the pioneer period, and by many today, as VT Park. In 1879, Levi Stewart's son-in-law, David K. Udall, along with several others located the first ranch within this aspen-lined valley extending north from the national park bound-ary. The OUO or VT outfit acquired the rights after the partners left in 1880. When the OUO dissolved in the 1880s, Brigham Young's son,

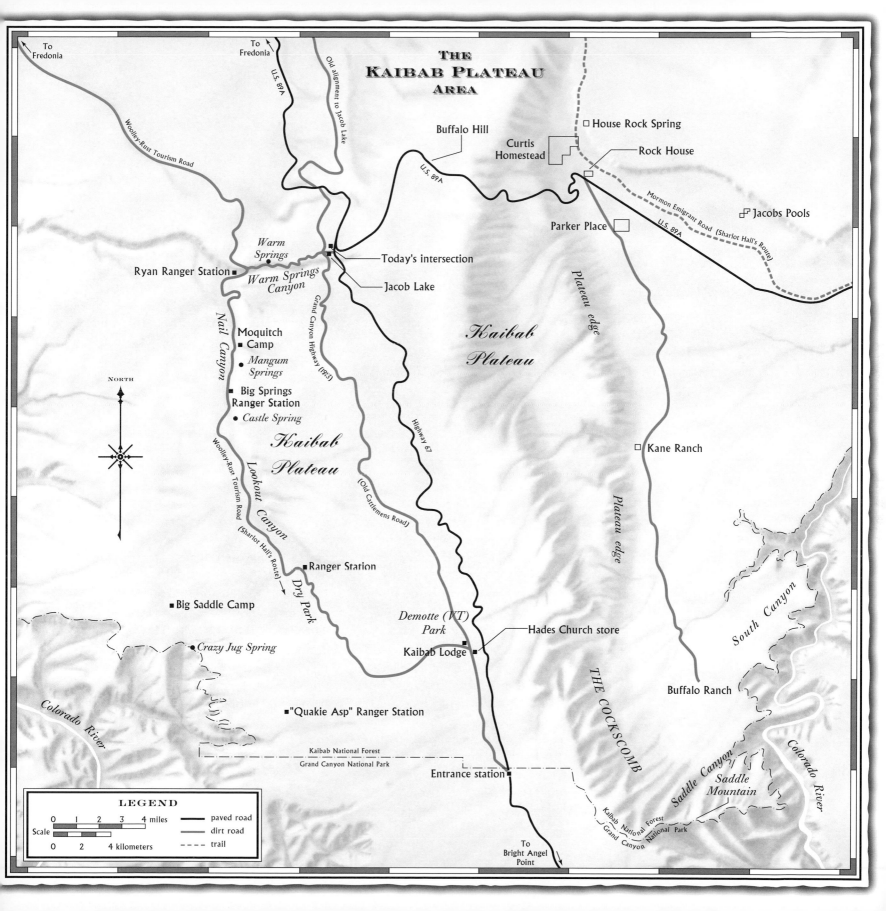

THE KAIBAB PLATEAU AREA

To Fredonia

To Fredonia

U.S. 89A

Old alignment to Jacob Lake

Woolley-Rust Tourism Road

Buffalo Hill

U.S. 89A

Curtis Homestead

House Rock Spring

Rock House

Jacobs Pools

Parker Place

Mormon Emigrant Road (Sharlot Hall's Route)

U.S. 89A

Warm Springs

Today's intersection

Ryan Ranger Station

Warm Springs Canyon

Jacob Lake

Moquitch Camp

Mangum Springs

Nail Canyon

Grand Canyon Highway (1923)

Kaibab Plateau

Plateau edge

Big Springs Ranger Station

Castle Spring

Kaibab Plateau

Highway 67

Kane Ranch

Lookout Canyon

Woolley-Rust Tourism Road

(Sharlot Hall's Route)

(Old Cattlemens Road)

Plateau edge

Ranger Station

Dry Park

Big Saddle Camp

Crazy Jug Spring

Demotte (VT) Park

Hades Church store

Kaibab Lodge

South Canyon

"Quakie Asp" Ranger Station

Buffalo Ranch

THE COCKSCOMB

Kaibab National Forest
Grand Canyon National Park

Colorado River

Entrance station

Saddle Canyon

Colorado River

Saddle Mountain

Kaibab National Forest
Grand Canyon National Park

To Bright Angel Point

LEGEND

| NORTH | | |

0   1   2   3   4 miles
Scale

0   2   4 kilometers

——— paved road
——— dirt road
- - - trail

Five cowboys of the early Arizona Strip cattle industry, ca. 1895. Left to right: unknown man; Duncan "Old Man" McDonald who ranched near the head of House Rock Valley; Taylor Button; Walt Hamblin, son of Jacob Hamblin, who also ran cattle in the valley; and Alexander Cram, the first House Rock Valley homesteader. Courtesy of Cecil Cram

John W. Young, acquired this spread along with most other church rights on the Kaibab Plateau, then the property transferred to B.F. Saunders in 1899. Cattle with the VT, Bar Z, and lesser brands continued to range on the Kaibab Plateau as far south as the North Rim at Cape Royal on the Walhalla Plateau well after the turn of the century and creation of the national park.[50]

There are few places in the American West where a cow will not go in search of grass and water, but Grand Canyon north of the Colorado River is one of them. One notable exception is the Esplanade, an inner-canyon bench akin to the eastern Tonto Platform and called the "sandrock" by cattlemen, which begins near the Powell Plateau and continues westward as a lower rim to the canyon's Inner Gorge.[51] Cattle as a rule probably would not descend the 1,500 vertical feet and more to the

Esplanade, either, if not persuaded by cowboys who, since the 1880s, valued the winter pasturage for its grass and ample waterpockets. Cattlemen improved half a dozen or more Paiute trails down to the sandrock and built some of their own to accommodate the footsore animals. A trail from Crazy Jug Point just east of Monument Point, Thunder River Trail from Little Saddle, and the Nail Trail farther west along the "fishtail" are just three examples of many northwest rim trails worn and maintained mostly by cowboys through the 1950s.[52]

Keeping a scorecard of which major companies owned what cows, springs, and brands is an interesting historical pastime, but tells little about the one-loop outfits and cowboys who simply worked for the owners. These men, whether footloose "rounders" or stable, married types with families in Kanab, Fredonia, or Bundyville, early on learned every square mile of the Arizona Strip and most of Grand Canyon's grassy benches and tributaries north of the Colorado River. Nearly all male North Rim pioneers worked livestock at some point in their lives and many descendants continued in the business while others started some of the first North Rim tourist enterprises.[53]

Ron Mace, a Fredonia cattleman and wrangler all his life, recalled driving small herds down to the Esplanade in late autumn and bringing out calves in early spring. Mace and other cowboys endured a bitter 1930-31 winter during which they had to drive cattle off the rim to the sandrock, trail or not, and stay with them from December through February. Even moderate winters required occasional rides down to make certain that grass and water remained sufficient. Cowboys other than Mace who worked regularly above and below the

canyon's edge west of the Powell Plateau included Carlos Judd, Billy and Tuffy Swapp, Ed and Sandal Findlay, Roy Woolley, Merle "Cowhide" Adams, Paul and Jense McCormick, Weaver White, Bob, Bill, and John Vaughn, and no doubt dozens of others who rode earlier for the Youngs, Saunders, and Nutter.[54]

Cowboys east of the Kaibab Plateau had a little easier time of it as cattle rarely found their way down Soap and Badger Creeks or other of the several steep tributaries within Marble Canyon south of House Rock Valley. Cowboys who combed this area from the 1880s through the turn of the century included Jacob Hamblin's son, Walt; Alexander, John, and George Cram; Ed Lamb Sr., Taylor Button, and Duncan MacDonald. Others, most of whom arrived from 1910 through the 1930s, followed the lead of Alex Cram who developed a well in House Rock Wash, erected a tent-cabin, then filed on the first House Rock Valley homestead in 1916. Moving up the wash from Alex Cram's place,

men and families who claimed water rights or homesteaded included the Mackelprangs; W.W. Seegmiller; Wannie Mace; Lorem, Ern, and Orson Pratt, who sold to the Anderson family; Roy Woolley; E.W. Parker, who sold to the Schoppmann family; and the Curtises who homesteaded several miles north of the rock house on U.S. Highway 89A, now owned by the Riches. Roy Woolley also obtained the old Kane Ranch at the southern foot of the plateau, the Bar Z brand, and whatever cattle the GCCC left behind when they vacated in 1924.[55]

Small outfits also ran cattle, sheep, and goats northeast of House Rock Valley on the three-hundred-square-mile Paria Plateau, known locally as the "sandhills." B.F. Saunders and the GCCC controlled the patented springs along the sandhills' western edge, but water-pockets proved sufficient for men like Dart Judd who ran goats on the sandy plateau from 1913 until the 1920s, Walt and Joe Hamblin, Jet and Six Johnson, Art and Frank Mackelprang, the

Edward Lamb Sr. and Taylor Button in House Rock Valley, 1892. NAU.PH.438-12

John Young's hunting party at the Kane Ranch, 1892. Left to right: Johnnie Baker, an exhausted English lord, unknown face, Ed Lamb Sr., Anthony Ivans, Al Huntington, unknown man, Buffalo Bill Cody (leaning on hitching post), two unknown men on cabin porch, Alex Cram, Dan Seegmiller, and Uncle Dee Woolley.

Courtesy of Cecil Cram

Broadbents, Johnny Adams, Bert Leach, Roy Woolley, A.T. Spence, Jim Glover, and the Bowmans. The only good route up to the sandhills ran past Two-Mile Spring, although some like Cecil Cram used a perilous path above Jacobs Pools to get stock down on occasion. Most used the sandy grassland as open range, but Joe Hamblin about 1900 dug an artesian well, filed a claim, and developed a small ranch later purchased by Adams, Spence, Woolley, then the Bowmans.[56]

Although ranchers had used House Rock Valley since the 1870s, no one at all lived east of the Kaibab Plateau except the Alex Cram family and the Johnsons at Lees Ferry until the middle 1920s. Alex Cram's son, Cecil, recalled the freedom of rounding up cattle along the Vermilion Cliffs to drive them west as far as Cedar City, and the nuisance of hauling potable water in wagons—later, automobile trunks—from Jacobs Pools. He also remembered the fateful day, 7 June 1928, when he and his father crossed the river at Lees Ferry, only to learn that on the next trip across three men and a Model T Ford sank to the bottom, ending the ferry's career in a heartbeat. It is difficult to imagine that for seven months following the accident, the Crams, Johnsons, and men working on Navajo Bridge had to travel west across the entire length of the Arizona Strip to the ferry near Searchlight, Nevada, then back again on more than six hundred miles of unimproved roads within three states—just to reach the south side of Marble Canyon!

In about 1920, a primitive automobile road south of today's U.S. Highway 89A replaced Hamblin's wagon road through House Rock Valley, but only the bravest nonresident travelers used it until a better realignment followed the opening of Navajo Bridge in January 1929. With promise of the new road and bridge, a few others joined the Crams in the valley, settling beneath the towering escarpment along the old emigrant road. After losing his ferry in 1928, Price Johnson homesteaded the site known today as Vermilion Cliffs. Bill and Blanche Russell arrived from New York to homestead Cliff Dwellers, named for a grotto near the top of the nearby cliffs and the stacked-stone cabins the Russells built; not, as some believe, for prior Prehistoric Puebloan occupants. After Bill died, Blanche sold the property to Art Greene who, with Earl Johnson and Vern Baker in the 1940s, built today's lodge and restaurant.[57]

The family of David "Buck" Lowery, an employee of Indian trader Lorenzo Hubbell, homesteaded Marble Canyon just north of Navajo Bridge in the late 1920s and built most of the facilities seen there today. Current owner Jane Bales Foster arrived in 1959, and not until 1968 and 1971 did she manage to get electric and telephone service to this still-lonely corner of the Arizona Strip.[58]

• • •

Only ranching among early Arizona Strip occupations touched Grand Canyon's North Rim and spilled over its edge because collecting then driving cattle did not require good roads. Aside from political indifference to improvements within the sparsely populated larger region, the topography of the North Rim would always make it difficult to build and maintain roadways to the very edge. The closer one nears the rim the greater the problem because, unlike at the South Rim, drainages flow into the canyon causing a ragged lip laced with steep tributaries. On the Kaibab Plateau, elevations average a thousand feet higher than the south side Coconino Plateau, increasing the severity of rain, snow, frost, and thaw which compound erosion and confound efforts to keep travelways open. Snow alone closes even today's black-topped roads six months of every year.[59]

Topography, climate, and the resultant lack of good roads hampered North Rim development but extended near-wilderness conditions which attracted another industry of sorts and some of the rim's more interesting individuals. The industry was sport hunting, not a traditional occupation by any means, but an activity which created a need for services. At first, hunters would use South Rim tourist operators to guide and supply them along the trailless plateau; ultimately, they would rely on men who knew the country best, the cowboys of the Arizona Strip.[60]

Subsistence hunting for mule deer on the Kaibab Plateau had long been an important activity of Southern Paiutes and later Navajos and Mormon settlers who had little trouble bagging their meat on the "Buckskin Mountain." Sport hunting began in 1892 through the efforts of the

TOURING BY WAGON

As the year 1912 and Arizona statehood approached, a few territorial residents feared that Utah politicians, always covetous of the Arizona Strip, might get their hands on it through redrawn state boundaries. Territorial historian Sharlot Hall was one of these, and to help advertise to Arizonans the potential of the land lying north of Grand Canyon, she embarked in 1911 on a summer tour of the isolated region still embraced by its pioneer period.

Hall started from Flagstaff in company of Al Doyle, a territorial resident since 1872 and long-time guide, in a light-weight Studebaker wagon powered by dependable horses, Mack and Dan. They took one variation of the sandy, wind-blown path to Lees Ferry that led up and over the saddle beside Sunset Crater and down to Tanner Crossing in its last year of use, then crossed Moenkopi Wash to the Mormon-Indian settlements at Tuba City. From this point north they traced the Mormon emigrant road, stopping as others had for forty years at Moenave, Willow Springs, Government Well, and Navajo Spring before descending the treacherous 1898 dugway to the Colorado River crossing. Along the way they saw no one except a few freighters and Navajos, but at the ferry they discovered Charles Spencer's hydraulic gold mining operators, working since the year before yet still failing to separate fine placer particles from the Chinle shale.

Hall and Doyle pressed on toward "civilization" through deep sand and rutted tracks in House Rock Valley, camping at the foot of the Vermilion Cliffs near precious water sources—Emmett Spring, Jacobs Pools, House Rock Spring—then managing the tortuous climb over the Buckskin Mountain to Navajo Well and the Utah towns of Johnson and Kanab. Along this segment of their journey they espied not a settlement, not a homestead, but only solitary cowboys, cattle, and a few sheep, buffalo, and cattalo, the latter animals ranging far north from their ranch at South Canyon.

At this point the pair may have concluded to let Utah have the region, as less than three hundred people lived within thousands of square miles and nothing of promise had been uncovered, but a trip to the North Rim may have changed their minds. They followed a "road" worn by cattlemen, miners, and lately tourist outfitters across sage flats that they felt (incorrectly) held promise for dry farming, past dormant copper mines at Ryan to the forest service station at Big Springs, then up Nail Canyon to the ponderosa-studded Kaibab Plateau. Here they enjoyed the company of forest rangers and cattlemen at VT Park, and the guide services of Uncle Jim Owens, who led them from their camp near Woolley Cabin to Bright Angel Point and the Walhalla Plateau before the sightseers returned to Kanab via Jacob Lake and Warm Springs Canyon.

Hall followed the remainder of the Mormon Trail to St. George, then picked up Jacob Hamblin's alternate emigration path south beyond the Grand Gulch Mine to Greggs Ferry and across the lower Colorado to Dolan Springs, Chloride, and the rail depot at Kingman. There she ended her seventy-five-day tour by rail to Prescott and the Salt River Valley. Her account of the adventure appeared in *Arizona, the New State Magazine* in 1913, prompting Governor Hunt to launch an official fact-finding automobile expedition over the same terrain the following year. By then Arizona had retained its strip of land north of Grand Canyon, despite its topographical, religious, and cultural ties to Mormon Utah. (You can trace Sharlot's trip by referencing the maps on pages 131 and 142.)

Recommended Reading:
Sharlot M. Hall, *Sharlot Hall on the Arizona Strip*, ed. C. Gregory Crampton (Prescott, Sharlot Hall Museum Press, 1998).

Above: Portrait of Sharlot Hall.
Sharlot Hall Museum P0565A

Uncle Jim Owens with his hunting dogs at another of his North Rim cabins, possibly at VT Park. Note the "dog-trot" breezeway architecture, a building style common in Jim's home state of Texas.
NAU.PH.568.5688

financially strapped yet always enterprising John W. Young.[61] When Young's fertile imagination contrived the idea of a dude hunting ranch on the Kaibab for British aristocracy, he convinced Buffalo Bill Cody, performing in England at the time, to round up a group of likely candidates for an exploratory trip. Dan Seegmiller of Kanab, one of several early regional tourism boosters, assembled wagons and supplies at Flagstaff to meet the train carrying an assortment of British nobles, United States army officers, and American capitalists. He led the group to John Hance's ranch near Grandview Point along the Flagstaff stage road, then down the Coconino Plateau to the Mormon emigrant road at Seth Tanner's crossing of the Little Colorado River. From that point, the hunters may have crossed paths with Mormon couples on their way to and from St. George as the party followed the emigrant road north to Lees Ferry, west to House Rock Valley and the Kane Ranch, then up the Kaibab Plateau to VT Park. Local cattlemen Dee Woolley, Alex Cram, Ed Lamb Sr., Walt Hamblin, and Anthony Ivans joined the unlikely group for the latter part of their pilgrimage.[62]

Early southwestern sport-hunting parties liked to bang away at anything that moved, but one has to wonder what targets the genteel aristocrats might have glimpsed along this mostly high-desert trek other than a few scattered range cattle. In fact, they may have seen little but a merciless sun, bleached landscape, and each and every one of their three hundred dusty miles travelled from "civilization"

at Flagstaff. There is something foreboding about this country even when crossed in an air-conditioned vehicle at fifty-five miles per hour, how much more so on a slow-motion trek by pampered nobility in open wagons. Whatever the case, the British lords had experienced enough of the Wild West, declined Young's invitation to invest, and rather than retrace their steps, they continued north to the nearest railroad by way of Mormon wagon roads.

Young's attempt to establish a formal hunting camp, about thirty-five years ahead of its time, proved a resounding failure, but small parties of vacationing dudes soon after approached the Kaibab Plateau for a week or two in pursuit of mule deer. Many came by way of Bill Bass's transcanyon trail system after 1896, often using his complete line of services which included transport from Ash Fork, supplies, stock, and guide. On these occasions, Bass kept in touch with his family by lighting signal fires at Point Sublime, indicating the party's safety and the number of days hence when saddle stock should be brought to the river for the return trip. At other times, hunters simply used the Bass trails and, after 1907, Grand Canyon's central corridor along the Bright Angel and Rust Trails.[63]

The nature of North Rim hunting changed when the United States Congress in June 1906 authorized the protection of Kaibab Plateau deer herds, and Teddy Roosevelt in November of that year created Grand Canyon Game Preserve. To implement their management mandate, the United States Forest Service prohibited deer hunting and at once declared war on any form of four-legged predator. By 1931, an estimated 800 mountain lions, 550 bobcats, 30 wolves, and nearly 5,000 coyotes lost their lives to deer-hunters-turned-"varmint"-killers, aided by government hunters, trappers, and one game warden who outdid them all, James T. "Uncle Jim" Owens.[64]

Uncle Jim, during his long North Rim tenure, became not only its most famed hunter, but also its first, longest-tenured, and best-liked resident. He was born at San Antonio, Texas, in 1857, and at eleven years of age began a first career as a cowboy for famed Texas cattleman Charles Goodnight. Helping Goodnight drive the first cattle herd to the Palo Duro Canyon area of the Texas Panhandle in 1876, Owens glimpsed the remnants of once vast buffalo herds and thereafter tended a vestigial few kept at Goodnight's ranch for sentimental reasons. In 1905 he met Charles Jesse "Buffalo" Jones—former frontiersman, Indian fighter, town founder, and buffalo-hunter-turned-conservationist—who, since 1886, had been trying to breed buffalo bulls with Galloway cattle to produce a hybrid meat animal called "cattalo." Thirty years as a cowboy proved enough for Owens so he threw in with Jones and his interesting experiment.[65]

Uncle Jim moved briefly to Wyoming and Montana then on to Yellowstone National Park where Jones served as game warden for the Sixth Cavalry in charge of the park. When Jones secured a federal permit to range buffalo east of the Kaibab Plateau in January 1906, Owens drove a herd of fifty-seven animals to their new home. The June 1906 buffalo drive from the railhead at Lund, Utah, across the Arizona Strip to House Rock Valley must have amused residents of Mormon towns along the way and bemused Owens and the three cowboys charged with the drive, but they arrived at the base of the Kaibab without mishap.[66]

Owens drove a second herd of thirty buffalos along the same trail in the following year to the ranch at the foot of Saddle Mountain just west of Marble Canyon. The ranch was included within the game preserve created later in 1906, then moved farther north in the 1940s to its present site through a grazing permit exchange with cattleman Roy Woolley. Cowboys of the 1920s and 1930s recalled as many as a hundred animals grazing throughout House Rock Valley as far north as the Vermilion Cliffs, but the slightly larger herd today ranges within a fenced 64,000-acre preserve.[67]

Uncle Jim was a partner in the buffalo enterprise from the very beginning along with Jones, Frank Onstott (or Ascott) from Texas, local ranchers Ernest Pratt and B.F. Saunders, and local man-of-all-interests Dee Woolley who anted up a hundred head of cattle for the breeding experiment. All original investors received shares in a company, never officially organized, in exchange for cash, livestock, supplies, or grazing/water rights, but the cattalo experiment languished. Buffalo and cattle mated despite no particular affection for each other and produced hybrids of the desirable size, but deliveries proved difficult because of offsprings' prominent humps. Male cattalo also tended to be sterile. The disappointed partners sold out one by one until the herd ended up in Owens' hands by the mid-1910s. Uncle Jim maintained the purebred buffalos at a loss until the late 1920s, occasionally driving the animals up to the Walhalla Plateau for summer pasturage, but usually keeping them on their preferred range in House Rock Valley.[68]

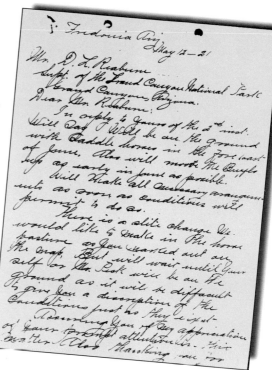

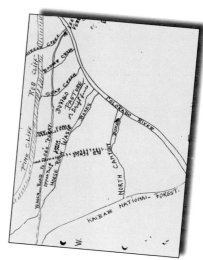

Uncle Jim's letter to Superintendent Raeburn working out grazing permit details for the 1921 season. Jim's buffalo preferred to roam the lower flats of House Rock Valley and it was a nuisance to try to keep them atop the plateau in summers, but Jim liked to please the park service and North Rim tourists. The sketch map accompanied Owens' letter. GRCA 5310, 5312

Owens is not as well remembered for his nearly twenty-year custody of Arizona's first buffalo herd as he is for his sixteen-year concurrent career as the North Rim's premier cougar hunter. Arriving in the year Roosevelt created the game preserve, Owens went to work as a "guard" for the United States Forest Service, and in 1907, became the reserve's first certified game warden, a position he held until 1919.[69] His official duties consisted of shooting, trapping, roping, or by other means removing predators from the Kaibab Plateau. The cougar, or mountain lion, was his primary prey and by his own account Owens killed more than 1,200, though others estimated his tally nearer 550. The numerical discrepancy may have arisen from his part-time job as a bounty hunter over a much larger region, ranging from southern Utah to the Black Mountains of Arizona, where he earned up to five hundred dollars per day eliminating everything from badgers, coyotes, wolverines, and cougars to grizzly bears.[70]

As a forest service game warden, Owens' duties allowed him to guide hunting parties at his own discretion, a labor which earned him and Grand Canyon's North Rim greater renown. He guided his most famous client, Teddy Roosevelt, on a cougar hunt while the ex-president toured Grand Canyon National Monument in 1913, a trip which Roosevelt made famous in the October 1913 edition of *Outlook* magazine. Two years earlier, Owens had led Arizona territorial historian Sharlot Hall on a sightseeing tour of the North Rim, an adven-

ture which Ms. Hall published in the well-read *Arizona, the New State Magazine.* Still earlier in 1908, Owens along with Lees ferryman Jim Emett and Buffalo Jones had guided western novelist Zane Grey to the Powell Plateau for a bit of lion roping. Grey published two books that featured Owens and Buffalo Jones: *The Life of a Plainsman* (1908) and *Roping Lions in the Grand Canyon* (1924).[71]

The improbable "sport" of lion roping required specially trained, English mixed bloodhounds who tracked, chased, then treed a cougar while men rode hell-bent through tall timber to keep up. Owens, who admitted he had never seen more than a half dozen cougars without his dogs, took special care of the hounds and especially leaders of the pack, Pot and Tub. Once they had the cougar up a tree, a member of the party—typically Jones, who loved the danger—shimmied up the trunk with a lasso hooked to a pole. The trick was to get the rope around the animal's neck, another around its hind legs, pull it out of the tree, tie the safe end down, lash all four legs together, clip its nails, and muzzle it before the eight- to ten-foot-long cougar killed man, dog, horse, or itself. Grey wisely stood clear with a camera then wrote about his adventure, which netted six, but Owens often returned from roping parties empty handed, lacerated, and shy a dog or horse. The cougars, if they survived the trauma, ended up in zoos around the world.[72]

In later years, as motorists began to approach the North Rim and Uncle Jim made the transition from warden to

independent guide, he posted a sign along the road near his cabin which read JIM OWENS CAMP. GUIDING TOURIST AND HUNTING PARTIES A SPECIALTY. COUGARS CAUGHT TO ORDER. RATES REASONABLE.[73]

As the 1920s rolled by, he gave up hunting cougars because he could no longer hear his baying hounds, and turned to less violent forms of tourism. His favored area surrounded his cabin near Bright Angel Spring, only one of at least a half dozen Owens homes, in what is known today as Harvey Meadow along the first mile of road to Point Sublime. From this base he could attract tourists driving the pioneer alignment of the North Rim approach road to the Wylie camp at Bright Angel Point, and also take care of his horse and buffalo herds which grazed eastward to Uncle Jim Point, the head of the Rust Trail, and on the Walhalla Plateau as far as Cape Royal.[74]

Approaching old age, and perhaps spooked by encroaching civilization which came with new park roads and tourist facilities, Uncle Jim sold his buffalo to the state of Arizona for ten thousand dollars and left the region in 1928 or 1929.[75] He went back to Texas to visit with Charles Goodnight and other old friends from his cowboy days, then moved to New Mexico where he died in the town of Afton at age seventy-nine on 11 May 1936.[76]

From 1906 to 1928 Uncle Jim made his living as buffalo herdsman, game warden, guide, and "arch-enemy of destructive animals" as Wylie Camp operator Thomas McKee later called him. Others remembered him simply as the ever-present resident on the plateau. His composite portrait reveals a spare man, barely five feet seven inches tall and 170 pounds, with a long face, firm jaw, and clear blue eyes. Old age added only a short white beard, white hair, and a slight stoop. He moved with the confidence typical of pioneers, with a touch of easy grace distinguishing him from most others. Those who knew him best say he was absolutely fearless of man, animal, or the elements. Scarcely a person over seventy-five years of age on the Arizona Strip today failed to meet the wide-ranging Owens at one time or another and all describe him, strangely enough, as a man kind to animals and people alike.[77]

Folklorists would have a fine time collecting Uncle Jim stories since he has become a legend with seemingly contradictory traits. Many over the years testified to his fondness for liquor and some contend he shot up El Tovar Hotel during one periodic binge, but others swear he never uttered an unpleasant word to or about anyone, was generous to a fault, and rarely if ever cussed, religious, yet it is unlikely that he ever saw the inside of a church. Some say in all sincerity that he once fell from a ledge, landed on a cougar's back, and rode it fifty yards before the animal streaked out from under him. All agree he was as honest as the day is long, once refusing a publisher's offer to write his autobiography because the story would be incomplete. Others confide that he rode with Jesse James and killed a man in Texas, the reason he left the panhandle and would not return until the closing years of his life. Cecil Cram describes him as a "rounder" for his free-spirited, unpredictable behavior, but with admiration; Anna Brown remembers him

Uncle Jim Owens, second from left, with cougar hunting party ca. 1920.
GRCA 5281

as a wonderful man for giving up his cabin when she and husband Joe showed up unannounced one cold night, yet a "stinker" for surreptitiously serving coyote stew one day at his cabin at White Sage Flat. Half a dozen cattlemen are proud to volunteer the simple fact that they met him once or twice.[78]

• • •

Most people today would condemn Uncle Jim's primary occupation, but he certainly did it well and by the early 1920s had created, at first glance, a land safe for livestock and mule deer. Much later, forest managers figured out that cattle of the 1880s and 1890s had actually created better deer habitat by overgrazing the plateau's natural timber-grass vegetation, encouraging the invasion of shrubs and annuals, ideal deer browse. Just as the deer population began to increase, the United States Forest Service took exactly the wrong measures by eliminating sport hunting and hiring men to kill off predators. The result was a deer population that had numbered less than four thousand in 1906 irrupted to between fifty and one hundred thousand by 1924, with tens of thousands dying of starvation during the winter of 1924-25.[79]

Authorities by 1920 decided that they had done something wrong, though they were not sure exactly what, and tried several creative solutions to thin the herd. Rather than eliminate predator control measures, the full effects of which most did not understand, the forest service and Arizona's Department of Conservation initiated a "trap and transplant" program similar in concept to Uncle Jim's occasional approach to cougars. Between 1924 and 1927, rangers captured and delivered fawns to four plateau dairy farms where they were raised on cow's milk until they could be shipped out of the region. After 1927, trapped fawns found homes among residents of Fredonia, Kanab, and VT Park. These measures proved ineffective because 50 to 70 percent of captured deer died before reaching the nearest railhead, and the number caught in the first place had negligible effects on herd size.[80]

The most famous of the failed schemes resulted in the one and only Great Deer Drive of December 1924, a plan that could only have originated in cattle country. George McCormick of Flagstaff agreed with local organizations to drive between three thousand and eight thousand deer across the canyon for two dollars and fifty cents per animal delivered. With federal approval, he recruited fifty-five Arizona Strip residents and seventy Navajos to form a skirmish line at South Canyon and beat the bushes toward the Nankoweap Trail, raising a din and theoretically herding deer before them. McCormick must have expected deer to behave like cattle and form an orderly line down Walcott's trail, swim the river, then reform and gain the South Rim over the Tanner Trail, duplicating, in fact, an earlier activity along the old Horsethief route which some say he knew quite well. After emerging from Saddle Canyon in a fierce rain storm, however, the men found not a single animal had made it even to the north edge. Forest Supervisor Rutledge, who participated in the adventure, commented with understatement that it was "the most interesting failure he had ever witnessed."[81]

To complement its creative ideas to reduce the deer population, the forest service in 1924 proposed wholesale slaughter through a series of mercenary hunts, but the state of Arizona challenged the federal government's right to massacre game animals. When the United States Supreme Court ruled against the state in 1928, the forest service promptly unleashed an assault reminiscent of 1870s buffalo hunts on the Great Plains. In December 1928, mounted government hunters, trailed by pack stock and buckboards, fanned out over the plateau and gunned down every deer within rifle range, more than 1,100 animals. Skins and meat presumably went to good use, but many condemned this type of slaughter. The forest service relented to public opinion the following year when Arizona's reorganized Game and Fish Department agreed to cooperate in managing annual sport hunts.[82]

Controlled hunting by sportsmen, along with kill data and observed effects on the range, proved an effective answer to plateau deer and range problems when combined with livestock reductions. The forest service conducted its first public hunt in late autumn 1924 when 270 hunters brought down 675 deer. The early years following an eighteen-year hunting hiatus produced trophies up to 225 pounds, field dressed, with antlers of thirty-two points and forty-eight-inch spreads. Even typical kills resulted in average dress weights of 150 to 208 pounds. Despite high success rates and as many as 10,000 hunters in a season, however, the deer population in 1949 stood at 57,000 and numbers remained fairly constant through the 1960s.[83]

Aside from accomplishing United States Forest Service objectives, sport hunting on the Kaibab Plateau brought a vigorous seasonal industry to the Arizona Strip and contributed to the rise of North Rim tourism. The number of hunters in the 1920s and 1930s far surpassed the number of local residents. Most were affluent and arrived with little more than a rifle and personal items, which translated into a healthy service business for Fredonia and Kanab stores, restaurants, hotels, and service stations. Because the forest service and state game wardens imposed strict controls, deer hunting also spawned five private hunting camps by 1926 which doubled as official checking stations on the east and west flanks of the plateau. These camps employed scores of local cowboys intimately familiar with the terrain to serve as requisite guides since, without help, out-of-state city dudes would have a hard time making it back to camp much less finding the best deer habitats.[84]

The first hunting camp may have been at Slide Reservoir, which opened in 1924 but disappeared by 1931.[85] Of the three other camps to open on the west side of the plateau, the first was probably Big Saddle, built by Hayden S. "Hades" Church and wife, Sytha, a few miles north of the rim above Crazy Jug Point. The Churches were true pioneer tourism operators on the Kaibab Plateau, opening a store, gas station, and saloon along the road to the North Rim at VT Park in the 1910s. Hayden earned his nickname by posting a cryptic sign along the road from Jacob Lake which read "Go to Hades," a phrase often directed his way when he told visitors that he came out each spring to paint the aspen trunks white for their touring enjoyment. Through the years the Churches could not help but stumble over literally thousands of deer that grazed the open valley, and when they caught wind of forest service plans, they hurriedly located Big Saddle Hunting Camp.[86]

Big Saddle and other hunting camps that soon followed closely resembled primitive tourism facilities found at the South Rim thirty years earlier. Canvas tents and tent-cabins served as the earliest accommodations. At Big

Saddle, the second and third generations of Churches—Jack, Mardean, and son Steve— added ten log or frame cabins and a 1,200-square-foot lodge to upgrade the hunters' experience as well as serve increasing numbers of hunters in the 1950s and 1960s. The forest service forced the family to remove all but the lodge, six cabins, and latrines after 1967, and the camp itself met its end about 1971 when rangers opened the plateau to guideless hunting and did not renew the Churches' use permit.[87] Camps at Pine Flat southwest of Big Springs, and Moquitch south of Ryan, probably never grew beyond the tent-cabin stage. Slim Waring operated Pine Flat and Elwin Pratt, Bob Vaughn, then Jack Butler ran Moquitch in the early years, but Jack and Mardean Church acquired all three west-side facilities by 1941. Moquitch closed about 1948 because hunters preferred camps at higher elevations. Pine Flat remained open until the late 1960s.[88]

Hunting camps of the 1920s through the 1960s also operated in an easy manner reminiscent of earlier tourist facilities at the South Rim, despite government controls normally associated with the end of a pioneer period. At Big Saddle, supplies for the fourteen- to thirty-day late autumn hunts had to be trucked in thirty to forty miles from Kanab or Fredonia along the poor dirt road through Nail Canyon, then on worse secondary roads. Operators hauled water to fill camp cisterns from Bee Spring five miles to the east or even farther from Big Springs. Wives arose long before sunup, often in bitter cold, to get the stoves going, coffee brewing, and breakfast on the table for as many as a hundred men, while guides slept fully clothed save boots and hat to keep from freezing. As guides saddled up for each day's hunt, the kitchen crew

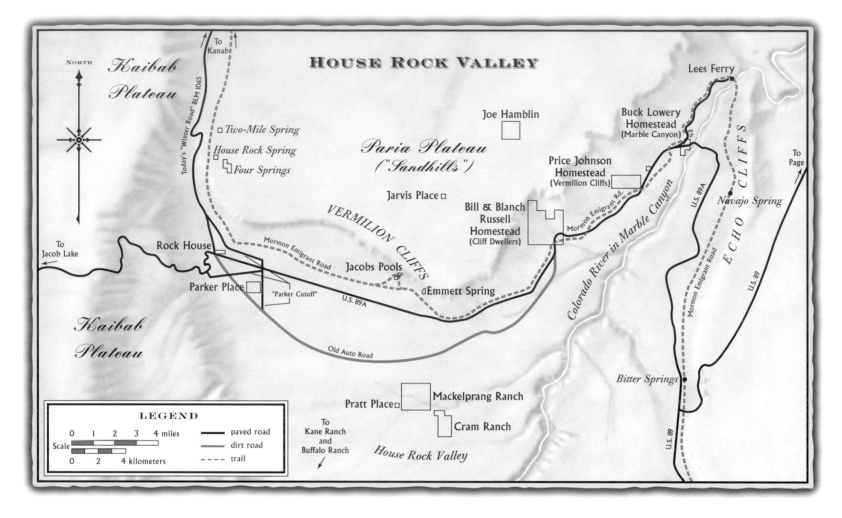

kicked reluctant hunters out of the warm cook shack with a sack lunch in hand, then fed them upon return in the late evening with steak, potatoes, beans, salad, cobbler, and hot coffee. One cabin offered a small saloon and slot machines for evening hours.

Mardean Frost Church recalled the hard work and frigid, lonely, early morning hours along with the amusing behavior of hunters and guides. Hunters paid five to six hundred dollars for room, meals, stock, and guide yet many spent the better part of a day lingering in the

cook shack for warmth and conversation while getting in the way of dinner preparations. Prominent guests like Clark Gable and Barry Goldwater acted no differently. Guides often led hunters along drainages of the irregular North Rim to catch deer moving down for the winter and rarely failed to set up a few good shots, but some of their charges seemed content to forego the shooting to admire the scenery. Many in fact gave away what deer they shot to Navajo and Paiute hunters, who camped nearby at Crazy Jug Spring during their annual plateau trips

for meat and pinyon nuts. Paiutes and Navajos camped separately, but mingled freely when they came to Big Saddle to trade, talk, and sell their handmade deerskin gloves.[89]

Guides worked hard for less than five dollars per day, though they earned as much as three hundred dollars in tips from the two to four hunters who stayed with them for an entire hunt.[90] They are also the most common subject of hunting camp stories today. Spike Heaton was one who did not like to get too far away from the cook shack, such that one of his parties complained that they never lost sight of the camp dump. "Walapai" Johnny Nelson was one of the more popular guides, but occasionally over imbibed and some mornings would miss the saddle when trying to mount up.

The Church family also ran the mule concession at North Rim, Bryce, and Zion after 1928. One story relates that as Walapai guided a group down the North Kaibab Trail in the 1960s, a young woman disrobed. When others complained and Mardean asked him later what he did about it, he replied, "I just rode backwards." Despite having to fire Walapai "fifty times per year" for various misdeeds, Jack and Mardean always hired him back, not only because hunters requested him by name but because the Churches considered him and other cowboy guides to be part of the larger regional family.[91]

Hunting camps on the east side of the plateau in the vicinity of the Great Deer Drive ran much the same as Big Saddle, Pine Flat, and Moquitch but on a smaller scale. The camp in the cockscombs near South Canyon Ranger Station opened by 1926 and served as many as twenty hunters per season until it burned in a forest fire in the 1960s. Another camp at Saddle Mountain opened early, perhaps at the same time as those on the western plateau, but shut down for awhile before reopening in 1953. Both camps operated in later years under Del and Sarah Hamblin and son, Ben, who upgraded early tents and cook shacks to include tent-cabins and a few frame cabins. Saddle Mountain Camp

closed about 1970 like Big Saddle when guideless hunting ended these pioneer forest service concessions.[92]

TOURISM ARRIVES

Mining, lumbering, agriculture, and even regionwide ranching had done little to overcome Mormon preferences for isolation and self-sufficiency on the Arizona Strip. Sport hunting on the slopes of the Kaibab Plateau, however, attracted visitors by the thousands to remote segments of Grand Canyon's North Rim and, as at the South Rim, offered promise of tourist developments at locations easily accessed from regional centers at Fredonia and Kanab. Ultimately, tourism would concentrate at a more distant point through concerted efforts of several prominent residents, but facilities could as easily have arisen almost directly south of these towns overlooking lovely, expansive, and more easily accessible areas.

The Thunder River environs held especial promise. John and Levi Stewart had approached within twenty miles of the rim as early as 1871 when they established their lumber mill and small ranch at Big Springs. Cattlemen had approached the North Rim directly south of the Stewart place at Indian Hollow, Little Saddle, Crazy Jug Point, and sites farther west by the 1880s, and not long after built a number of trails to the sandrock Esplanade and one trail, along Dutton's path, to Surprise Valley and Bonita Creek. European-American discovery of Thunder River, probably by a regional cattleman, is

placed at 1904. Thus, by the turn of the century and before federal regulation had arrived, the Thunder River rim area, less than sixty miles from Fredonia by wagon road and cattlemen's trail, lay waiting for some entrepreneur like Bill Bass or Pete Berry to gaze upon the truly picturesque landscape and aspire for control. Such an individual never arrived.

Tourism in the Thunder River area instead awaited the United States Forest Service, hunting camps, and the National Park Service, by which time the period of unregulated development had passed and most had acquired a sense that Thunder River should remain backcountry. Coincident with the first seasons at Big Saddle Hunting Camp in 1925 and 1926, park service ranger Edward Laws and forest service workers improved the old cattlemen's trail from Little Saddle to the Esplanade, then along the sandrock rounding the upper Deer Creek drainage to access the Redwall Limestone break where Dutton's party had descended in 1880, then across Surprise Valley as far as Thunder Spring. In 1939, a park service crew consisting of local residents Weaver White, Ferris Pratt, Raymond Pointer, and Reece Locke completed the trail alongside the half-mile-long river to its confluence with Tapeats Creek at Camp Cove, the pioneer name for today's Upper Tapeats campground. Ed Laws soon returned and stocked the stream with trout fry.[93]

Despite these few improvements made in the 1920s and 1930s, the Thunder River area remained virtually a personal wilderness reserve for cattlemen and other

NPS ranger Ed Laws beside the 1928 north entrance station, still in use today. This July 1930 photograph shows the old dirt road connecting VT Park and Bright Angel Point, replaced in 1930-31 by today's automotive road that passes beside the station. GRCA 3884

Because the United States Forest Service and National Park Service chose to direct tourism elsewhere, the Thunder River area including its rimside trailhead never succumbed to development other than hunting facilities at Big Saddle, five miles distant. In 1949, park superintendent Harold C. Bryant estimated that fewer than two hundred people had ever visited the robust spring and turbulent river, and that was fine with administrators who were content to maintain it as a wilderness area. So few used the trail in the 1940s and 1950s that those who did confused and debated the origins of Thunder River and Tapeats Creek, partly because of their disbelief that a river, perhaps the shortest in the world, could flow into a creek. Visitation increased beyond a few per year only after the 1960s, when commercial rafters began to make the several-mile ascent beside Tapeats Creek and backpackers coincidentally rediscovered the old horse trail down from Little Saddle. Today, most backcountry hikers bypass the old cattlemen's trail to the Esplanade and instead use the Bill Hall Trail from Monument Point, a shortcut developed during the 1950s.[95]

• • •

Even fewer early visitors disturbed near-wilderness conditions of the North Bass Trail, its trailhead area at Swamp Point, and nearby Powell Plateau, another promising development site less than ten air-miles southeast of Big Saddle Hunting Camp. Bill Bass had led tourists and hunters into the area from 1896 through the late 1910s, but his trail system on both sides of the Colorado River quickly deteriorated after he moved to Wickenburg since no one other than a few backcountry rangers and feral burros cared to walk the primitive

residents of Fredonia, Kanab, and Bundyville. Hunting camp operator Hades Church did advertise excursions in a limited way, however, and Jack Church continued the service in association with routine hunting and concession activities. In these instances, a few flexible hunting guides doubled as tourist guides and wranglers as they drove the Church family's saddle stock down to the Esplanade for winter forage following autumn hunts, and retrieved them in the spring to prepare for summer concessions at Zion, Bryce, and Bright Angel Point. While at the bottom, they paused a few days to informally entertain guests with a few days of fishing and evening campground stories about the time they used chains to catch the river's "monster" trout, and other such whoppers. Billy and Tuffy Swapp, Ron Mace, and Johnny Nelson were just a few of the guides who led handfuls of tourists and a few friends to this enchanted place.[94]

paths. In 1925, National Park Service rangers responded to criticism that they had not opened up the northwest side of the park by improving the twenty-mile-long Powell Saddle Trail from the North Rim checking station at VT Park to Swamp Point. In the same year, they built a winter patrol cabin at Muav Saddle and reconstructed the upper trail from Swamp Point, beyond the cabin, and up to the Powell Plateau.[96]

These improvements more or less mimicked those in the Thunder River area and served the same purpose, allowing access to a backcountry area while discouraging full scale development. The North Bass Trail below the Coconino Sandstone remained unimproved, and was so difficult to follow that rangers sent to plant fifty thousand trout eggs in perennial Shinumo Creek in the late 1920s chose instead to dump them in upper White Creek. When the fish failed to thrive in the typically dry creek bed, chief ranger Jim Brooks and rangers Art Brown and Ed Laws returned in 1930 with another batch. They made it all the way to Shinumo Creek this time, but only after others had improved the trail. The area was virtually abandoned after 1930 until backpackers rediscovered, rerouted, and renovated the trail through use during the 1960s.[97]

Sport hunting and park service improvements brought only a few visitors to Thunder River and Swamp Point after the 1920s, and both areas, though laced with extensive trails and blessed with remarkable scenery, remain by design backcountry areas to this day.

Developments at today's single center of tourist activity, Bright Angel Point, came about through the efforts of small businessmen to attract the sightseeing public, a quarter century after like entrepreneurs had done the same at the South Rim. Grand Canyon's success as a transportation barrier accounted for the fact that in the first years of the new century, as the South Rim bristled with visitors and Ralph Cameron struggled with the Santa Fe Railroad and United States Forest Service for control, Bright Angel Point, a scant ten air-miles away, remained empty. When developers did arrive, they came from the Arizona Strip and southern Utah, maintained enterprises independent of southside concessioners, and developed in many respects a separate national park with almost no influence from the southside other than the controlling arm of federal agencies headquartered at Grand Canyon Village.

• • •

The Bright Angel Point story begins with the paradox that Mormon pioneers usually did not engage in nontraditional enterprises, yet were initially responsible for North Rim tourism. The explanation is that the few church members who took an interest in development at the turn of the century were among those who believed in greater interaction with the outside world and sensed no moral dilemma in extracting dollars from the travelling public. One of the earliest of these was Dan Seegmiller, the Kanab resident who shuttled John Young's English aristocrats from Flagstaff to the Kaibab Plateau and offered buggy

rides from Kanab to the North Rim on an irregular basis well into the 1900s. Others provided similar services to occasional travelers, but the man who more than anyone believed in attracting regional tourism, then made it happen, was Edwin Dilworth "Uncle Dee" Woolley.

Uncle Dee came from the same mold as Buckey O'Neill and John Young, men who would try anything that promised a dollar and shrugged off occasional failure. He was born in 1844, came west with his family and Brigham Young at the age of three, and moved to St. George soon after its founding in 1861. By the middle 1860s, Dee and older brother Franklin worked as lonely freighters along Jacob Hamblin's wagon road east from St. George, and served in several militia campaigns against the Navajo. After the wars, in which Franklin was killed, the younger brother remained on the Arizona Strip, and by 1880, began his forty-year romance with regional tourism. To finance and advance his passionate avocation, Woolley retained a commanding position as president of the Kanab stake and earned a good living as a merchant and cattleman.[98]

Uncle Dee passed up few opportunities to promote regional tourism, as evidenced by his failed interests in John Young's noblemen and Jim Owens' buffalos, but his most important contribution began in 1903 when he formed the Grand Canyon Transportation Company with local residents Thomas Chamberlain, T.C. Hoyt, Jim Emett, and E.S. Clark. The company had many stated purposes, among them regional road improvements, but one of its

Easily portaged canvas (and sometimes wood or steel) rowboats were used to cross the Colorado prior to Rust's and Bass's cable systems. Here Dave Rust gives pointers to Ellsworth and Emery Kolb near the mouth of Bright Angel Creek, 1906. NAU.PH.568-966

primary goals entailed construction of a trail from the head of Bright Angel Canyon to the Colorado River, a cable crossing and trail to link up with the Bright Angel Trail, and a tourist camp near the mouth of Bright Angel Creek. To complete all three tasks Woolley hired his son-in-law, David Rust, as company foreman.[99]

David Rust was born in Payson, Utah, in 1874. He was raised on a dirt-poor homestead near the remote Mormon village of Kaneville, Utah, but his mother insisted he attend Brigham Young Academy in Salt Lake City and he later earned a degree in English literature at Stanford University. Rust married Dee Woolley's daughter, Ruth, in 1903, and settled down to teach school in Fredonia before his father-in-law recruited him into the tourism business in June 1906.[100] Others had been along Bright Angel Creek from the river to the North

Rim before Rust—including Dan Hogan, Wash Henry, Lannes Ferrall, the François Matthes topographical party, and a few prospectors and hunting parties—but only Matthes had scratched out a path and no one had invested the time and money to build a good tourist trail until Rust arrived in July 1906.

Personally supervising five to six men during July and August 1906, Rust spent six weeks wielding pick and shovel to cut a saddle trail from the trailhead, about one mile west of Greenland Spring, to the bed of Bright Angel Creek below the Redwall Limestone cliffs. Construction posed no particular problem below the Redwall, since the creek drains in a gentle gradient from this point to the Colorado River, but simple tools and cost-conscious managers ensured that the trail crossed the shallow creek nearly a hundred times within the lower granite gorge before reaching its destination. Word of Rust's mission must have spread quickly, as two tourist parties came by during the first three weeks of construction.[101]

Building any trail proved difficult during the pioneer years, but did not approach the time, cost, and energy required to erect a dependable cable system across the Colorado River. Although Dee Woolley ordered cables and equipment from Salt Lake City in 1905, pieces did not begin to arrive until October 1906. Hauling a five-hundred-foot-long cable down the new trail and hand braiding support strands at the river seemed easy compared to stringing them across the river with only a rowboat then building abutments and balancing the 1,500-pound cable car properly. Almost a year passed before the system became operational, and not before Rust had nearly lost his hands to the installation and his life to recurrent pneumonia. He captured the mood of the entire experience in his description of one day's work on 1 April 1907:

A sad day for us, a heart breaker. We had salty coffee for breakfast, but that isn't the trouble. Just as we finished the platform landing … we load the cage with about 2000# of stone and start her across. All goes lovely and jubilant until the car is nearly half way over, then buzz! whang! ka-plash. She sinks out of sight—the river eats it up like the monster she has proved herself … We pull on the slack and go to camp sad, sad!

Rust retrieved the cage from the river despite his pneumonia, then labored another six months to finish the system. On 21 September 1907, Rose Evans and Lida Bilveal became the first tourists to cross on the cable car.[102]

While Rust and his employees completed the cable system they went to work on a trail on the south side of the river which Rust called the Wash Henry Trail. It is uncertain whether this was the trail which climbed the steep slope straight south from the cable terminus to the Tonto Platform—a path soon called the Cable Trail, rebuilt by the National Park Service in 1925 as the bottom segment of the South Kaibab Trail—or another that skirted the cliffs downriver along the route of today's Colorado River Trail to Pipe Creek, but in either case, it connected with the county's Bright Angel Trail to Grand Canyon Village. Rust often climbed to the village during cable installation to meet with Ralph Cameron and arranged a reciprocal-use agreement that marked the opening of the central tourism corridor in late 1907. He also surveyed the site called Rust Camp, less than a mile up Bright Angel Creek, and may have filed a claim to the location, though he never patented the parcel or any claim on either side

of the river. Rust dug irrigation ditches and planted a garden and cottonwood trees at his camp, some of the latter towering today over Phantom Ranch, but facilities never amounted to more than a few tents with nearby corrals.[103]

Dee Woolley, Dave Rust, and others of the transportation company worked hard to improve their trail, camp, cable system, and overall tourist enterprise in 1908 and 1909. They opened a livery and out-fitting business in Kanab, built the Woolley Cabin near the Rust trailhead, and often guided customers the entire distance from town to camp, an operation similar in scope to Bill Bass's 1890s business from Williams and Ash Fork. It was necessarily a part-time endeavor, however, limited by winter snows which blocked travel to the Kaibab Plateau and by the men's several occupations. Rust himself continued to teach school most of a year at Fredonia until 1928, edited Kanab's *Kane County Standard* newspaper which diligently lobbied for better roads and tourism during the 1920s, and served several terms in the state legislature. This explains why Rust Camp, later called Roosevelt Camp and Woolley Camp by some, never developed beyond the tent stage, and why passersby during the 1910s, who approached from the south-side trail, open year round, often described it as abandoned. Actually, Rust and company operated their business and

David Rust at an abutment of his cable system across the Colorado, ca. 1910.
GRCA 16001 (Rust Collection)

Arizona Governor Hunt (fifth from left) sent a party from Phoenix to the Arizona Strip in 1914 to assess regional resources. He visited in 1923, pictured here at Will Rust's lodge or Uncle Jim's cabin at VT Park. GRCA 7120

fix the worst spots and cache gasoline and supplies at Panguitch, Johnson, Kanab, Ryan, and VT Park. He recruited his nephew Gordon Woolley to lead the expedition and on 26 June 1909, bade the automotive explorers farewell at Salt Lake City.

Gordon Woolley's two-vehicle caravan set out from Salt Lake City with his wife, Ollie, and their four children, a chauffeur, and two friends rounding out the main party. A roadster crammed with axes, picks, shovels, and other turn-of-the-century road equipment led the way. The family followed in a convertible touring car and managed to make Kanab in only three days, a ride which takes today's motorist along U.S. Highway 89 perhaps seven to eight hours at a leisurely pace. North of Kanab, the adventurers crossed a one-and-one-half-mile segment of sand dunes by repeatedly spreading a canvas tarp and driving ahead several yards at a time. Just east of Kanab, they crossed a gully by pressing straw and tarp against its slippery banks. At about this point, Uncle Dee met the party—how he got there is anyone's guess—and entered Kanab shouting from the hood of the lead car to the many skeptics who had scoffed at his idea, "I told you so!" The party spent three recuperative days at Kanab giving rides to the townsfolk, not a dozen of whom had ever seen an automobile.

maintained the camp during summers until 1917, when spring floods wrecked the cable cage. Rust continued to lead occasional groups to his camp until the National Park Service arrived in 1919.[104]

• • •

Dee Woolley made one more direct contribution to tourism which epitomized his vision as well as the dismal condition of regional roads in 1909. With the transportation company's business off the ground, Uncle Dee thought it appropriate to sponsor the first automobile trip to the North Rim. The problems: there were no maps, no automotive roads, no service stations, and few automobiles between there and Provo, Utah, hundreds of miles to the north. Undeterred by minor inconveniences, Woolley made his own maps of the old wagon road from Provo south to Kanab, noting every gully, dugway, sand hill, curve, and stream along the way. He also sent a party ahead in wagons to

The expedition left Kanab for the head of the Rust trail along a path first worn by cattlemen. Striking southeasterly from Fredonia, they made thirty-five miles the first day, spending much of their time rebuilding road segments across sage flats while running out of gasoline, a problem solved by an enterprising threshing machine operator who happened by and sold them five gallons of the rare fuel for a dollar apiece. On the second day, they bounced along a better wagon road past abandoned mines at Ryan, up Nail Canyon, and beyond the United States Forest Service ranger station at Big Springs, then climbed the Kaibab Plateau through Dry Park and continued to the cattle ranch at VT Park. Here they picked up the even poorer road long used by cattlemen and since 1907 by the transportation company southward through Little Park to Fuller Canyon and on to the cabin at Rust's trailhead.[105]

The 1909 Woolley automotive jaunt, like the Hogaboom expedition from Flagstaff to Grandview in 1902, proved that automobiles could make it to the chasm's edge, but did not exactly incite a traffic jam. Real traffic awaited road improvements of the 1920s. Still, the imaginative Uncle Dee Woolley had pointed the way once again and, until his death in 1920, campaigned relentlessly for a regional railway and better roads.

David Rust also kept his interest in regional tourism, helping to organize good roads associations, successfully promoting convict road gangs, and guiding tourists over a broad area ranging from Zion National Park to Rainbow Bridge. Colorado River historian Dock Marston credited Rust with starting commercial river rafting in the canyons of the Colorado by charging for such trips in Glen Canyon, his favorite haunt, during the 1920s.[106] Rust moved his family to Provo, Utah, in 1928, but continued to spend summers outfitting from the Pace

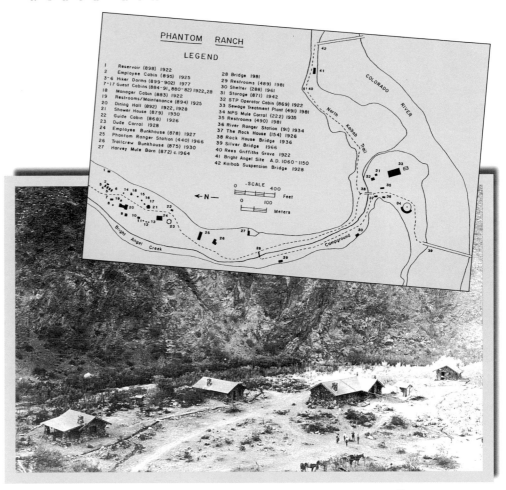

Phantom Ranch and sketch map depicting structures built between 1922 and 1981. Rust Camp and the original Phantom Ranch were located within today's complex approximately one-half mile up Bright Angel Creek. Rust's 1907 cable system and the 1921 wooden suspension bridge were located beside today's Kaibab Suspension Bridge. Map courtesy of its creator, Teri Cleeland, U.S. Forest Service archaeologist and historian.

GRCA 4440

The 1921 and 1928 Kaibab suspension bridges. A rider is making a final crossing on the older bridge.

GRCA 10141

THE HOUSE ROCK VALLEY GAS WAR

ouse Rock Valley never really had a "road," hardly needed one until persistent needling by North Rim tourism boosters prompted the government to extend U.S. Highway 89 (today's 89A) to the Arizona Strip during the early 1930s. North Rim tourism operator Thomas McKee wrote of a man in the 1920s who had glimpsed El Tovar from Bright Angel Point, a mere ten miles away, and decided to drive his Packard around the grand crevasse via the old emigrant road to have a closer look. He never made it to Lees Ferry, though they found him alive within a week. McKee himself, a veteran driver of horrific pathways, once spent four and one-half days making the trip to Flagstaff by the same route.

Considering the absence of a road constructed for automobiles, few regional residents (fewer still owning autos), and almost no tourist traffic, one may find it incredible that there were two gas stations, their owners fighting for every vehicle that passed, maybe a half-dozen per day. Dean Cutler had a little store and two gravity gas pumps in front of the rock house still standing north of today's highway at the base of the Kaibab Plateau. E.W. Parker had a little shack on his homestead several miles southeast and no store, just a pump he picked up somewhere and used to make a little money.

Cutler clearly had the advantage: a store as well as gasoline alongside what passed for the main road, improved only slightly for autos by the early 1920s. Parker, however, held the job of Coconino County highway worker; not that the county did any work, but he had the title and a scraper. One day he decided on his own authority to move the road around a little bit to improve his business.

The old auto road came west from Lees Ferry to Marble Canyon, generally as it does today, but then swung as far as several miles south of today's U.S. Highway 89A to avoid the worst of the valley's sand. It ran south of the Parker place then angled northwest past Cutler's rock house—a former headquarters of the Grand Canyon Cattle Company—and up the valley toward House Rock Spring (where the real "Rock House," a houselike rock pile noted by Powell's second crew, is located). A wagon road also climbed the Kaibab Plateau to Jacob Lake roughly where it does today, placing Cutler at something of a favorable crossroads.

Parker found this situation intolerable, so he rebuilt the road from Lees Ferry to angle up to his gas pump, then sharply north and northwest up the valley, totally bypassing Cutler's store. He effectively placed the crossroads at his own place by also rebuilding the

road to the plateau, placing it a couple hundred yards south of Cutler's rock house then up the plateau to regain the original alignment (near today's first scenic pullout). To prevent motorists from wandering off the new roads, he lined them with old tin cans.

Cecil Cram, who related this story, cannot recall Dean Cutler's reaction to Parker's effrontery, but the new alignments remained in place until the federal government commissioned today's road a few years later, which again passes alongside the old rock house and bypasses the Parker place several hundred yards to the south. Only on the Arizona Strip could one man change an entire road system as late as the 1920s!

Note: See map on page 142.

Above: This gravity gasoline pump from southern Utah was the type used on the Arizona Strip from the 1910s into the 1960s. Courtesy of Mike Anderson.

Ranch at Torrey, Utah, and leading parties into Wayne's Wonderland, an area encompassing scenic Kane, Garfield, and Wayne Counties in southern Utah. He witnessed the flooding of Glen Canyon shortly before his death in 1963 and, tourism booster to the end, approved of the action that would bring even more visitors to the remote region he loved so much.[107]

• • •

Woolley, Rust, Uncle Jim Owens, and cattle companies operating from VT Park all had a hand in steering visitors to the vicinity of Bright Angel Point, as did the United States Forest Service when it became apparent that tourism would unfold on the Kaibab Plateau. Beginning in the mid-1910s, managers of the Kaibab National Forest began to publish brochures for "campers and tourists" that advertised mileage between key points, cultural and scenic attractions, roads and trails, and the very few services available. In 1913, they built the Grand Canyon Highway, a fifty-six-mile road that traced an old cattle and lumbermen's trail from the north forest boundary up LeFevre Canyon, past ranger stations at Jacob Lake and VT Park, to the Bright Angel Ranger Station at Harvey Meadow. The grandiose name and advertisement as an "excellent auto road having only a few grades that exceed 10 percent" belied the reality. Contemporary travelers revealed little more than an improved wagon road, but it may well have seemed a boulevard compared to other plateau alternatives. Besides the road and an offer of limited telephone service from any of five plateau ranger stations to Fredonia, forest rangers concentrated on warning the public of fire dangers and helping out in emergencies.[108]

In 1915, Aldus "Blondie" Jensen and wife Melissa Brown Jensen moved into the Woolley Cabin to begin the first saddle concession near Bright Angel Point. The Jensens led guests down the Rust trail to the river, handing them off to Fred Harvey muleskinners if they wanted to continue to the South Rim, while taking on Harvey guests who chose to visit the North Rim. They charged a hefty forty-nine dollar fee for both one-way and round trips, but only six dollars for day trips to Roaring Springs, and variable rates for other rides within the canyon or along its edge. Like Bill Bass, the Jensens communicated with the South Rim by lighting fires at a certain time each night, indicating the number of riders who would cross the river the following day. South Rim concessioners similarly alerted the Jensens. In 1917, the couple discontinued their informal tent accommodations for overnight guests in favor of Thomas and Elizabeth Wylie McKee, who arrived with a United States Forest Service agreement to operate a formal Wylie Way Camp near the fire tower at Bright Angel Point.[109]

First tourist concession at the North Rim of Grand Canyon: Uncle Dee Woolley's cabin near Blondie Jensen Spring and the head of David Rust's trail, 1910. NAU.PH.568.1224

Tent-cabins preceded rustic log and wood frame cabins as individualized Grand Canyon tourist accommodations. Interiors varied greatly. The cozy room at left is from Cameron's Hotel and Camps or Bright Angel Camp at Grand Canyon Village. The cruder interior on the right greeted visitors to Louis Boucher's Dripping Springs camp. Elizabeth McKee's, James Thurber's, and Bill Bass's tent-cabins probably resembled the one on the left, though more simply furnished. Prices during 1891-1928 ranged from one dollar and fifty cents to three dollars per night. GRCA 15801, 15802

Wylie Way camps represented an intermediate-type tourist facility, a step above uncontrolled camps of the pioneer period but a few steps below accommodations western park managers hoped to achieve like El Tovar Hotel. The concept originated with W.W. Wylie at Yellowstone National Park about the turn of the century. Its distinguishing feature was the tent-cabin: a wood-frame, floor-and-wall structure of one to three rooms with a peaked, canvas-tent roof. Tent-cabins could be decorated nicely, as those built later at Hermit Camp, or left rather spartan, but in either case, kept occupants high and dry in foul weather. Other standard camp features included a central dining tent or cabin, corral and livery later replaced by an automotive garage, communal campfire, and fixed-price guided tours to reveal wonders of the particular park. Wylie's blueprint for low cost national park concessions would be copied at Bass Camp and Hance Ranch at the turn of the century and Hermit Camp after 1913.[110]

Wylie brought his concession concept south from Yellowstone to southern Utah in 1917 when he established a camp at Mukuntuweap

National Monument, redesignated Zion National Park in 1919. These were years when the nascent National Park Service had begun to work hand-in-hand with western railroads to develop the parks, and specifically to work with the Union Pacific Railroad to upgrade facilities within southern Utah parks and at Grand Canyon's North Rim. The cooperative arrangement coincided purposefully with federal legislation which allocated seventy-five million dollars for national automotive roads, fostered creation of state road commissions, and made available the engineering expertise of the federal Bureau of Public Roads. Railroads typically required, often demanded, regional road improvements before millions of dollars were invested in park infrastructure and nationwide advertising. But with a "circle tourism route" already envisioned to encompass Zion, Bryce, Cedar Breaks, and the North Rim by 1917, the Union Pacific requested camps at the former and latter locations.[111]

W.W. Wylie established his concessions in 1917 and, since he stayed to operate the Zion facility, recruited daughter Elizabeth McKee to

run the North Rim camp. The McKees and forest service rangers selected a spot beside the rim less than fifty yards north of today's Grand Canyon Lodge, and between 1917 and 1922 the camp accommodated as many as twenty-five guests with ten tent-cabins and a central kitchen-dining room. Curtains partitioned each cabin into two bedrooms and a sitting room, furnished with a table, wash bowl and water pitcher, chairs, metal beds, and bedding for which the guest paid one dollar and fifty cents per night and one dollar per meal.

Elizabeth McKee managed the facility and business, handling with a few employees not only the typical domestic requirements of a primitive hostelry but all contracts and most correspondence with federal land managers. Renewing annual permits over a ten-year period, she negotiated each year with forest service supervisors then the park's first five superintendents as well as park service director Stephen Mather and acting directors Horace Albright and Arno Cammerer. Thomas McKee filled the role of all male pioneer concessioners, helping to manage the business, building facilities, and guiding guests by horseback, wagon, and later automobile over horrible roads to Point Sublime, Skidoo Point, and Cape Royal. Although the McKees dominated guide

services to these points before 1922, the Jensens, by 1921 in partnership with local cattleman Bob Vaughn, continued to offer guided trips to more remote sites and along the Rust trail.[112]

The McKees also maintained an informal business relationship with Uncle Jim Owens, who had left the United States Forest Service in 1919 to develop a small tourist business of his own. Operating from his home at Bright Angel Spring, the Woolley Cabin, and the Greenland Lake Cabin, Uncle Jim led multiday horseback trips for cougar hunters and sightseers from Cape Royal on the east to Kanab Creek on the west at an all-expense cost of ten dollars per day. He also grazed his buffalo within visitors' sight on the Walhalla Plateau and on two thousand acres at Uncle Jim Point, an aspect of Grand Canyon tourism that tickled Stephen Mather who hoped that the "James T. Owens Herd" would one day belong to the National Park Service. Owens also led parties down Rust's trail to the river, and planned a formal tourist camp at Cape Royal in 1921 until Mather rejected his request.[113]

Tourism at Bright Angel Point caught on by 1922 as meager regional road improvements nudged annual visitation upward to nearly three thousand persons. Formerly, most visitors reached Grand Canyon's northern brow by the

Left: The McKees began to replace tent-cabins with wood frame cabins like this one in 1926. Courtesy of David Scott

Center: Wylie Camp cabins at Bright Angel Point, 1926. Courtesy of David Scott

Right: Thomas and Elizabeth McKee (left), Wylie Camp proprietors, 1917–26. Also Brighty the burro, the McKee's son, and other camp workers during the 1919 tourist season. The McKees were residents of Pasadena, California, who operated the Wylie Camp each summer from late May through September. Courtesy of Mrs. Martha Krueger

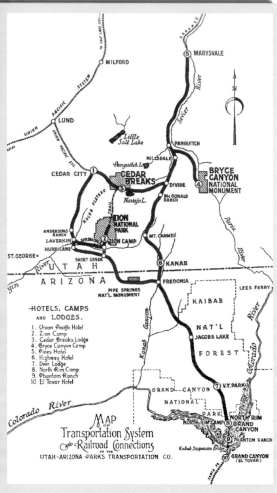

Map accompanying the 1924 Parry brochure. By 1928, the Union Pacific controlled accommodations and tourist transport over this entire grid, advertised as a "circle tourism route." The Union Pacific, like the Santa Fe south of Grand Canyon, invested millions in first-class hotels and park infrastructure in return for park service concession monopolies.

Chauncey and Gronway Parry were, in 1922, the first to establish regular auto- motive stage service to Bright Angel Point. The enterprising brothers were independent tourism operators, but closely tied to the Union Pacific Railroad and its subsidiary Utah Parks Company until bought out by the latter company ca. 1925.

GRCA 5313

place with plain log cabins and a central lodge and dining room … in charge of kindly people who keep it clean and serve excellent meals."[115] This camp developed into the Kaibab Lodge by the late 1920s, and though it opened with sleeping accommodations for only sixteen, it soon rivalled the McKees' facility.[116]

Competitive struggles similar to those at the South Rim soon erupted among the McKees, Will Rust, the Parrys, and the Jensens, although they remained less virulent because none of the people involved owned the land from which they operated. Still, the bickering that simmered each winter via poisonous letters and resumed each summer between 1922 and 1927 required park rangers to act as occasional referees, and convinced park managers that Stephen Mather's plan for concession monopolies had merit.

Disputes revolved around the aggressive Parrys, who charged one hundred and twenty- five dollars for an eight-day, all-expense-paid trip along the emerging circular tourism route and understandably cut corners wherever possible. They found it more economical to drive customers out to Cape Royal in company touring buses, a service which the McKees also offered with their own vehicles, and preferred to lodge passengers with Will Rust who apparently charged less than the McKees' increased cabin and meal rate of six dollars per day.[117] The McKees also argued with Jensen and Vaughn over the three-and-one-half-mile shuttle ride between the Wylie camp and the Woolley Cabin at the Rust trailhead, a service for which the McKees charged but Vaughn provided free. Although the approach road as far as Harvey Meadow had been improved in 1913, scenic roads to Skidoo Point, Cape Royal, and Point Sublime remained what cattlemen had worn—

twice-weekly stage along a 135-mile route from Marysvale to Kanab, then by whatever con- veyance they could secure for the remaining 80 miles to Bright Angel Point. In 1922, Gronway and Chauncey Parry, brothers who owned a hotel, car dealership, and transportation company in Cedar City, expanded their scenic automobile tours to include trips to the North Rim.[114] Also in that year, Will S. Rust, an older brother of David Rust, opened a tourist camp outside the national park boundary at VT Park, which an early visitor described as a "primitive

steep, high-centered, rutted-dirt wagon tracks—and it is a wonder anyone would argue over their use at any price![118]

Services from Fredonia continued to improve in 1923, when Dee Woolley's grand-niece, Nina Nixon Bowman, and her husband, Harold, opened a general store and gasoline station in a ten-by-twelve-foot frame building along the Grand Canyon Highway at Jacob Lake. When the forest service and state highway department built two new automotive highways in the early 1930s, one connecting Fredonia with House Rock Valley, today's U.S. Highway 89A, and one branching south toward Bright Angel Point, today's Arizona Highway 67, the Bowmans moved to their current location at the junction of these roads. In 1934, the Bowman store at its new location became the first and only year-round service operation on the Kaibab Plateau.[119]

In 1924, the National Park Service began to spend its first few dollars on North Rim management. Congressional appropriation acts prior to that year specifically prohibited park administrators from spending money on the north side, although superintendents since 1920 had sent across one or two rangers who spent summer seasons based at whatever plateau cabin happened to be vacant.[120] The United States Forest Service during these first few transition years helped where it could, particularly with fire control, with its rangers still working from stations at Jacob Lake, VT Park, Big Springs, Dry Lake, and Quaking Aspen. When park appropriations began to flow a bit more freely in 1924, crews started blading the former wagon tracks to Point Sublime and Cape Royal, although these improvements were intended only to give better access to forest fires and

Watercolor of the original Grand Canyon Lodge completed in 1928, by G.S. Underwood. The new lodge, reconstructed in 1937, varies considerably from the original architecture, although both were built in the rustic style. Massive beams within today's lodge contain fireproof steel inserts in the event history repeats itself. GRCA 9781

mitigate insect infestations. Park rangers also built an administrative cabin, warehouse, barn, and machine shed at Bright Angel Point near the Wylie Camp, while park service landscape engineers and Bureau of Public Roads engineers began surveys for scenic automotive highways to Cape Royal and Point Sublime.[121]

Elizabeth McKee became sole owner of the Wylie Camp when she bought her father's interests in winter 1923-24 and made plans to expand the business despite her concern for year-to-year permits. For the 1925 season, the McKees added tent-cabins to accommodate forty overnight guests and hauled in canvas, lumber, and furniture to build more according to demand. They improved their relationship with the Union Pacific which, through its Utah Parks Company subsidiary, now owned transportation services still operated by the Parrys. Cabin and meals remained six dollars per day and Thomas McKee led parties out to Cape Royal, Point Sublime, and VT Park in the family Dodge

Dining room of the original Grand Canyon Lodge (stereoscope image).

GRCA 13652

Interior of 1928 standard guest cabins at Grand Canyon Lodge. These cabins are still in use, though with improved utilities and other safety modifications.

GRCA 13651

sedan and two seven-passenger Buick touring cars. The condition of the roads, though improved in 1924 and 1925, is reflected in the initial forty dollar fare for these auto excursions. Stephen Mather turned down Elizabeth's request to set up additional camps at Cape Royal and Point Sublime, but allowed her to outfit visitors who wanted to stay overnight at these scenic overlooks.[122]

More than two thousand automobiles brought seven thousand visitors to Bright Angel Point in 1925, and although many carried their own camping equipment, enough clung to the older practice of staying with concessioners to tax the McKees' limited facilities. Understanding that increased visitation foreshadowed a Union Pacific takeover, yet assured compensation if it happened, the McKees in 1926 built a wood frame lodge containing a lobby, rest rooms, and general store which they connected to the camp's central dining room with a roofed passageway. They increased overnight capacity to one hundred persons by erecting more than twenty frame cabins and otherwise improved the camp by installing electric lights and "fly proof and sanitary" pit toilets. Visitation in 1926 justified the expansion, as nearly three thousand automobiles brought eleven thousand tourists to Bright Angel Point during the five-month season.[123]

The McKees waited impatiently through winter 1926-27 to receive their permit for the 1927 season, then learned that the time had come to hand over the reins to the Union Pacific. Park superintendent Eakin notified

Elizabeth that for the first time, the park service would be accepting bids for the concession. The McKees readily understood that envisioned facilities far surpassed their modest means. In May 1927, the Utah Parks Company paid twenty-five thousand dollars for the Wylie Camp, purchased the Jensen and Vaughn saddle concession, and bought whatever rights remained with the Parrys, consolidating all North Rim tourist services under one management roof. Utah Parks operated the Wylie Camp through the 1927 summer season while building Grand Canyon Lodge. When the lodge opened in June 1928, park rangers moved the McKee cabins to today's campground area, where a few remained until demolished in 1946.[124]

Although hunting camps kept the pioneer spirit alive in remote North Rim locations through the 1960s, the era ended at Bright Angel Point with completion of the Utah Parks-dominated circle tourism route between 1927 and 1930. As at the South Rim during the late 1920s and early 1930s, federal and state road agencies replaced antiquated wagon roads with modern automotive highways that, north of the great chasm, connected Zion, Bryce, Cedar Breaks, Pipe Spring, and Grand Canyon's North Rim. The railroad subsidiary responded immediately with more than three million dollars in tourist facilities at several of these parks and stepped up national promotional campaigns which soon attracted tens of thousands of visitors to the formerly isolated region.

The National Park Service left concession infrastructure to the Utah Parks Company, but did its part to upgrade the touring experience by entirely reconstructing its entrance and scenic roads. Contractors completed the twenty-one-mile Cape Royal Road and three-mile Point

Imperial spur between 1927 and 1929, along the exact path driven by today's visitors. After Congress extended the park's northern boundary in 1927 to the slight saddle separating VT and Little Parks, rangers built the log checking-station which is still used today. Contractors replaced the 1913 Grand Canyon Highway alignment from Little Park to Harvey Meadow with a new thirteen-mile entrance road in 1930.[125]

The park service further hastened the end of the pioneer period by reconstructing its trail corridor connecting the South Rim with Bright Angel Point. In 1925, workmen finished the South Kaibab Trail from Yaki Point to Bright Angel Creek to bypass the county's south side toll trail to the Fred Harvey Company's Phantom Ranch. Park crews made a few improvements to David Rust's trail through the creek's granite gorge between 1922 and 1926 and named it the Kaibab Trail, then in the latter year began a formal project to rebuild and relocate the increasingly popular path. Working in the cooler winter months, crews eliminated all but seven of nearly one hundred creek crossings, then turned left at Roaring Springs Canyon to complete an entirely new trail segment directly approaching facilities at Bright Angel Point. The rechristened North Kaibab Trail, finished on 21 May 1928, just days before the opening of Grand Canyon Lodge, bypassed the pioneer tourism locale of David Rust's upper trail, the Woolley Cabin, and Uncle Jim Point.[126]

Grand Canyon Lodge surpassed National Park Service expectations. Union Pacific architect Gilbert Stanley Underwood designed, and the Utah Parks Company built, the 250-by-225-foot rustic style lodge of native stone and ponderosa pine with an oversized central lobby, dining hall, and recreation room. Exterior wings enclosed a curio store, soda fountain, barber shop, rest rooms, baths and showers, kitchen, and storage rooms. Its south face at the canyon's edge consisted of a glass-enclosed lounge, and exterior terraces with an observation tower and massive outdoor fireplace for evening gatherings. Guests stayed in 120 individual one- and two-bedroom cottages of harmonious log and stone, extending north from the two exterior wings. An early morning fire on 1 September 1932 destroyed the five-hundred-thousand-dollar main building, but spared the cabins which are still used by today's visitors. Utah Parks rebuilt the lodge on its original site and it has remained open each summer season, except for the Second World War years, since 1 June 1937.[127]

As a gesture to the end of the pioneer period at Grand Canyon's North Rim, park superintendent Minor Tillotson brought together local and national dignitaries for dedication ceremonies at Grand Canyon Lodge on 15 September 1928. With new tourist facilities, trails, and park roads underway and better approach roads on the horizon, he had much to celebrate in the first year of his superintendency. Only the state's delay in completing Navajo Bridge marred the event, as guests from the chasm's south side had to arrive on muleback via the central trail corridor or take the long way around by automobile or train via Searchlight or Needles, California. Tillotson could take pride, however, in the park's own Kaibab Suspension Bridge over the Colorado River, completed less than two months before the celebration.[128] As at the South Rim, federal control, monopolistic concessions, and massive construction projects in the face of escalating tourist numbers signalled the end of pioneer enterprises at Grand Canyon's northern edge.

Influential men of the early park service and Grand Canyon National Park. Right to left: Stephen Mather, first NPS director; Daniel Hull, NPS landscape architect; George Goodwin, NPS engineer; Walter Crosby and Dewitt Raeburn, Grand Canyon superintendents. Photographed at the Powell Memorial, 1921. GRCA 9612A

AFTERWORD
Living at the Edge

In spring 1995, Jim Babbitt and I led a group of backpackers down the South Bass Trail as part of the Grand Canyon Field Institute's third season of educational programs. Advertised as a hike concerned with human history, we described remains of human constructions: debris at Bass Camp, Indian ruins along the way, Rock Camp, the trail itself. Steve Verkamp came along and helped identify historic sites for the rest of the party, made up of doctors from Colorado and New England, an avid avocational historian from Prescott, and three wonderful people from England, all but one first-timers to Grand Canyon backcountry. Everyone seemed genuinely interested in our stories, listened, pondered, and questioned, but at the same time seemed distracted. It finally occurred to me that we were competing with a near-wilderness slice of the canyon itself. And we were losing.

It is difficult for a historian to accept that people in the past and their works are incidental in some landscapes. I had always thought of the Bass transcanyon corridor as a human construction, although recognizing as mentioned a lot of words ago that the chasm itself draws visitors; that people are an effect and not the cause of attention. Still, the hypnotic gaze of our companions, directed always toward some natural feature, made me think about natural aspects versus the historic possibilities of our surroundings.

What if William Bass, the personification of all canyon pioneers in my opinion, had found the money and power to fulfill his dreams? What if he had built his hotel at Havasupai Point, visible for dozens of inner-canyon miles, or patented his mining claims, subdivided, built condos along his trail, and a tramway to reach them? What if one of the dozen would-be dam builders had drowned the canyon near here creating a lake that stretched up Bass and Shinumo Canyons? Marinas and lakeside villas? Paved roads from Williams and the village would have approached a concession village at Bass Camp; another might have appeared at Swamp Point with a good road from Fredonia and similar developments along the still lovelier fourteen-mile path of the North Bass Trail. I am convinced that Bill Bass would have promoted it all had he the means; confident that Pete Berry and James Thurber would have followed within their own spheres of influence. And Ralph Cameron?

The end of Grand Canyon's pioneer period, like the end of similar times at many of our western parks, is defined by the death of such unchecked developmental dreams, but not all of them died at once. The National Park Service had secured a tenuous grip on park matters by the middle 1920s and even in these early years spurned Coney-Island type developments, but had not yet acquired the revulsion they and most others feel today for access at the price of irreplaceable ecosystems. The decline of small businessmen had also heralded ascendance of mega-concessioners with oodles of money, cash-register minds, and developmental visions not all that dissimilar from those of Stephen Mather. What did they and the park's first administrators consider?

At the North Rim, they planned little more than is seen today. No serious thought was ever given development of the Thunder River and North Bass areas, or for that matter, anywhere west of today's entrance road other than a good road to Point Sublime. To the east, Mather considered permanent facilities at Cape Royal proposed by Jim Owens and Elizabeth McKee, but rejected them in favor of informal campgrounds at the cape and Neal Spring. The Utah Parks Company for its part was content to develop Bright Angel Point, recognizing that Grand Canyon Lodge and a few scattered campsites would satisfy relatively light visitation for years to come.

The South Rim was another matter. As soon as the park acquired Bill Bass's properties, administrators planned an automotive road to replace wagon tracks toward Supai. This scenic drive and its spur roads would have afforded vistas along the southwestern rim and ended at Manakacha Point overlooking the village of Supai, where tourists with binoculars could peer down on residents of the small reservation. Administrators suggested overnight facilities at Bass Camp along the way, perhaps renovations to Bass's structures or a formal campground. To the east of the village, they conjured facilities at Grandview and favored a good hotel at Desert View.

Although a gravel-surfaced automotive road was built westward toward Bass Camp and the Havasupai Reservation, ideas for decentralized South Rim services had dissipated by the early 1930s. Avoidance of the developmental nightmares of pioneer concessioners, however, had little to do with administrators' early decisions. The Santa Fe and Harvey company heavily influenced choices, calculating the costs of maintaining far-flung enterprises against the likelihood that tourists would come in sufficient numbers to justify expense. Their budget for the early 1930s allocated millions of dollars toward South Rim capital improvements, but earmarked more than 90 percent for central corridor improvements. Although they budgeted the remainder for access to

and facilities within Havasu Canyon—with thoughts, perhaps, toward finishing the road down from Topocoba Hilltop—they, like the Utah Parks Company, decided that centralization would prove most cost effective. The National Park Service fortunately shaped their earliest plans within others' economic parameters, deciding, in what would become their general strategy for the next sixty years, to expand services at Grand Canyon Village as required, reconstruct and maintain the central corridor trails, and improve automotive access.

Automotive access in fact became the insatiable goal of park superintendents who were frantic to accommodate but, paradoxically, also to attract the onslaught of Henry Ford's Model Ts. Mesmerized as most other Americans by the automobile phenomenon, and supported by Stephen Mather's preferences, J.R. Eakin and Minor Tillotson beginning in 1925 supervised reconstruction of all park approach, entrance, scenic, and service roads. A state approach highway directly north from Williams replaced pioneer roads emanating from U.S. Route 66, while the concurrently constructed South Entrance Road, now running beneath Shuttlebus and Center Roads, superseded numerous wagon paths through Long Jim Canyon, Rain Tank, and Rowe Well to Grand Canyon Village. Another approach highway from Cameron coupled with a new East Entrance Road within the park replaced Fred Harvey's primitive Navahopi Road up the Coconino escarpment. East Rim Drive, purposely built

closer to the rim with several spurs to scenic overlooks, replaced the dirt road from Desert View and James Thurber's interior stage extension to the village. West Rim Drive replaced the Santa Fe's Hermit Rim Road, marking a temporary end of south side reconstructions in 1935.

Despite the mad flurry of road building and simultaneous reconstruction of central corridor trails, a new Bright Angel Lodge, and other service buildings, administrators could keep no better pace with popular demand than pioneer concessioners until the 1930s economic depression brought a brief respite. Fewer visitors and Tillotson's building projects coincided with arrival of the Civilian Conservation Corps and emergency relief funds to create, quite by accident, the type of relaxed park experience all had hoped to achieve. Between 1933 and 1942, five companies of CCC recruits, fully a thousand eager young men, along with men and funds of the Public Works Administration and Works Progress Administration applied finishing touches to building projects like masonry walls and culverts still glimpsed along roads and scenic turnouts. They also built trails and service roads, performed trail and road maintenance, assembled service structures and cattle fences, landscaped, cleaned ditches, even raked excess pine needles from heavily used visitor areas. Free of maintenance responsibilities and with fewer visitors, rangers found time to interact and conduct interpretive programs like daily automotive caravans on North and South Rim scenic drives.

The 1930s, ironically, marked the golden era for Grand Canyon National Park and many other western parks, but it did not last long beyond the Depression. The Second World War prolonged the dearth of visitors but also stripped the park of funding and personnel, thus, infrastructure deteriorated. After the war, instead of rejoicing as one might expect for a return to normalcy, Superintendent H.C. Bryant lamented that "everyone who had a trip planned and interrupted by the war immediately resumed his plans, in many instances starting the same day."

Parents of the baby boomers, more than ever in love with their automobiles and again, as in the 1910s, encouraged to "See America First," inundated the national parks during the postwar period. The rush prompted a ten-year, billion-dollar national park rebuilding program termed Mission 66, which, at Grand Canyon, sparked another round of construction between 1953 and 1968 resulting in a reconfigured road system to relieve pressure from the village and modest decentralization in the form of a new service area surrounding a new visitor center. Rustic architecture also gave way during this period to steel and concrete, a result of shifting artistic preferences coupled with cheaper building materials and the high cost of postwar labor, resulting in the inconsonant mix of old and new seen at the South Rim today.

Between 1925 and 1935, 1953 and 1968, and in more recent years to accommodate the baby boomers themselves, Grand Canyon's rims reverberated with jackham-mers, backloaders, and dump trucks rejuvenating park infrastructure to satisfy ever escalating numbers of visitors. Trail construction along with additions of the Maswik, Kachina, and Thunderbird Lodges as well as other village service structures added to the din. Still, it may surprise many to learn that despite efforts to satisfy annual visitation that has irrupted from tens of thousands in the 1920s to five million by the 1990s, developed areas within the national park have considerably diminished from pioneer days. More than 99 percent of today's visitors are deliberately routed along entrance roads to scenic drives stretching from Hermits Rest to Desert View, Bright Angel Point to Cape Royal, and to central corridor trails, all present in more primitive forms seventy-five years ago. Gone are most scars of myriad wagon roads and pioneer facilities at Bass Camp, Hopi Point, Grandview, and Hance Ranch, as are earlier campgrounds at Grandview, Neal Spring, and Cape Royal.

This is how National Park Service administrators planned it once they moved beyond thoughts of decentralization, and why, three-quarters of a century after the agency's arrival, field institute backpackers can still marvel at something resembling a natural landscape far less impacted than in Bill Bass's time. But reclaiming then keeping a natural environment within the park's dual mission of access and preservation remains a dilemma posing ever more difficult choices. Recurrent plans dating to 1909 address increasingly complex problems: motorized rafts along the Colorado River reverberating throughout the Inner Gorge; riparian ecosystems, now creations of Glen Canyon dam; airplane and helicopter overflights; and air pollution, emanating from as far away as Los Angeles, are but a few. Then there is the old challenge of spiraling visitation, which is not so much a problem of people, who, after all, simply love and need their national parks, but the two million or more vehicles that bring them here each year. These are all distinctly modern problems that could not occur to early explorers, exploiters, and settlers of the Grand Canyon region, and would have been far beyond their ability and inclination to resolve.

END Notes

Organizational Acronyms Used in Notes

ASHPO	Arizona State Historic Preservation Office
BIA	Bureau of Indian Affairs
BLM	Bureau of Land Management
GLO	General Land Office
GPO	Government Printing Office
GCA	Grand Canyon Association
GCNPRL	Grand Canyon National Park Research Library
GCNHA	Grand Canyon Natural History Association (now GCA)
GCNP	Grand Canyon National Park
HAER	Historic American Engineering Record
NPS	National Park Service
USDA	United States Department of Agriculture
USDI	United States Department of the Interior
USFS	United States Forest Service
UASC	University of Arizona Special Collections
WPA	Works Progress Administration

CHAPTER ONE

Earliest Residents

1. Bertha P. Dutton, *American Indians of the Southwest* (Albuquerque: University of New Mexico Press, 1983), 4; David Lavender, *The Southwest* (Albuquerque: University of New Mexico Press, 1980), 22–23; GCNHA, "New Discoveries in Grand Canyon," *Regarding* (Spring 1994): 10–11.

2. David Grant Noble, *Ancient Ruins of the Southwest* (Flagstaff: Northland Publishing, 1981), 25, 62; Richard W. Effland Jr., A. Trinkle Jones, and Robert C. Euler, *Archeology of the Powell Plateau: Regional Interaction at Grand Canyon* (GCNHA, 1981), 12f; Dutton, 4.

3. Noble, 25–29; Effland, 8, 13; Lavender, 27–28; Douglas W. Schwartz, *On the Edge of Splendor: Exploring Grand Canyon's Human Past* (Santa Fe: School of American Research, no date), 53–63.

4. Noble, 25–29; Effland, 13.

5. Dutton, 34; Schwartz, 69–72.

6. Mardean Frost Church, interview by Michael F.

Anderson, tape recordings, 22 May 1992 and 9 February 1994, Kanab, Utah; Walapai Johnny Nelson, interview by Michael F. Anderson, tape recording, 9–10 February 1994, Fredonia, Arizona; Dutton, 63–64.

7. USDA, USFS and USDI, BLM, *Man, Models, and Management: An Overview of the Archaeology of the Arizona Strip and the Management of Its Cultural Resources* (1989), by Jeffrey H. Altschul and Helen C. Fairley, 147, 149–150, 152; Dutton, 157–159; Schwartz, 27. Altschul and Dutton posit an early arrival and probable interaction with pueblo peoples while Schwartz indicates a later appearance, about A.D. 1400, following a two-hundred-year occupational hiatus.

8. Angus M. Woodbury, *A History of Southern Utah and Its National Parks* (Salt Lake City: Utah State Historical Society, 1950), 117; Dutton, 159–161; Mardean Frost Church interviews.

9. Stephen Hirst, *Life in a Narrow Place: The Havasupai of the Grand Canyon* (New York: David McKay Company, 1976), 40–43; Dutton, 178–79. Schwartz, 34–38, identifies another culture called the Cohonina who occupied roughly the same territory as the Pai from A.D. 700 to 1100. These people lived similarly to their Prehistoric Pueblo neighbors to the north and east and may have joined with later arrivals from the west, the Cerbat, to become the Havasupai.

10. Henry F. Dobyns and Robert C. Euler, "A Brief History of the Northeastern Pai," *Plateau Magazine* (January 1960): 49–57; Dutton, 189–91.

11. Henry F. Dobyns and Robert C. Euler, *The Havasupai People* (Phoenix: Indian Tribal Series, 1971), 2–5; Leslie Spier, *Havasupai Ethnology* (New York: The Trustees, 1928), 94–97; Frank Hamilton Cushing, *The Nation of Willows* (Flagstaff: Northland Press, 1965), 34; George Wharton James, *The Indians of the Painted Desert Region* (Boston: Little, Brown & Company, 1903), 217.

12. Michael F. Anderson, "Natural Disasters within Traditional Societies: Floods and the Havasupai Indians," paper presented to the Arizona Historical Society's 1994 convention at Casa Grande, Arizona; BIA and the Havasupai Tribe Planning Committee, "Secretarial Land Use Plan for Addition to Havasupai Indian Reservation," bound report, 12 March 1976, GCNPRL.

CHAPTER TWO

The Spanish

1. John Francis Bannon, *The Spanish Borderlands Frontier: 1530–1821* (Albuquerque: University of New Mexico Press, 1970), 12–17; David Lavender, *The Southwest* (Albuquerque: University of New Mexico Press, 1980), 37–40. Antilia was a legendary island containing seven cities founded by seven Spanish bishops in the eighteenth century. Authors often refer to these as the Seven Cities of Cíbola, or Seven Cities of Gold, for their legendary wealth. For all the early Spanish knew and hoped, mainland America might be Antilia.

2. Lavender, 41; Bannon, 18.

3. Bannon, 18–19; Lavender, 42.

4. J. Donald Hughes, *In the House of Stone and Light: A Human History of the Grand Canyon* (GCNHA, 1978), 19–20; Pedro de Casteñeda, *Relacion de la Jornada de Cíbola*, trans. and ed. by George Parker Winship in *Fourteenth Annual Report of the Bureau of Ethnology: 1892–93* (Washington: GPO, 1896), 489–90.

5. Baltazar de Obregon, "Chronicle, Commentary, or Relation of the Ancient and Modern Discoveries in New Spain and New Mexico, Mexico, 1584," trans. and ed. by George P. Hammond and Agapito Rey, in *Obregon's History of 16th Century Explorations in Western America* (Los Angeles: Wetzel Publishing Company, 1928), 268–313.

6. Bannon, 153–64. Juan Bautista de Anza from 1773 to 1776 pioneered a route from Sonora to California known as the Devil's Highway and became governor of New Mexico soon thereafter. He should not be confused with his father of the same name who was also a military man in central and northern Mexico.

7. Elliott Coues, trans. and ed., *On the Trail of a Spanish Pioneer: The Diary and Itinerary of Francisco Garcés (Missionary Priest) in His Travels through Sonora, Arizona, and California, 1775–1776* (New York: Francis P. Harper, 1900), 314–425.

8. Coues, 336–47. Dr. Andrew Wallace, in a conversation with the author, 29 December 1995, stated that his and Dr. Robert Euler's research place the priest at a waterhole south of the present town of Peach Springs, not

at the more famous water source mentioned by Coues several miles north of town along the present road to Diamond Creek.

9. Coues, 347–48, states that Garcés reached a point along the rim likely near the end of the old stage road from Flagstaff, which would be the vicinity of Grandview Point.

10. Coues, 357–64, 381–92. The Hopi joined with other tribes in a successful 1680 regional revolt that killed hundreds of Spanish colonists and drove the remainder south to El Paso. Spaniards reconquered New Mexico between 1692 and 1700, but never again subdued the Hopi, who thereafter maintained an aloof though nonviolent relationship with most foreigners and steadfastly rejected religious overtures.

11. Coues, 374–80; Fray Angélico Chávez, trans., and Ted J. Warner, Ed., *The Domínguez-Escalante Journal: Their Expedition Through Colorado, Utah, Arizona, and New Mexico in 1776* (Provo, UT: Brigham Young University Press, 1976), 3.

12. Chávez, 3–5; Leroy R. Hafen and Ann W. Hafen, *Old Spanish Trail: Santa Fe to Los Angeles* (Glendale, CA: Arthur H. Clark Company, 1954), 59–61.

13. Hafen, 61–72; Chávez, 70–71.

14. The party carried an alidade, an early version of the sextant, to plot a rough latitudinal position from the sun. They had no way to measure longitude accurately, however, thus were uncertain of the remaining distance to Monterey.

15. Chávez, 82–84.

16. Chávez, 84–94, explains that a San Benito was a garish white cassock worn by errant priests as punishment. *Salsipuedes* translates "get out if you can."

17. Chávez, 94–116. The priests managed to get lost again south of the Colorado, but a party of Southern Paiutes showed them the correct trail to the Hopi.

The Trappers

18. Hafen, 93; Americans operating mainly from the Missouri settlements had been trapping illegally in the Spanish Northwest since 1810, but specific movements of these shadowy "Taos trappers" are, understandably, little known today. See Bil Gilbert, *Westering Man: The Life of Joseph Walker* (Norman: University of Oklahoma Press, 1983), 71–79, and generally, David J. Weber, *The Taos Trappers* (Norman: University of Oklahoma Press, 1971).

19. Hafen, 96–100; Gilbert, 171–73, 247. Joe Walker (1798–1876), a burly six-foot-four-inch tall Scots-Irish adventurer and one of the West's premier guides, expressed his desire to raft the canyons of the Colorado from Wyoming to the Mohave villages in 1839 and 1842, but apparently never got the men and equipment together to do it.

20. Harrison Clifford Dale, ed., *The Ashley-Smith Explorations and the Discovery of a Central Pacific Route to the Pacific, 1822–1929* (Cleveland: Arthur H. Clark Company, 1918), 138–53.

21. John Wesley Powell, *Canyons of the Colorado* (Flood and Vincent, 1895; repr., *The Exploration of the Colorado River and Its Canyons* New York: Dover Publications, 1962), 142–43. Powell mistakenly believed that Ashley's boat had swamped within the Green River's Red Canyon, not to be confused with the Red Canyon tributary to Grand Canyon hundreds of miles downstream.

22. Richard Batman, *James Pattie's West: The Dream and the Reality* (Norman: University of Oklahoma Press, 1986), 168–74.

23. Batman, 174–78.

24. Batman, 178–79, 350, speculates that the party may have left the river farther south of Mohave Valley.

25. James Ohio Pattie, *The Personal Narratives of James O. Pattie of Kentucky*, ed. by Timothy Flint and Reuben Gold Thwaites (Cleveland: Arthur H. Clark, 1905), quoted in Hughes, 39.

26. Batman, 179–81, 350, again speculates that the men may have reached the area of Desert View, descended an old Indian alignment of the Tanner Trail, then left the region via the Little Colorado River gorge. If true, Young, Yount, and Pattie would be the first white men known to reach the Colorado within Grand Canyon.

27. George R. Brooks, ed., *The Southwest Expedition of Jedediah S. Smith: His Personal Account of the Journey to California, 1826–1827* (Glendale, CA: Arthur H. Clark Company, 1977), 56–65; Angus M. Woodbury, *A History of Southern Utah and Its Parks* (Salt Lake City: Utah State Historical Society, 1950), 126–27.

28. H. Lorenzo Reid, *Brigham Young's Dixie of the Desert: Exploration and Settlement* (Zion Natural History Association, 1964), 25–42; Woodbury, 126–30. The Hafens give a detailed history of the trail; Woodbury offers a good summary; and Reid is excellent for a discussion of the trail in Mormon history.

29. Forbes Parkhill, *The Blazed Trail of Antoine Leroux* (Los Angeles: Westernlore Press, 1965), 37–40.

30. Parkhill, 65–68.

31. Parkhill, 85–104, 111–16, 134–35, 145–50, 183–97.

32. Parkhill, 161–62, 164, 209, 216. The "spear wounds" did not come at the end, but accumulated over the years. General Johnston's march resulted from Mormon attempts to control the Utah Territory, created in 1850. The march elicited much excitement and even guerrilla warfare as Johnston approached Salt Lake and precipitated the Mountain Meadows Massacre. Joe Walker is another trapper who was officially asked his preference for a transcontinental route. He had travelled the entire thirty-fifth parallel route from Los Angeles to Albuquerque in January 1851, months before Sitgreaves,

and agreed with Leroux that it offered the best water, grass, and terrain.

Government Surveyors

33. One of many definitions for the "American Southwest" might be, simply, the former "Spanish Northwest." A concise historical/geographical consideration of the region is D.W. Meinig's *Southwest: Three Peoples in Geographical Change, 1600–1970* (New York: Oxford University Press, 1971), though Meinig defines the region much more narrowly. The 1853 Gadsden Treaty with Mexico ceded more territory south of the Gila River, completing the general path of today's international boundary.

34. W. Turrentine Jackson, *Wagon Roads West: A Study of Federal Road Surveys and Construction in the Trans-Mississippi West, 1846–1869* (Lincoln: University of Nebraska Press, 1964), 28, 35–36. Need for a central route was also predicated by United States-Mormon tension, since the Old Spanish Trail ran through territory tightly controlled by church members.

35. Andrew Wallace, "Across Arizona to the Big Colorado: The Sitgreaves Expedition of 1851," *Arizona and The West* (Winter 1984): 325–64; Hughes, 28; Parkhill, 145–51; Jackson, 28. Camp Independence was under siege in association with a local Indian revolt at the time of Sitgreaves's arrival, adding to the trip's hazards.

36. Jackson, 241, 244.

37. Jackson, 245–55.

38. Dan W. Messersmith, *The History of Mohave County to 1912* (Kingman, AZ: Mohave County Historical Society, 1991), 158, 161. Portions of old U.S. Route 66 across northern Arizona can be driven today. An eighty-six-mile segment is the loop road north of Interstate 40 from Seligman through Peach Springs to Kingman. Jack Beale Smith, in *John Udell "The Rest of the Story": With an Adventure on the Beale Wagon Road* (Flagstaff: Tales of the Beale Road Publishing Company, 1987), details the travels of several wagon trains along the road in 1858.

39. Joseph C. Ives, *Report Upon the Colorado River of the West, Explored in 1857 and 1858* (Washington: GPO, 1861), 80–82. Ives's orders also were to find a route into Mormon Utah from the southwest, thus his side trip toward Las Vegas and the Old Spanish Trail. Mormon scouts, including Thales Haskell and Jacob Hamblin, shadowed the party during the latter part of its river exploration and reportedly stirred up trouble among the Mohave, Paiute, and Hualapai Indians toward the Ives party and early travellers along the Beale Road. See Smith, 33–35, and Ben W. Huseman, *Wild River, Timeless Canyons: Balduin Mollhausen's Watercolors of the Colorado* (Fort Worth, TX: Amon Carter Museum, 1995), 44–46.

40. Ives, 85–113; Huseman, 46–53.

41. Ives to Captain A.A. Humphreys, 1 May 1860, letter of transmittal accompanying the Ives report.

42. Ives, 110.

43. Wallace Stegner, *Beyond the Hundredth Meridian: John Wesley Powell and the Second Opening of the West* (Boston: Houghton Mifflin Company, 1953), 43–46.

44. Stegner, 46–47. Richard Quartaroli, a historian of the Grand Canyon region, notes that the boats were a "Whitehall" type, a pattern long in use, but Powell specified size, materials, and reinforcement. They would prove heavy and clumsy, but strong enough for three of four to survive the journey.

45. Powell, 152–57, 211, 234; Stegner, 91.

46. Powell, 277–87. Powell's party was met by a Mr. Asa and his two sons who had been called by the church to establish a town at the Virgin's mouth (Rioville).

47. Powell, preface to the 1895 publication by Flood and Vincent. Powell mixed details of his first and second expeditions to create a romantic account of a single trip, a forgivable act for a novelist but roundly condemned by later river historian Robert Brewster Stanton in *Colorado River Controversies* (Dodd, Mead and Company, 1932; repr., Boulder City, NV: Westwater Books, 1982) and by others.

48. As late as 1949 only one hundred people had run the river through Grand Canyon, but many left journals and a dozen or more have been published. David Lavender's *River Runners of the Grand Canyon* (GCNHA, 1985) is a fine survey of significant early river trips is.

The Railroad

49. Robert Brewster Stanton, *Down the Colorado*, ed. Dwight L. Smith (Norman: University of Oklahoma Press, 1965), 223–27.

50. ASHPO, "Transcontinental Railroading in Arizona, 1878–1940," prepared by Janus Associates, December 1989, 3–4, 16–17; James E. Babbitt, "Surveyors Along the 35th Parallel," *Journal of Arizona History* (Autumn 1981): 325–48. The federal government granted early railroad companies millions of acres of land astride their tracks as an incentive to invest the enormous capital to build. Atlantic and Pacific owners received alternate (odd-numbered) sections extending twenty miles north and twenty miles south of their line. It was in their interest to quickly attract a large population who would not only ride the rails and ship freight, but also purchase or lease these lands.

51. Messersmith, 141–45; ASHPO, 17–18, 22–23. The Santa Fe became sole owner of the Atlantic and Pacific about 1897 and absorbed it into its larger corporation, the Santa Fe Pacific.

52. ASHPO, 18. A few settlements like Williams, the Mormon community of Sunset near today's Winslow, and the Hispanic community of Horsehead Crossing near today's Holbrook existed before the railroad arrived, but the location of the track and station always dictated subsequent town development.

53. A.P.K. Safford, Charles H. Binley, and John G. Campbell, *Resources of Arizona Territory* (San Francisco: Francis and Valentine, 1871), Arizona Collection, Hayden Library, Arizona State University, Tempe, 10.

54. Roman Malach, *Early Ranching in Mohave County* (Mohave County Board of Supervisors, 1978); Frank J. Tuck, comp., *History of Mining in Arizona* (Arizona Department of Mineral Resources, 1955), 2; Robert Clark Euler, "A Half Century of Economic Development in Northern Arizona," (M.A. Thesis, Northern Arizona University, 1947), 29–30, 58, 76–77, 83; Messersmith, 103–104, 129–30.

CHAPTER THREE

Southwest

1. Henry P. Walker and Don Bufkin, *Historical Atlas of Arizona*, 2d ed. (Norman: University of Oklahoma Press, 1986), 39; Philip Fradkin, *A River No More: The Colorado River and the West* (New York: Knopf, 1981; repr., Tucson. University of Arizona Press, 1984), 325–26, 328–30; Clifford E. Trafzer, *Yuma: Frontier Crossing of the Far Southwest* (Wichita, KS: Western Heritage Books, 1980), 43–45, 52–57, 74, 77, 82–83, 88–90. The practical head of navigation during normal flows was Hardyville, near the point where Ives ended his river expedition and the exact site of today's Bullhead City, but during high flows, steamers could reach the Mormon community of Callville near the mouth of Las Vegas Wash above today's Hoover Dam. Beginning in 1852, flat-bottomed steamboats plied the lower Colorado from the Gulf at Puerta Isabel (established 1865) to Hardyville until Laguna Dam was built above Yuma in 1909.

2. See Jack Beale Smith's *John Udell "The Rest of the Story:" With an Adventure on the Beale Wagon Road* (Flagstaff: Tales of the Beale Road Publishing Company, 1987), 27–35, for a description of the troubles encountered by the Rose and Bailey emigrant parties with Hualapai and Mohave Indians in 1858.

3. Dan W. Messersmith, *The History of Mohave County to 1912* (Kingman, AZ: Mohave County Historical Society, 1991), 38–42; Will C. Barnes, *Arizona Place Names* (1935; repr., Tucson: University of Arizona Press, 1988), 283, 498–99; William S. Collins, Melanie Sturgeon, and Robert M. Carriker, *The United States Military in Arizona, 1846–1945* (Phoenix: ASHPO, 1993), 15. Hoffman's detachment started its march at Fort Tejon near Los Angeles and was guided across the desert and along the Colorado without mishap by the ubiquitous Joe Walker. See Bil Gilbert, *Westering Man: The Life of Joseph Walker* (Norman: University of Oklahoma Press, 1983), 244–45.

4. Gilbert, 267–74; Messersmith, 42, 73, 90; Barnes, 197; Roman Malach, *Cerbat Mountain Country: Early Mine Camps* (Arizona Bicentennial Commission, 1975), 5, 7. Congress created Arizona Territory in February 1863; Walker's party made their discovery in May 1863 and set up a camp named Walker; soldiers arrived in summer 1863 to establish nearby Fort Whipple; and by the end of the year there were a thousand residents at Walker, which became the territorial capital in January 1864 and was officially renamed Prescott in May 1864.

Mohave County was one of four original territorial counties and was enlarged to include the Arizona Strip east to Kanab Creek in 1889. Coconino County was created from the northern two-thirds of Yavapai County in 1891. These two counties encompass all of northern Arizona considered in this and later chapters.

5. Roman Malach, *Peach Springs in Mohave County* (Bicentennial Commemorative Publication, 1975), 25–29, 31–41; Messersmith, 42–44, 75, 77, 129, 134–35; Roman Malach, *Early Ranching in Mohave County* (Mohave County Board of Supervisors, 1978).

6. George H. Billingsley, "Geology of the Grand Canyon," (Museum of Northern Arizona and GCNHA, 1974), 170–78, in *Reference File—Mines and Mining*, GCN-PRL; A. Humphreys, letter, 19 March 1934, *Reference File—Havasupai Reservation*, GCNPRL. The Charles Spencer mentioned here was a former army scout, interpreter, guide, and mail carrier who died in 1886, not the Charles Spencer later associated with gold mining at Lees Ferry.

7. "History of Mining Work in Havasupai Canyon," handwritten extract from a report of J.E. Busch and H.A. Ferris, GLO, [1921]; R.O. Giddings, letter, 11 August 1926; Dan E. Davis, "Notes on Mining Operations in Grand Canyon," manuscript, [1950s]; all in *Reference File—Mines and Mining*, GCNPRL.

8. "History of Mining Work"; Billingsley; "Conclusions regarding Havasupai Mining Claims," handwritten extract from the report of J.E. Busch and H.A. Ferris, [1921], *Reference File—Mines and Mining*, GCNPRL.

9. "History of Mining Work"; Congress, House, *A Bill granting right of way to the Williams and Cataract Canyon Railroad Company across the Supai Indian Reservation in Arizona*, 57th Cong., 1st sess., H.R. 11848.

10. "History of Mining Work"; E.F. Schoeny, General Warranty Deed, 8 March 1957; James M. Siler to Region Three Regional Director, letter, 22 July 1957; latter two documents in File *L3023 Schoeny 1957*, GCNPRL.

11. Dan Hogan's copper and uranium Orphan Mine and copper mines on Horseshoe Mesa belonging to Pete Berry and Ralph Cameron compete with the Havasu mines for most intensive use and longest duration.

12. Budge Ruffner, "The First? Resort," *(Phoenix) Arizona Republic*, 31 March 1974; ASHPO, "Transcontinental Railroading in Arizona, 1878–1940," prepared by Janus Associates, December 1989, 20–21.

13. Fisher; *The Grand Cañon of the Colorado*, 298.

14. Malach, *Peach Springs*, 9–11; File *Farlee, Julius H. and Cecilia M. (Raney)*, Mohave County Museum, Kingman, Arizona. An item in the *(Kingman) Mohave County Miner*, 7 January 1883, notes that Young and

Farlee had also opened a feed yard, saloon, and restaurant in town; thus, the Farlees with a partner had established businesses in Peach Springs by late 1882.

15. Malach, *Peach Springs*, 7, 17; Mary Wager Fisher, "A Day in the Grand Canyon," *Outing* (July 1893): 261–64; Dorothy Osterman, "Peach Springs, 1874 to 1916," manuscript, no date, Vertical files, Mohave County Museum, Kingman, Arizona. Given his age (to have fought in the Civil War), it is likely Julius, too, spent his final years at Peach Springs and preceded Cecilia in death. He was apparently a well-known and respected man as his movements were reported in the local newspaper and he was mentioned as a possible Republican candidate for the territorial legislature. See *Mohave County Miner*, 1 April 1883, 6 May 1883, 13 May 1883 for more information on the man and his activities.

16. Malach, *Peach Springs*, 7, 17; *Mohave County Miner*, 25 March 1883. It is occasionally said that the Atlantic and Pacific or Atchison, Topeka and Santa Fe may have owned the Farlee Hotel. In a letter from Bill Burk, Manager of Public Relations, Atchison, Topeka and Santa Fe Railroad Company, to George F. Getz, 18 February 1969, *Diamond Creek File*, Mohave County Museum, Burk says he searched railroad files and found no connection with the hotel. Advertisements also indicate that the Farlees, probably in partnership with Young, owned the hotel.

17. Ruffner; Mary Wager Fisher, "A Day in the Grand Cañon," manuscript, [1880s], *Reference File—Diamond Creek Hotel*, GCNPRL; Robert Morrow, "The Diamond Creek Hotel," transcript of a speech, ca. 1970, File Diamond Creek, Mohave County Museum. Farlee and partner Young apparently filed on the stage road as a toll road—see *Mohave County Miner*, 6 May 1883.

18. Ruffner; Fisher; *The Grand Cañon of the Colorado*, 300; photo included in Malach, *Peach Springs*; Johnnie Nelson, page 2 of a questionnaire concerning the hotel, 11 March 1939, *Reference File—Diamond Creek Hotel*, GCNPRL.

19. Fisher; *The Grand Cañon of the Colorado*, 300–304.

20. Ruffner; Malach, *Peach Springs*, 17; Works Progress Administration, *Arizona: A State Guide* (American Guide Series, 1940), 323; Ancel E. Taylor to Robert E. Morrow, letter, 22 March 1969; Ancel E. Taylor, "Peach Springs, 1881 to 1967," manuscript, [1969]; Photograph of Camp Powell and caption, Negative #4098; latter three sources in vertical files, Mohave County Museum, Kingman. The WPA source indicates that the hotel was carried off piece by piece by Indians and ranchers after it was abandoned, which is consistent with Taylor's account.

21. Malach, *Peach Springs*, 11–13; Osterman, "Peach Springs"; Taylor, "Peach Springs."

22. Lon A. Garrison, "Notes Taken From W.W. Bass Material at Wickenburg, Arizona–January 30–31 and February 1, 1952 (Garrison notes)," *Trails Miscellaneous File*, GCNPRL, 2, 13; James R. Fuchs, *A History of Williams, Arizona: 1876–1951* (Tucson: University of Arizona Press, 1953), 35–37. Fuchs mentions that the town had 260 registered voters in 1882, the year railroad gangs arrived, and 35 in 1884, the year the gangs moved west. This boom and bust pattern was typical of Atlantic and Pacific railroad towns during the period from 1881 to 1883.

23. *Williams Coconino County Arizona*, Sanborn fire insurance maps, 1892, 1901, 1910, Arizona Collection, Hayden Library, Arizona State University, Tempe.

24. Garrison notes, 1, 2, 7, 13, 20. Most material on the Bass family is taken from Michael F. Anderson, "North and South Bass Trails Historical Research Study, Grand Canyon National Park, Arizona," 1 November 1990, GCNPRL. Original sources are noted hereafter, however, except for appendices compiled and conclusions drawn by Anderson. A concise published source on Bass and his trails is James E. Babbitt and Scott Thybony, *South and North Bass: Grand Canyon Trail Guide*, ed. by Rose Houk and Pam Frazier (GCNHA, 1991).

25. Garrison notes, 3, 13, 19; William Wallace Bass, *Adventures in the Canyons of the Colorado* (Grand Canyon: by the author, 1920), 36; Nell Murbarger, "Trail-Blazer of Grand Canyon," *Desert Magazine* (October 1958); 5–9.

26. Garrison notes, 10, 19; George Wharton James, *In and Around the Grand Canyon* (Boston: Little, Brown and Company, 1905), 244–46; Stephen Maurer, *Solitude and Sunshine* (Boulder, CO: Pruett Publishing Company, 1983), 1. The author's research revealed that Bass constructed more than fifty miles of inner-canyon trails and nearly two hundred miles of roads leading to and along the rim.

27. Garrison notes, 10; Lisa D. Madsen, "The Grand Canyon Tourist Business of the W.W. Bass Family," (M.A. Thesis, University of New Mexico, 1980), 15–16.

28. Garrison notes, 8, 11, 14, 16; Madsen, "The Grand Canyon Tourist Business," 42. The Bass Camp register for 1885–95 was destroyed in a fire in 1895, but later entries suggest fewer than thirty tourists per year. Bass had grand dreams, like a majestic hotel at Havasupai Point, but never fulfilled them.

29. Anonymous manuscript to Dr. Harold Bryant, [ca. 1937–41], 8, 10, *Historical File*, GCNPRL; James, *In and Around*, 194; Murbarger.

30. James, *In and Around*, 120.

31. J. R. Eakin to Carl Hayden, letter, 3 July 1924, *Bass Claims File*, GCNPRL; Anderson, Appendix B, lists valuations of Bass holdings within the park in 1924.

32. Garrison notes, 9; *Florence Arizona Enterprise*, 21 November 1891. Bass leased Farlee's Peach Springs and Grand Canyon Stage Line in 1891 after Farlee discontinued regular service.

33. James, *In and Around*, 54–60.

34. Garrison notes, 9–10; Murbarger; "The Ash Fork Route," undated advertising brochure published by Bass's Grand Canyon Stage Line, Special Collections, University of Arizona, Tucson, Arizona. The author visited the Caves with Tom Carmony of Tempe in 1994 and noted the outline of the tent foundation and considerable debris. Bass's Williams and Ash Fork roads converged near this point, then continued almost due north through Pasture Wash to Bass Camp. A spur off this road was built by Bass and/or Sanford Rowe to Rowe Well between 1891 and 1900 and became known as the Ash Fork Road to Grand Canyon Village.

35. James, *In and Around*, 61–64; Garrison notes, 7.

36. Garrison notes, 7. "Tent houses," more commonly called tent-cabins, were an improvement to dirt-floored canvas tents and are discussed in connection with the Wylie Camp at the North Rim.

37. James, *In and Around*, 335–38; anonymous manuscript to Dr. Bryant, 8, 10.

38. Traffic studies of the 1950s and 1960s indicate that the average tourist visit had declined to less than six hours. Imagine the facilities it would require to accommodate a week-long stay for 1996's five million annual visitors!

39. James, *In and Around*, 257–58; "The Ash Fork Route," 17. James recounts Bass's relationship with the Havasupai, and was one of those fascinated by his visits to Supai.

40. Garrison notes, 4, 6, 11, 14; Lisa Madsen, "Women and the Grand Canyon," undated manuscript, GCNPRL, 3.

41. Garrison notes, 11, 14–16; Murbarger; James, *In and Around*, 85; Madsen "The Grand Canyon Tourist Business," 39; Anderson, Appendix A, details Bass's GCNP mining claims, all filed between 1891 and 1908, with locations, dates, and partnerships. James actually wrote his first canyon book, *In and Around the Grand Canyon*, from a nearby cliffside grotto called Author's Amphitheater.

42. James, *In and Around*, 156–58.

43. Author's field observations, June 1990; Stephen Maurer, "Grand Canyon's Bass Corridor," manuscript, [ca. 1986], GCNPRL.

44. Garrison notes, 10; James, *In and Around*, 199—photograph of the craft; *Williams (Arizona) News*, 14 September 1939.

45. James, *In and Around*, 87. Bass probably used Shinumo Camp during the 1890s and perhaps the 1880s as it is a natural camping area, but improvements as those described by James were effected nearer the turn of the century.

46. George Wharton James, *The Grand Canyon of Arizona* (Boston: Little, Brown and Company, 1910), 89.

47. Barbara H. McKee, "A Large Cliff Dwelling," *Nature Notes*, 7 October 1933, GCNPRL; F. E. Matthes, "Breaking a Trail Through Bright Angel Canyon," *Nature Notes*, 21 November 1927, GCNPRL.

48. Large cattle outfits often used homestead laws, but also mining claims, to secure regional water sources. Lumbermen used variant forms of the homestead principle like the Timber Culture Act to reserve forest segments. Within Grand Canyon, mining claims were the preferred mechanism.

49. Anderson, 78–81, Appendix A. It was easy to make a claim by marking an area of allowable size with stone monuments, posting a claim notice (usually in a tobacco tin), and recording the claim with the county the next time one travelled to the county seat. A patent, however, which transformed the parcel from federal to private land, required proof of commercial-grade mineral deposits or use as an actual millsite, a plat map approved or drawn by a government inspector, and evidence that claims had been worked consistently. Since enforcement was fairly relaxed, many Grand Canyon mining claims were patented, but far more were simply abandoned and quite a few legally extinguished when investigations showed that claim/patent requirements had not been fulfilled.

50. Garrison notes, 7; Madsen, "Women," 2.

51. Madsen, "Women," 6, 13–15.

52. Park Superintendent Peters to the Director, letter, 10 July 1920, *Privileges: W.W. Bass—GCNP Files*, Series RG 79/E6/CF 1907-39, National Archives, Washington, D.C.; Madsen, "Women," 14; author's field observations, May 1990. See Santa Fe Railroad to M.R. Tillotson, letter, 10 August 1937, and work order from Tillotson, 16 August 1937, *Bass Claims File*, GCNPRL, concerning the camp's demolition.

53. *(Flagstaff) Coconino Sun*, 28 June 1902; Al Richmond, *Cowboys, Miners, Presidents and Kings: The Story of the Grand Canyon Railway* (Williams, AZ: Grand Canyon Railway, 1989), 84; "Excerpts from Report Made Jan. 25, 1910 to Forest Supervisor F.C.W. Pooler on Roads and Trails in Grand Canyon Division," manuscript, no date, *Miscellaneous—Old Roads & Trails in the Park 1923–1944 File*, GCNPRL.

54. Per the author's conversation with Steve Verkamp in May 1995, the White House stood in a flat area between two ponderosa pines, on the south side of Forest Road 328, perhaps 150 yards west of the railroad tracks. The Lauzons lived in this home after Ada and Bill moved to Wickenburg, and it stood at least into the 1950s or 1960s.

55. Anderson, Appendix A; H.R. Lauzon, "Is There Gold in the Canyon?" *Grand Canyon Nature Notes*, 10 January 1934; Garrison notes, 9, 15, 18–19; Edwin D. McKee, "Copper Deposits of Grand Canyon," *Nature Notes*, 31 July 1930; Madsen, "The Grand Canyon Tourist Business," 65; Madsen, "Women," 20.

56. Superintendent Eakin to Carl Hayden, letter, 3 July 1924, *Bass Claims File*, GCNPRL.

57. Stephen Mather to Clarkson, letter, 29 July 1925, *Bass Claims File*, GCNPRL.

58. For details on negotiations among the Basses, National Park Service, Santa Fe, and Fred Harvey Company, 1919–26, see Anderson, 85–101. The railroad had already paid Bass five thousand dollars for an option, so the equal checks were for ten thousand dollars each.

Southeast

59. Platt Cline, *They Came to the Mountain: The Story of Flagstaff's Beginnings* (Flagstaff: Northland Publishing, 1976), 49–106 passim.

60. Quoted in Cline, 119.

61. Cline, 119, 125, 127–31, 136, 193–202, 229, 252.

62. George S. Tanner to Don Webster, letter, 4 April 1977; P. T. Reilly to Don Webster, letter, 21 August 1977; both in *Reference File—Tanner, Seth and Tanner Trail*, GCNPRL. Tanner was born in New York in 1828 and came west with his family and Brigham Young in 1847. He was a miner and farmer in California for nearly a decade before returning to Utah in 1858. He was still living in 1917, but had been long retired from Grand Canyon prospecting.

63. P. T. Reilly letter, 21 August 1977; Harvey Butchart to Don Webster, letter, 31 August 1977, both in *Reference File—Tanner, Seth and Tanner Trail*, GCNPRL; *Superior (Arizona) Sun*, 13 April 1917, notes Tanner's 1877 canyon claims. Nancy Brian's *River to Rim: A Guide to Place Names Along the Colorado River in Grand Canyon from Lake Powell to Lake Mead* (Flagstaff: Earthquest Press, 1992), 47, adds that McCormick bought Tanner's mine in 1903 and renamed it the Copper Blossom. Brian's book is recommended as a recent guide to the origin of many canyon place names.

64. J. Donald Hughes, *In the House of Stone and Light: A Human History of Grand Canyon* (GCNHA, 1978), 47. The cabin was intact as of 1995.

65. George Wharton James, *In and Around the Grand Canyon* (Boston: Little, Brown and Company, 1905), 242–43; George McCormick to Eddie McKee, letter, 6 June 1932, *Reference File—Tanner, Seth and Tanner Trail*, GCNPRL. McCormick in his letter claims to have built the upper section from Lipan Point some time after 1900. Little was uncovered of Bedlins and Bunker other than they were contemporary prospectors. French, too, was a prospector who married Emma Lee in 1879 shortly after John D. Lee's execution and lived with her at Winslow from 1887 to 1897. See Juanita Brooks, *Emma Lee* (Logan, UT: Utah State University Press, 1978), 97–105.

66. Butchart letter, 31 August 1977; Harvey Butchart, interview by Michael F. Anderson, tape recording, 5 January 1994, Sun City, Arizona; H. C. Bryant, memorandum, 17 January 1944, *Reference File—Boucher, Louis*, GCNPRL; James, 243–46.

67. Today's developments at Desert View originated in the late 1920s and early 1930s following construction of East Rim Drive.

68. [Andy Ashurst] journal, [ca. 1920], and transcript of Ashurst materials, undated, *Reference File—Ashurst*, GCNPRL; Andy Ashurst to Lon Garrison, letter, 22 December 1951, *Reference File—Hance, Captain John*, GCNPRL; *Arizona Daily Sun*, 28 April 1975; Cline, 90–92. See *Coconino Sun*, 2 March 1901, for an account of Ashurst's death.

69. "Rules and Regulations of the Grand Cañon Mining District," Record of Mines, Book 1, pp. 225–27, County Recorder's Office, Flagstaff, Arizona.

70. Grand Canyon mining records after 1891 are found in the Coconino County Recorder's Office, Flagstaff. *Coconino Sun*, 13 June 1891, identifies the reaction to Stanton's report. Ralph and Niles Cameron and several others joined Ashurst a little before Stanton's report in the late 1880s. Few Grand Canyon mining claims were recorded in the name of a single person; more often there were two to four partners.

71. J. A. Pitts to Andrew Ashurst, letter, 30 July 1947, *Reference File—Ashurst*, GCNPRL; *(Flagstaff) Coconino Sun*, 3 December 1891.

72. Transcript of Ashurst materials, Exhibit No. 2.

73. Hughes, 48–49; Margaret M. Verkamp, *History of Grand Canyon National Park*, ed. Ronald W. Werhan (Grand Canyon Pioneers Society, 1993), 10; Teri A. Cleeland, "To Hull and Back," in U.S. Forest Service Cultural Resources Management Report No. 10, *People and Places of the Old Kaibab* (September 1990). Frank C. Lockwood in *Arizona Characters* (Los Angeles: Times-Mirror Press, 1928), 169–70, dates the Ayer trip to February 1883 in company with Ayer's brother and a friend, Colonel Montague, perhaps an earlier trip made by Ayer without his wife.

74. Cleeland, 43; Gordon Chappell to Regional Historian, memorandum, 29 June 1983, copy in Professional Services, GCNP; Russell Wahmann, "The Grand Canyon Stage Line," in *(Flagstaff) Sun*, 15 February 1974; H. C. Bryant memorandum, 17 January 1944. See *Coconino Sun*, 5 May 1892, 12 May 1892, 26 May 1892, 17 May 1894, 9 August 1894, for more information on the formation of the Grand Canyon Stage Line and stage stops. Early records reveal that "Grandview" was most often spelled in two words: "Grand View," but the modern spelling is used throughout this book.

75. Cleeland, 43–45; Vanessa Christopher, "Hull Cabin to 1901: A Historical Context of the Grandview Area," research paper, 1993, author's possession. See *Arizona Champion*, 8 January 1887, 12 March 1887, 23 April 1887, 10 November 1887, for early dreams of a railroad from Flagstaff. The U.S. Forest Service took possession of Hull's cabin and reservoir in June 1901 and thereafter barred southeastern tourist operators from using the valuable water source. This seemingly arbitrary closure was one of several forest service actions which convinced pioneer tourist operators that the government agency was in collusion with railroad interests. See F.W. Rankin, Forest Ranger, to P.D. Berry, letter, 6 June 1901, Accession #1031, GCNP Museum Collection.

76. Cleeland, 45–46.

77. Frances Hance Rose to Lon Garrison, letter, 31 July 1948; Ruth Thayer, "Fact or Fiction? The Hance Brothers of Yavapai and Coconino Counties," research paper, 1963; Lon Garrison, "John Hance—Famous Guide, Trail Builder, Miner and Windjammer of Grand Canyon," manuscript, 24 August 1948; all in *Reference File—Hance, Captain John*, GCNPRL. Jim Shirley, interview by Michael F. Anderson, tape recording, 2 February 1994, Sedona, Arizona. Bill Bass was another who never served in the military but was called "the Captain" or simply "Cap."

78. Thayer; George W. Hance, "Highlights of Territorial Indian Wars Recalled by Noted Pioneer of Arizona," in *(Phoenix) Arizona Republic*, 15 April 1931.

79. Debra Sutphen, "Grandview, Hermit, and South Kaibab Trails: Linking the Past Present and Future at the Grand Canyon of the Colorado, 1890–1990," (M.A. Thesis, Northern Arizona University, 1991), 7; Andy Ashurst letter, 22 December 1951; Cline, 98.

80. *(Flagstaff) Arizona Champion*, 18 September 1886; see *Champion*, 22 January 1887, for notice of John Hance's homestead and 16 March 1889 for another Hance advertisement.

81. Wahmann, in *(Flagstaff) Sun*, 1974; Andy Ashurst letter, 22 December 1951.

82. James, 248–50. Some have also called the new trail the Red Canyon Trail, as its lowest segment descends Red Canyon to the river.

83. Garrison, *"John Hance—Famous Guide."*

84. Garrison, "John Hance—Famous Guide."

85. Garrison, "John Hance—Famous Guide"; "Captain John Hance and the Grand Canyon," *University of Arizona Bulletin* (1 July 1942): 41–52.

86. Garrison, "John Hance—Famous Guide."

87. Andy Ashurst letter, 22 December 1951.

88. *Coconino Sun*, 10 October 1895, 7 November 1895; Will C. Barnes, *Arizona Place Names* (1935; repr. Tucson: University of Arizona Press, 1988), 450; Verkamp, 11, 19.

89. "Captain John Hance and the Grand Canyon"; George A. Reed to Lemuel A. (Lon) Garrison, letter, 15 August 1948, *Reference File—Buggeln Hotel*, GCNPRL. The cemetery was located far from the village when established in 1919, but facility expansion after the 1950s now finds it adjacent to the Shrine of the Ages near the park visitor center—the town has moved, not the cemetery.

90. H.C. Bryant memorandum, 17 January 1944; J.J. Byrne, Santa Fe General Passenger agent, to James W. Thurber, letters, 23 September 1897 and 3 May 1898, reference files, GCNPRL; *Coconino Sun*, 16 April 1898, 14 October 1899; Wahmann, in *(Flagstaff) Sun*, 1974. The stage delivered nine hundred tourists to the southeastern rim during the entire 1899 summer season.

91. Wahmann, in *(Flagstaff) Sun*, 1974; Gordon Chappell memorandum, 29 June 1983; "Grand Canyon of the Colorado," *Catholic World* (December 1899): 305–320; G. A. Neef, "The Grand Canyon of the Colorado," *Southwest Illustrated Magazine* (October 1895): 127; H. C. Bryant memorandum, 17 January 1944; Dean Smith, *Brothers Five: The Babbitts of Arizona* (Tempe: Arizona Historical Foundation, 1989), 102–103. Two more stage stops were located along the road during the pioneer period. The Red Horse Station, a prominent landmark on early maps, sat about a mile up Red Horse Wash from Moqui Station; its main building was moved sometime between 1896 and 1903 to Grand Canyon village where it became the first floor of Ralph Cameron's hotel. A station or rest stop also existed at Little Springs, about a mile from Fern Mountain Ranch. Moqui Station may never have been much more than the plaster-lined masonry water tank still found at the site. Its name on early maps most frequently is given as Moqui Tank. The Fern Mountain homestead is wonderfully preserved—the only extant stage station approaching Grand Canyon—and is owned today by the Nature Conservancy.

92. Russell Wahmann, "Grand Canyon Stage Line," *Desert Magazine* (January 1975): 32–35; William E. Austin, "Reminiscences on Travel by Stage to the Grand Canyon," manuscript, undated, reference files, GCNPRL; *Catholic World* article; *Coconino Sun*, 5 May 1892, 12 May 1892.

93. George A. Reed letter, 15 August 1948; Neef; H.C. Bryant, memorandum, 26 June 1942, *Reference File—Buggeln Hotel*, GCNPRL; Byrne letters, 23 September 1897 and 3 May 1898; *Coconino Sun*, 16 April 1898. It is possible that Hance built the cabin and barn near the head of his old trail at an earlier date, but the author believes this cabin beside the barn may well have been Hance's original cabin, moved to this site by Thurber. See Endnote 96.

94. *Coconino Sun*, 22 June 1901; Hughes, 50; H.C. Bryant, Press release, 2 August 1948, *Reference File—Hance, Captain John*, GCNPRL; Verkamp, 31. Photographs taken ca. 1907 show three major structures standing beside each other at Hance Ranch: the one-room cabin, which is certainly the original built by Hance since it is identical to earlier photos picturing Hance beside it; the larger log dining room/kitchen, very likely built by Thurber and Tolfree since narrative sources indicate they built such a structure, but possibly built by Buggeln as another source suggests; and the two-story frame building known to have been built by Buggeln.

95. Buggeln genealogy, *Reference File—Buggeln Hotel*; Arno Cammerer to J. R. Eakin, letter, 11 September 1925, both in GCNPRL.

96. Buggeln genealogy; H.C. Bryant press release; GCNP Superintendent to Southwest Regional Director, memorandum, date stamped 23 April 1964, copy in author's possession, identifies razing the Hance Ranch properties in 1957. This memo states that the original Hance cabin had been removed prior to the park service acquiring the property. A 1941 plat map confirms that the cabin was missing from its original site, and the author speculates that it may have been moved to the head of the old Hance Trail (perhaps by Thurber for Hance's use as noted earlier, perhaps at a later time). H.C. Bryant's press release of 1948 clearly mentions the Hance one-room cabin standing in 1948, and it seems that Dr. Bryant, who was a keen historical observer, could only be referring to the cabin that *is* indicated on the 1941 plat map at the head of the old trail.

97. Sutphen, 26; Arizona State Board of Health, Certificate of Death of Peter D. Berry, filed 30 September 1932, and Certificate of Death of Ralph J. Berry, filed 11 March 1919, copies in *Reference File—P.D. Berry*, GCNPRL; Berry genealogy, *Reference File—P.D. Berry*, GCNPRL; Scott Ingersoll, "Black Monday: Death and Reprisal in Old Flagstaff," *Northern Arizona Visitor's Guide* (Summer 1987): D10–D12.

98. Lon Garrison, "Historical Data on Pete Berry," notes taken in an interview with Ray Berry, 4 October 1951, *Reference File—P.D. Berry*, GCNPRL.

99. Emery Kolb to Miss Hamilton, letter, 31 December 1973; Lemuel Garrison to Miss Leslie Hamilton, letter, 15 January 1974; both in *Reference File—P.D. Berry*, GCNPRL; Sutphen, 28–29.

100. *(Flagstaff) Arizona Champion*, 19 July 1888; Sutphen, 30.

101. Berry Daybook entry, 3 June 1892, Berry papers, GCNP Museum Collection, quoted in Sutphen, 28.

102. Wayne C. Leicht, "Minerals of the Grandview Mine," *The Mineralogical Record* (September/ October 1971): 215–21; H.H. Smith to J.E. Kintner, letter, 11 August 1926, *Reference File—Mines and Mining*; P.D. Berry, interview by Mr. Waesche and Mrs. Sevey, notes, 19 July 1932, *Reference File—P.D. Berry*; plat maps filed with Mineral Survey #3592 A and B, *Reference File—Grandview Hotel*, latter three sources in GCNPRL.

103. Sutphen, 31–36; Berry interview, 19 July 1932; H.H. Smith letter, 11 August 1926. The partners apparently did charge tolls for the trail's use in early years, but how much and to what extent is unknown. See Ralph Cameron to P.D. Berry, letter, 17 November 1897, Accession #14829, GCNP Museum Collection.

104. Sutphen, 39–40; Berry interview, 19 June 1932; See *Coconino Sun*, 16 January 1896, 13 February 1896, 27 February 1896, 16 April 1896, for reports on ore shipments from the Last Chance Mine. See *Coconino Sun*, 25 January 1902, for the partners first leasing the Grandview Trail and associated mines to Barbour in August 1901. The lease and sale were forced by partner Ed Gale, who patented the properties in late 1900 in his name alone and warned Berry that the matter would go to court if they did not all sell out soon. See Ed Gale to P.D. Berry, letters, 5 December and 23 December 1900, Accession #1031, GCNP Museum Collection.

105. Berry interview, 19 July 1932; H.H. Smith letter, 11 August 1926; Photographs, GCNP Museum Collection, #826 and #8808.

106. Berry interview, 19 July 1932; Photograph, GCNP Museum Collection, #6255; Photograph, Huntington Library, Pierce #9744; Fred Lynch, "An Automobile Trip to the Grand Canyon of Arizona," *Out West* (1911), copy in *Reference File—History—General GRCA —1911 Auto Trip to Grand Canyon*, GCNPRL; Sonja Sandberg, "Grandview Hotel: A Brief History," manuscript, February 1976, *Reference File—Grand View Hotel*, GCNPRL. The hotel was built of mud-chinked logs, had plank as well as mud floors, windows on the rim side only, and gable roof. The complex included a laundry, blacksmith shop, saloon, and storage sheds. A U.S. Post Office operated from the hotel building from 1902 to 1913. See *Coconino Sun*, 30 July 1896, for comment on Grandview tourism.

107. *Coconino Sun*, 11 June 1896.

108. Sutphen, 41–44; James, 126–29; Grandview business cards, 1901–2, *Reference File—Grand View Hotel*, GCNPRL; See *Coconino Sun*, 19 February 1898, for discovery of the caves in 1896. George James describes the excitement of easterners rubbing elbows and sharing meals with colorful miners at Horseshoe Mesa.

109. Berry interview, 19 July 1932; Sutphen, 46; Sandberg; *Coconino Sun*, 30 March 1901, 23 July 1904.

110. Advertising flyer, ca. 1905, Accession #15170, GCNP Museum Collection.

111. Berry interview, 19 July 1932; Sutphen, 46–48; Sandberg.

112. Berry interview, 19 July 1932; Sandberg; A.J. Cooke to Leslie Hamilton, letter, 29 January 1974, *Reference File—Grand View Hotel*, GCNPRL. Exact purchase prices: $48,618.34 for Berry's 159.68 acres and buildings; $25,618.30 for the Grandview Hotel, millsites, and mining claims.

113. Certificates of Death for Pete and Ralph Berry; Gordon E. Beck to Leslie Hamilton, letter, 28 June 1974, *Reference File—P.D. Berry*, GCNPRL. Ralph Berry's ranch was patented by 1917 as homestead entries 398 and 21636 in Section 30, T30N, R5E, about five miles southeast of the Grandview Hotel and two miles southeast of the Hull's cabin. The property passed to R.W. and Mary G. Berry, who sold it to a Mrs. J. Laura Starke Belknap in April 1937. See homestead entry survey, 3 August 1917, Accession #1031, GCNP Study Collection and Warranty Deed, *Reference File—P.D. Berry*, GCNPRL.

114. A.J. Cooke letter, 29 January 1974; GCNP Superintendent to Southwest Regional Director memorandum, 23 April 1964; F.A. Kittredge, Memorandum for the Files, 12 August 1940, *Reference File—Hearst Properties*, GCNPRL. Aside from the Summit Hotel, the latter source identifies the "Hearst Cabin" and two other log buildings on the Hearst properties in 1940: two built about 1902 by Berry or the Canyon Copper Company as a blacksmith shop

and an employee bunkhouse, and one built by Berry in 1905 as a saloon, later used by Dick Gilligand, Hearst's caretaker after the Berrys left. Many other outbuildings were also identified, all razed by the NPS by 1959.

115. Sutphen, 54–63; F.A. Kittredge, memorandum, 12 August 1940, *Reference File—Hearst Properties*, GCN-PRL. The Congressional Act of 26 February 1931 and an amendment of 28 March 1934 were passed specifically to expedite condemnation proceedings within federal lands. It was a revision of a 1918 Condemnation Act passed for military purposes. See Sutphen, 58, 70–71.

116. GCNP Superintendent to Southwest Regional Director memorandum, 23 April 1964; see also Kittredge memorandum, 12 August 1940.

Southcentral

117. The Havasupai word "Vesna" is spelled "Vesnar" in one source. George Wharton James notes that the man was also known as Pu-ut. He has also been called Big Jim "Gvetna" with variations of that spelling. Whites at the canyon simply referred to him as Big Jim.

118. George Wharton James, *The Grand Canyon of Arizona: How to See It* (Boston: Little, Brown and Company, 1910), 33, 62; Leslie Spier, *Havasupai Ethnology* (New York: American Museum of Natural History, 1928), 94; C.H. McClure, "In the Matter of the Bright Angel Trail," affidavit, April 1902, Cameron Papers, Box 5, UASC, Tucson, Arizona. Affidavits taken in 1902–4 concerning Cameron's lawsuits are in this same collection and are hereafter noted by individual name.

119. Minor R. Tillotson and Frank J. Taylor, *Grand Canyon Country* (Stanford University Press, 1935), 30, 63–64.

120. C.H. McClure affidavit, UASC; Gale Burak to Mike Anderson, letter, 17 January 1992, author's possession.

121. Manuscript, no date, no author, *Origin and Development of Supai Camp 1976* File, GCNPRL. Supai Camp still exists, but is no longer considered an "Indian camp." It is located just west of Rowe Well Road, about one mile south of West Rim Drive.

122. May Rowe Curties to Charles Shelvin, letter, 30 January 1934, *Reference File—Rowe Well*, GCNPRL; Jeanne and Fred Schick, interview by Michael F. Anderson, tape recording, 2 February 1994, Sedona, Arizona.

123. Tillotson and Taylor, 63–64; Curties letter, 30 January 1934; J. Donald Hughes, *In the House of Stone and Light: A Human History of the Grand Canyon* (GCNHA, 1978), 57; F.A. Kittredge, historical memorandum for the files, 22 March 1941, GCNPRL. Navajos, Hopis, and Havasupais continue to interact at the South Rim, but live in standard NPS or concessioner housing or elsewhere outside park boundaries. The year of Big Jim's death was not uncovered in historical records, but photos place him in the vicinity as late as 1947. The author is confident that his relatives

still live and interact at the South Rim, but did not confirm the fact.

124. Edward W. Murphy to Edwin D. McKee, letter, 13 April 1933; H.C. Bryant, memorandum for history files, 28 March 1949; John W. Stockert to Katherine M. Stoker, letter, 15 February 1965; all in *Reference File—Boucher, Louis*, GCNPRL; *(Flagstaff) Coconino Sun*, 10 July 1908; USDI, NPS, "Grandview and Hermit Trails Historical Research Study, Grand Canyon National Park, Arizona," by Debra Sutphen, manuscript, 1 June 1990, copy in Professional Services, GCNP, 34–36, 40–41. Remains of Boucher's stone cabin are still encountered along the lower trail, along with a nearby mining adit.

125. Debra L. Sutphen, "Grandview, Hermit, and South Kaibab Trails: Linking the Past, Present and Future at the Grand Canyon of the Colorado, 1890–1990," (M.A. Thesis, Northern Arizona University, 1991), 73; *Coconino Sun*, 8 August 1903.

126. James, 47; *Coconino Sun*, 10 July 1908.

127. Stockert letter, 15 February 1965; Sutphen thesis, 84–86; Hughes, 54. The Santa Fe preserved Boucher's nickname by naming its western developments Hermit Road, Hermits Rest, Hermit Trail, and Hermit Camp.

128. *Arizona Daily Sun*, 13 May 1957; H.C. Bryant, memorandum to the history files, 17 January 1944, *Reference File—Dan Hogan*, GCNPRL; Matt Dodge and John W. McKlveen, "Hogan's Orphan Mine," *True West Magazine* (November–December 1978): 6–10, 42.

129. Dodge and McKlveen; Clyde M. Brundy, "Orphan with a Midas Touch," *Denver Post Empire Magazine*, 27 November 1977; H.C. Bryant memorandum, 17 January 1944. These men built the tank and the trail as described, but the author found no evidence that they named it the Waldron Trail, though it appears on a 1913 map by that name.

130. Dan N. Magleby to David N. Magleby, technical memorandum with claim map, March 1961, *Reference File—Orphan Mine*, GCNPRL.

131. USDI, NPS, collection voucher for a permit obtained by F.D. Schemmer of Prescott, 15 August 1951, *Reference File—Orphan Mine*, GCNPRL.

132. Dodge and McKlveen.

133. Dodge and McKlveen; Magleby memorandum, March 1961; USDI, NPS, "Briefing Statement," 1 November 1976, *Reference File—Orphan Mine*, GCNPRL. The NPS in the 1930s tried but failed to buy the claim, then routed the new West Rim Drive south of the facility so as not to benefit Hogan's planned establishment.

134. Dodge and McKlveen; Brundy; Magleby memorandum, March 1961; *Arizona Republic*, 2 August 1964; NPS "Briefing Statement," 1 November 1976. In 1955, the mining company built an 1,800-foot-long tramway which dropped steeply—as much as 57 degrees—from facilities at the rim 1,100 vertical feet to horizontal shafts at the bottom of the claim.

135. *(Flagstaff) Arizona Daily Sun*, 13 May 1957.

136. "Location of Rowe Well June 1890," undated and unsigned manuscript, *Reference File—Rowe Well*, GCNPRL. The site over the last century has interchangeably been called Rowe Well, Rowes Well, and Rowe's Well.

137. "Location of Rowe Well"; USDI, NPS, "Grand Canyon National Park Rowe Well Properties," plat map, 1936, NPGC–5103, Denver Service Center—Technical Information Center, Denver, Colorado. The Lucky Strike and Little Mamie were contiguous claims a few yards southeast of the Highland Mary. See also Al Richmond, *Rails to the Rim: Milepost Guide to the Grand Canyon Railway* (Flagstaff: Northland Printing, 1990), 57–58.

138. Curties letter, 30 January 1934; *Coconino Sun*, 14 April 1892; John Woods affidavit, UASC.

139. Winfield Hogaboom, "A Prehistoric Motor Tour," *Touring Topics* (January 1924): 16–18, 30–31; *Coconino Sun*, 4 January 1902, 18 January 1902, 25 January 1902, 8 February 1902. By 1912, automobiles were making the seventy-mile trip along the Grandview road in three hours, and this road continued in use until abandoned about 1928 in favor of the new automotive approach road from Williams.

140. Rowe Well Properties plat map, 1936; "Camp at Rowe's Well," business card, no date, *Reference File—Rowe Well*, GCNPRL. Edward Hamilton, 1868–1940; Maude J. Hamilton, 1872–1933.

141. Hughes, 56–57; Richmond, *Rails to the Rim*, 57 58; Jeanne and Fred Schick interview.

142. M.R. Tillotson to the Director, letter, 15 August 1930, Miscellaneous Construction D30—*Desert View Cameron Approach Road May 1929–December 1931*, GCNPRL; the Director (Horace Albright) to the files, 18 April 1932, *Misc Construction D30—Desert View Cameron Approach Road January 1932–January 1933*, GCNPRL; Jim Shirley, interview by Michael F. Anderson, tape recording, 2 February 1994, Sedona, Arizona.

143. H.C. Bryant memorandum, 17 January 1944. Thurber probably worked with Sanford Rowe to build and maintain the road through Shoski Canyon and north to the rim since it benefitted both men. Rowe operated from Williams, lodged his guests several miles from the rim, and had a separate trail, later road, to Rowes Point thus the two were not in direct competition.

144. Hughes, 67. The author assumes that the cabin built by Lester and Motz became the Bright Angel Hotel. See Endnote 146 for a partial analysis of the very first structure to be built at the southcentral rim.

145. Ralph Keithley, "He Stayed With 'Em While He Lasted," *Arizona Highways* (January and February 1943); James H. McClintock, *Arizona* (S.J. Clarke Publishing Company, 1916), 345, 523.

146. Ralph Keithley, *Buckey O'Neill* (Caxton Printers, Ltd., 1949), 200–201, pages copied in *Reference File—O'Neill* ("Buckey"), GCNPRL; Keithley; [Mary Colter] to Charlotte Hall, letter, 22 February 1937, *Reference File—O'Neill, W.O.* ("Buckey"), GCNPRL. A note attached to Keithley's pages in the O'Neill reference file states that the *bunkhouse* formerly served as the Red Horse stage station, implying that O'Neill moved it to the rim site. Bill Suran in his letter to the author, 30 January 1995, and most others say that Ralph Cameron moved the Red Horse structure to the rim area about 1900. The author is inclined to believe that O'Neill may have moved the structure, but if so, Cameron quickly acquired it after O'Neill's death in 1898, using it as the first floor of the Cameron Hotel which opened soon thereafter.

F.A. Kittredge's memorandum of 22 March 1941 contends that Buckey's *office* was the first structure built along the southcentral rim, while Colter's (unsigned) letter to Sharlot Hall casts doubt on O'Neill erecting the structure and states that it was long used as the lobby of the first Bright Angel Lodge (Thurber's Bright Angel Hotel, renamed the Bright Angel Lodge after 1906 when the Santa Fe acquired it). The author speculates that the "Buckey O'Neill office" on the rim may have been Thurber's cabin built by Lester and Motz, and simply used freely by O'Neill on his occasional canyon visits. Cabin sharing was a common, generous gesture during the pioneer era; building nearly on top one another's properties was not, and it is unlikely that Thurber would have built his Bright Angel Hotel immediately beside another's cabin with so much land available. The frame structure pictured beside the log cabin in all photographs from the late 1890s to the early 1930s was likely an early Thurber addition to his original cabin. The frame building was torn down to make room for the second (today's) Bright Angel Lodge, built in 1935.

In any event of original ownership, both the rimside log cabin and the relocated log Red Horse stage station (acquired by Cameron by 1903) date to 1895–98, and both in modified form are now cabins within the Bright Angel Lodge complex and the oldest extant buildings at Grand Canyon Village.

147. Keithley.

148. Margaret M. Verkamp, *History of Grand Canyon National Park*, ed. Ronald W. Werhan (Grand Canyon Pioneers Society, 1993), 12–13; Hughes, 60; Al Richmond, *Cowboys, Miners, Presidents and Kings: The Story of the Grand Canyon Railway*, 2nd ed. (Flagstaff: Northland Printing, 1989), 4–6. See *Coconino Sun*, 8 January 1887, 12 March 1887, 23 April 1887, 10 November 1888, 20 July 1889, 22 October 1891, 3 December 1891, 16 June 1892 for newspaper accounts of more plans for an early Flagstaff-to-Grand-Canyon railroad.

149. USDI, NPS, "History of Legislation Relating to the National Park System Through the 82nd Congress," comp. Edmund B. Rogers, 1958, copy in GCNPRL.

150. Clippings from the *Williams News* and *Phoenix Republican* for July 1897 detail the mining district's development and are collected in *Reference File—Mines and Mining*, GCNPRL.

151. Richmond, 6–22 passim; Rogers' "History of Legislation," Part I, 1–4, identifies the railroad congressional bills including HR 9956 (passed May 1898) granting the right-of-way. Senate Bill 4428 identifies the railroad's destination as Lombard, the name apparently chosen by Lombard, Goode and Company for the depot and town now called Grand Canyon Village, though the official name is simply Grand Canyon. The right-of-way extended from the village along the rim eastward as far as the Little Colorado River.

152. Keithley; Lowell Parker, "'Rough Rider' Buckey O'Neill's Blurred Legend," in *Arizona Republic*, 23–24 January 1978.

153. The Bass family's reaction to the railway is described in Chapter Three, South Rim. The railway did not *immediately* end other enterprises, but did drain the life out of these marginal businesses and, as the primary means of transport from 1901 to 1926, focused development at its terminus. When automobile arrivals began to outnumber railway arrivals in 1926 and modern roads replaced pioneer paths all along the South Rim, some entrepreneurs considered reopening facilities away from the village. The NPS considered ideas for distributed growth to offset village overcrowding in the late 1920s and early 1930s, but decided against it and has remained steadfast in that decision with few exceptions.

154. Jo. Conners, *Who's Who in Arizona* (Tucson: Arizona Daily Sun, 1913), 499–500.

155. Ralph H. Cameron and John Marshall affidavits, UASC; Platt Cline, *They Came to the Mountain: The Story of Flagstaff's Beginnings* (Flagstaff: Northland Publishing, 1976), 156–57.

156. C.H. McClure, Ralph H. Cameron, and John Marshall affidavits, UASC.

157. John Woods and George Campbell affidavits, UASC.

158. C.H. McClure and Ralph H. Cameron affidavits, UASC. Cameron by the first years of the new century held nearly forty claims along the entire trail from rim to river.

159. *Coconino Sun*, 14 December 1901, 25 January 1902, 8 August 1903; T. E. Pollack affidavit, UASC; letterhead advertisement on letter, 24 April 1905, Cameron Papers, Box 4, File 5, UASC; Bruce Babbitt, *Grand Canyon: An Anthology* (Flagstaff: Northland Press, 1978), photographs, 124, 240. Per Bill Suran letter, 30 January 1995, Cameron may have opened the hotel earlier, perhaps as early as 1898–1900, but no hotel records or other evidence have been found prior to 1903.

After the Railroad

160. USDI, NPS, "History of Legislation Relating to the National Park System Through the 82nd Congress," comp. Edmund B. Rogers, 1958, Part I, 1.

161. Grand Canyon Game Reserve, created in 1906, prevented private entry two years earlier, but applied mostly to North Rim events considered in later chapters.

162. It was common in the West to "squat" on a piece of unsurveyed, unoccupied public domain. When the federal government got around to surveying the land thus opening it to private use through homesteading, squatters were usually forgiven their "preemptive" action and allowed to acquire the parcel. "Closing" an area to "private entry" means that no new claims to the land are allowed, but historically, the rights of those already there are usually protected by a guarantee, called grandfathering, often written into a law. Laws creating Grand Canyon National Monument and National Park contained such grandfather clauses.

163. Most Grand Canyon claims were filed between 1900 and 1908 and the number skyrocketed as the latter year approached.

164. USDI, "Decision of the Department of the Interior in regards to the Grand Canyon Railway Company v. Ralph H. Cameron," 11 February 1909; C.C. Spaulding to Ralph Cameron, letter, 31 March 1909; both in Cameron Papers, Box 4, File 5, *Grand Canyon Correspondence, January 1903 – April 1909*, UASC.

165. J. Donald Hughes, *In the House of Stone and Light: A Human History of the Grand Canyon* (GCNHA, 1978), 68; USDI, "Decision of the Department of the Interior," 11 February 1909. The author's own admittedly incomplete research revealed perhaps a hundred Cameron claims, but a strategically placed claim, such as one that contains isolated water sources like at Indian Garden or Dripping Springs, can mean control of a much larger area. Western cattlemen, especially, made such strategic claims.

166. Hereafter, the terms Santa Fe and "railroad" are used to express the decision makers of the larger Santa Fe Pacific corporation as well as the subsidiary Grand Canyon Railway. Santa Fe managers made decisions of any magnitude. The Fred Harvey Company and Santa Fe were separate companies, but closely connected. During the pioneer period at least, the Santa Fe, not the Harvey company, invested the money to build Grand Canyon infrastructure.

167. Margaret M. Verkamp, *History of Grand Canyon National Park* (Grand Canyon Pioneer Society, 1993), ed. Ronald W. Werhan, 23, states that the Atlantic and Pacific loaned [Thurber] money to build the Bright Angel Hotel and that the Santa Fe Pacific maintained it after 1897. The loan may have occurred, but other sources noted later, including Verkamp, 29, suggest that Thurber then Buggeln owned the building. The railroad and Thurber/Buggeln probably had close but independent business relationships like that between the Santa Fe and Fred Harvey Company.

168. Bill Suran to Mike Anderson, letter, 30 January 1995, author's possession.

169. USDI, "Decision of the Department of the Interior," 11 February 1909.

170. Verkamp, 29. Cameron would probably have imposed the toll earlier, but had to clear up his right to do so with the Department of the Interior, who notified him that he had such a right in January 1903.

171. *(Flagstaff) Coconino Sun*, 30 September 1905, 14 April 1906, 21 April 1906.

172. *Coconino Sun*, 10 October 1904.

173. Ralph Cameron to L.L. Ferrall, letterhead, 13 July 1905, Cameron papers, Box 4, File 5, UASC; *Coconino Sun*, 2 September 1905, 16 June 1906; Platt Cline, *They Came to the Mountain: The Story of Flagstaff's Beginnings* (Flagstaff: Northland Publishing, 1976), 157. Burton served as county assessor, 1906–12. Ralph served only one term as supervisor, 1905–07, but had friends who served on the board from 1905 to 1910.

174. Verkamp, 31. Numerous letters in the Cameron papers, Box 4, Files 5–7, UASC, from Ferrall to Cameron from 1905 to 1911 illustrate the men's close relationship. Ferrall's wife, Louisa (1864–1939), was Grand Canyon postmaster during these years and another Cameron friend and informant. Lannes Ferrall (1861–1928) succeeded his wife as postmaster in 1916, serving into the 1920s. The couple retired to Phoenix, Arizona by the late 1920s.

175. *Coconino Sun*, 28 February 1907, 11 April 1907, 2 May 1907, 22 January 1909; Cameron to Ralph E. Pearce, letter, 31 March 1909, Cameron Papers, Box 4, File 5, UASC.

176. R. H. Cameron, "A Word to the Tourist," advertising letter, [ca. 1904], *Reference File—Cameron, Ralph H.*, GCNPRL.

177. George Wharton James, *In and Around the Grand Canyon: The Grand Canyon of the Colorado River in Arizona*, [rev. ed.] (Boston: Little, Brown and Company, 1905), 344; Thomas Smith, Frank Cornette, and Lannes Ferrall affidavits, UASC.

178. Verkamp, 24; *Coconino Sun*, 21 March 1902.

179. Cameron's hotel registers in the Cameron papers, Box 5, UASC, begin in 1903. The author analyzed and totalled these to obtain the given numbers. See also miscellaneous correspondence in Cameron papers, Box 5, File *Grand Canyon Legal Papers 1903, 1906–07, 1909–1912*, UASC; and *Coconino Sun*, 11 June 1904.

180. Verkamp, 26; Jim Shirley, interview by Michael F. Anderson, tape recording, 2 February 1994, Sedona, Arizona; Cline, 157; Superintendent's Annual Report, 1919–20.

181. "Speech by Emery Kolb on his 90th birthday," typed manuscript, 15 February 1971, *Reference File—Kolb, Emery and Ellsworth*, GCNPRL; "Conversation with: Emery Kolb," *Western Gateways* (Winter 1967): 40–46; William C. Suran, *The Kolb Brothers of Grand Canyon* (GCNHA, 1991), 7–9, 11, 14. The brothers photographed parties about to descend the Bright Angel Trail, using a fixed camera mounted in a studio window. Emery would then jog down to Indian Garden to develop the film and jog back up to beat the mule parties to the top so they could receive their photos the same day. The historic Kolb Studio is under restoration by the Grand Canyon Natural History Association, in 1995 renamed the Grand Canyon Association.

182. Suran, 10. The Buggelns had children, but none were born at the village. The family moved to the Grandview area in 1906–07.

183. *Arizona Republic*, 12 December 1976. Kolb's materials are available to researchers at Northern Arizona University's special collections library.

184. *Coconino Sun*, 17 May 1902, 24 May 1902, 6 June 1903, 2 April 1904, 1 October 1904.

185. Lesley Poling-Kempes, *The Harvey Girls: Women Who Opened the West* (New York: Paragon House, 1989), 167–68; USDI, NPS, *Architecture in the Parks: National Historic Landmark Theme Study* (Washington, D.C.: GPO, 1986), 91.

186. See Poling-Kempes for Harvey operations at Grand Canyon and the Fred Harvey-Santa Fe relationship which lasted from the late 1870s to 1968.

187. USDI, NPS, *Architecture in the Parks*, 91–93.

188. USDI, NPS, "Grand Canyon Village Historic District," National Register nomination by James W. Woodward, Jr., Janus Associates, Inc., 19 May 1989, copy in Professional Services, GCNP, 7.11, 8.3. Structures built from 1905 to 1908 and still standing are the mule barn, livery stable, blacksmith shop, and carpenter shop. See the above document, or Timothy Manns, *A Guide to Grand Canyon Village Historic District* (GCNHA, no date), for comprehensive lists of extant historic structures.

189. Observations of the early village are based primarily on USDA, USFS, "A Townsite Plan for Grand Canyon National Monument," by Forest Supervisor W. R. Mattoon, 18 July 1910; and USDA, USFS, "A Working Plan for Grand Canyon National Monument," by Forest Examiner W. R. Mattoon, 23 June 1909; both in GCNPRL.

190. USDA, USFS, *A Plan for the Development of the Village of Grand Canyon, Arizona*, by Frank A. Waugh (Washington, D.C.: GPO, 1918), 8.

191. USDA, USFS, "A Townsite Plan," 13.

192. See applications for Grand Canyon post office, 1902, 1904, *Reference File—Post Office*, GCNPRL; Arno Cammerer to Superintendent Crosby, letters, 7 and 8 September 1922; Crosby to the Director, letter, 1 December 1922; J.R. Eakin to the Director, letter, 1 November 1924; Cammerer to Eakin, letter, 12 November 1924; M.R. Tillotson to the Director, letter, 17 December 1927; all in *Reference File—Post Office*, GCNPRL.

193. Owen Wister, foreword to Ellsworth Kolb, *Through the Grand Canyon from Wyoming to Mexico* (New York: MacMillan, 1914); Suran, 8–9. Suran writes that the USFS denied the Kolbs a special use permit at Santa Fe urging, which explains why they set up their tent and later studio on Cameron mining claims and helps illustrate the polarization between Cameron and his associates and the USFS-railroad interests.

194. Previously noted USFS plans of 1909 and 1910 amply illustrate the agency's early attempts to manage the new national monument. Note that Pinchot actually disliked the concept of "preservation" and argued with many, including John Muir, over its application to public lands.

195. Berry to Cameron, letter, 9 January 1914, Cameron papers, Box 4, File 7, UASC.

196. USDA, USFS, "A Working Plan," 11, 13. Bass, physically far removed from struggles at the village in the early years, actually maintained a good relationship with the USFS and the railroad until about 1908–10.

197. Michael F. Anderson, "North and South Bass Trails Historical Research Study, Grand Canyon National Park, Arizona," 1 November 1990, GCNPRL, 78–82; Pete Berry to Niles Cameron, letter, 11 May 1910, Cameron Papers, Box 4, File 7, UASC.

198. L.L. Ferrall to Ralph Cameron, letter, 23 July 1909, Cameron Papers, Box 4, File 5, UASC; L.L. Ferrall to Ralph Cameron, letters, 14 December 1909, 16 December 1909; Niles Cameron to Ralph Cameron, letters, 17 December 1909, 18 December 1909; Bill Bass to Sid Ferrall, letter, 24 April 1910; Pete Berry to Niles Cameron, letter, 11 May 1910; Pete Berry to Ralph Cameron, letter, 9 January 1914; Ralph Cameron to Pete Berry, letter, 3 February 1914; all in Cameron Papers, Box 4, File 7, UASC.

199. Niles to Ralph Cameron letter, 18 December 1909.

200. Ferrall to Cameron letters, 23 July 1909, 14 December 1909, 16 December 1909.

201. An *arrastra* is a circular grinding mill usually powered by mule or burro harnessed to the spoke(s) of a revolving central stamp. The concept, imported from Mexico, is the simplest, cheapest, and one of the earliest types of hard-rock mills.

202. USDI, "Decision of the Department of the Interior," 11 February 1909.

203. *Coconino Sun*, 28 May 1909; USDA, USFS, "A Working Plan," 59–62. The road segment from the village west to Hopi Point had been improved by the railroad in 1907–08. The entire Hermit Rim Road was designed for buggies and preceded today's automotive road, West Rim Drive, by more than twenty years. See USDI, NPS, HAER, "West Rim Drive," by Michael F. Anderson, September 1994, draft copy in GCNPRL.

204. USDA, USFS, "Special Use Permit to Santa Fe Land Improvement Company," 3 May 1909, Cameron Papers, Box 4, File 5, UASC. This is one early example of

how the USFS and NPS also used the corporate giant to their own ends, as the permit reads like an invitation for legal warfare—a war in which the forest service could stand to one side and hope for a favorable result.

205. Cameron to Pinchot, letter, 7 August 1909, Cameron papers, Box 4, File 5, UASC; Assistant Forester Overton Price to Cameron, letter, 20 December 1909; Forester Henry S. Grave to District Forester, Albuquerque, letter, 7 April 1910; Bill Bass to Sid [Farrell], letter, 28 April 1910; Cameron to Secretary of Agriculture James Wilson, letter, 1 July 1910; Ferrall to Cameron, letter, 6 June 1911; all in Cameron Papers, Box 4, File 7, UASC. Construction apparently started before the permit was actually issued, perhaps in 1909, but progress was slow as graders reaching each Cameron claim had to go around and resume on the opposite side and the railroad was plagued by injunctions to stop work.

206. Ferrall to Cameron, letters (2), 6 June 1911; Ferrall to Cameron, telegram, 6 June 1911; Cameron to Ferrall, telegram, 12 June 1911; Cameron to Judge Edward M. Doe, letter, 27 March 1912; all in Cameron papers, Box 4, File 7, UASC; Superintendent's Annual Report, 1919–20.

207. Debra L. Sutphen, "Grandview, Hermit, and South Kaibab Trails: Linking the Past, Present and Future at the Grand Canyon of the Colorado, 1890–1990" (M.A. Thesis, Northern Arizona University, 1991), 92–93.

208. USDI, NPS, HAER, "West Rim Drive," 3; *Superior (Arizona) Sun*, 16 February 1923. Even as late as 1922, only 250 road-miles in the entire state of Arizona had better than gravel surfacing. Most of these 250 miles were of concrete in urban areas; only 29 miles were water-bound macadam like Hermit Rim Road; and 3 miles were of the modern, automobile-resistant, asphalt-bound macadam.

209. Sutphen, 87–89.

210. Sutphen, 91, 93, 98.

211. A cable tram operated from the village to Indian Garden for a short time ca. 1930 to facilitate construction of a water pipeline, and three cable systems spanned the Colorado during the pioneer era: Bill Bass's two and David Rust's. The Harvey tram to Hermit Camp was built as a permanent structure, but was removed in 1936 along with the camp.

212. Virginia L. Grattan, *Mary Colter: Builder Upon the Red Earth*, 2d ed. (GCNHA, 1992), 25–35. Lookout Studio was the railroad's attempt to compete directly with the Kolb Studio, both of which offered books, photographs, and views of the canyon.

213. USDI, NPS, "Grand Canyon Village Historic District," 7.11–7.12.

214. Cameron to L.L. Ferrall, letter, 13 July 1905, Cameron Papers, Box 4, File 5, UASC; USDI, NPS, *Architecture in the Parks*, 123–33.

215. Verkamp, 25. USDA, USFS, "A Townsite Plan," released in July 1910 identifies, but does not name, only two village hotels. These would have to be El Tovar and Bright Angel Hotel. No mention at all is made of Cameron's hotel which, with Verkamp and other sources, suggests it closed in 1910.

216. Emery Kolb to Cameron, letter, 16 November 1908; Louisa Ferrall to Cameron, letter, 11 November 1908; both in Cameron papers, Box 4, File 5, UASC.

217. USDI, NPS, "History of Legislation," 4–6; Sutphen, 80.

218. Cameron to Pete Berry, letter, 3 February 1914, Cameron Papers, Box 4, File 7, UASC.

219. *Coconino Sun*, 24 May 1912, 13 December 1912, 26 December 1913.

220. Jo. Conners, *Who's Who in Arizona* (Tucson: Arizona Daily Star, 1913), 499–500; Arthur Warner, "Canyons and Camerons: A United States Senator Defies the Government," *The Nation* (28 October 1925): 481–83; Teri Cleeland, "The Cross-Canyon Corridor Historic District in Grand Canyon National Park" (M.A. Thesis, Northern Arizona University, 1986), 28, 31; *Arizona Republic*, 12 September 1959.

221. Verkamp, 36; Warner.

222. Hughes, 88.

223. Congress, House, Congressional Record, "Speech of Hon. Carl Hayden of Arizona in the House of Representatives," 68th cong., 1st sess., 11 March 1924, a report concerning H.R. 3682 involving roads and trails in the national parks; Sutphen, 105–33 passim. The South Kaibab Trail was briefly called the Yaki Trail in 1924–25, since construction began at Yaki Point, but retained this alternate name for only a few years.

224. Warner; *Los Angeles Times*, 27 June 1926.

225. *Arizona Republic*, 25 January 1952, 12 September 1959; Cline, 156.

226. Ample evidence of this support is found in numerous letters within the reference files at GCNPRL written by NPS personnel in the early 1920s. Residents consistently resisted NPS regulations, and administrators attributed this to alliances with Ralph Cameron and other old-timers like Bass, Berry, Rowe, and Hamilton.

227. Harold K. Steen, *The U.S. Forest Service: A History* (Seattle: University of Washington Press), 114–22; Darrell Hevenor Smith, *The Forest Service: Its History, Activities and Organization* (Washington, D.C.: Brookings Institute, 1930), 63. The USFS began to consider historic preservation after the 1906 Antiquities Act required them to do so, but not until the movement to create the NPS in the 1910s did they begin to take tourism seriously, and not until the 1920s or later did they consider recreational use to be more than the bottom rung on the multiple-use ladder.

228. Excellent biographies of Mather and Albright are Donald Swain's *Wilderness Defender: Horace M. Albright and Conservation* (Chicago: University of

Chicago Press, 1970) and Robert Shankland's *Steve Mather of the National Parks* (New York: Knopf, 1970).

229. Horace Albright, *The Birth of the National Park Service: The Founding Years, 1913–33* (Salt Lake City: Howe Brothers, 1985), 18, 26–29, 35, 46, 71f, 104–105, 264–65. For a fine overview of the railroad-NPS relationship, see Alfred Runte, *Trains of Discovery: Western Railroads and the National Parks* (Niwot, CO: Roberts Rinehart Publishers, 1994).

230. For background on the NPS relationship with the Bureau of Public Roads and histories of regional roads see USDI, NPS, HAER, "Zion National Park Roads and Bridges," by Michael F. Anderson, August 1993, draft copy in Professional Services, GCNP; and seven HAER reports by Anderson concerning Grand Canyon roads, titled by road name, September 1994, draft copies in GCNPRL.

231. Superintendent's Annual Report, 1919–20.

232. Superintendent's Annual Report, 1919–20.

233. Superintendent's Annual Report, 1920–21.

234. Superintendent's Annual Report, 1922–23. Park visitation from 1920 to 1923 increased by 26 percent, while automobile arrivals increased 127 percent.

235. Superintendent's Annual Report, 1921–22; Elizabeth J. Simpson, *Recollections of Phantom Ranch* (GCNHA, 1984).

236. Fred Harvey Company to the Secretary of the Interior, letter, 4 March 1930, *Santa Fe Buildings 1924–1935*, GCNPRL.

237. Superintendent's Annual Reports, 1922–23, 1923–24; USDI, NPS, "Grand Canyon Village Historic District," 8.8.

238. USDI, NPS, "Grand Canyon Village Historic District," 8.9–8.12; USDI, NPS, "Grand Canyon National Park General Plan Community Development," village plan map, 24 June 1924, copy in Professional Services, GCNP.

CHAPTER FOUR

Regional Discovery

1. USDI, NPS, "History of Legislation Relating to the National Park System Through the 82nd Congress," comp. Edmund B. Rogers, 1958, Part I, 6–10; U.S. Congress, House, H.R. 18785, 14 September 1914, 63d cong., 2d sess.; H.R. 11869, 19 February 1916, 64th cong., 1st sess.; H.R. 15937, 28 January 1921, 66th cong., 3d sess. A spur line from the San Pedro, Los Angeles and Salt Lake Railroad reached St. Thomas, Nevada—now under Lake Mead—after 1900, still fifty miles west of the Grand Wash Cliffs and no nearer by developed roads than railheads at Lund and Cedar City.

2. A good church history is Leonard J. Arrington's and Davis Bitton's *The Mormon Experience: A History of the Latter-day Saints* (New York: Random House, 1980;

reprint, Knopf, Inc., 1979). A detailed history of the migration west is Wallace Stegner's *The Gathering of Zion: The Story of the Mormon Trail*, 2d ed. (Salt Lake City: Westwater Press, Inc., 1964).

3. Ironically, the United States acquired the Utah region with the Treaty of Guadalupe Hidalgo in May 1848, less than a year after Mormon arrival. A political State of Deseret did exist from 1849 to 1851, but church leaders dismantled it following Utah's territorial designation in 1850. See Dale L. Morgan, *The State of Deseret* (Logan: Utah State University Press, 1987).

4. Mormon leaders issued a "call" when families were needed to settle a new area. A call ranked somewhere between a request and an order. Most considered it their religious duty and few refused to obey, despite leaving extended families, friends, and property behind. The idea of a political state died early, but a theocratic state with close economic ties among church members remains strong even today.

5. H. Lorenzo Reid, *Brigham Young's Dixie of the Desert: Exploration and Settlement* (Zion Natural History Association, 1964), 57–61; Angus M. Woodbury, *A History of Southern Utah and Its National Parks* (Salt Lake City: Utah State Historical Society, 1950), 136.

6. Hazel Bradshaw, ed., *Under Dixie Sun: A History of Washington County by Those Who Loved Their Forebears* (Daughters of the Utah Pioneers, Washington County Chapter, 1950), 117–27, 255, 281, 346, 348; Woodbury, 143, 145–48.

7. Woodbury, 138–41; Reid, 87–88. John D. Lee, 1812–1877. The Mountain Meadows Massacre occurred west of Pine Mountain in southwestern Utah in September 1857 along one of two alignments of the Old Spanish Trail. The Fancher wagon train, bound for California during years of Mormon-U.S. conflict (1857–58), exchanged hostile words with town residents from Salt Lake City southward, and a joint Mormon-Indian force ultimately attacked and massacred all but a dozen or so children. Lee did not order the massacre—regional Indians called him "cry-baby" for the rest of his life for wanting to stop it—but he was the field commander and became the church scapegoat, although Brigham Young and others helped him avoid arrest. The remote nature of this region and the church's tight communications and security networks made it possible for him to avoid federal marshals for seventeen years. See Juanita Brooks, *John D. Lee: Zealot—Pioneer Builder—Scapegoat* (Glendale, CA: Arthur H. Clark, 1973), 200–217, for a concise account. A larger work is Brooks' *The Mountain Meadows Massacre* (Norman: University of Oklahoma Press, 1962).

8. Adonis F. Robinson, ed. and comp., *History of Kane County* (Salt Lake City: Utah Printing Company, 1970), 6–7, 104, 302–303, 420, 445, 457; Woodbury, 141–43; *Deseret Evening News*, 21 September 1870, transcribed in "Correspondence, Fort Kanab, Sept. 10, '70," *Miscellaneous File*, Zion National Park archives.

9. San Bernardino represented a giant leap in the line of march when it was purchased and settled by Mormons in 1850. Littlefield, along this westward march, was the first Mormon town founded in Arizona. One reason Hamblin, 1819–1886, is well remembered is that he had four wives and twenty-four children. Some four thousand descendants came to the family reunion about 1960, per Mardean Church, Hamblin's great-granddaughter, interview by Michael F. Anderson, tape recording, 9 February 1994, Kanab, Utah.

10. Hamblin spoke with such a soft voice that all in his presence quieted to hear what he had to say. More than once alone among dozens of Indians in a hostile situation, he escaped death through his quiet, confident demeanor.

11. Brooks, *John D. Lee*, 263. Deep sand in House Rock Valley would be a constant travel hazard until the Arizona Highway Department and Bureau of Public Roads built today's automotive highway in the 1930s.

12. Woodbury, 164–66; USDA, USFS and USDI, BLM, *Man, Models, and Management: An Overview of the Archeology of the Arizona Strip and the Management of Its Cultural Resources*, by Jeffrey H. Altshul and Helen C. Fairley, 1989, 162–69. Fairley's Chapter 5, "History," is an excellent regional account and is hereafter noted as Fairley. See also W.L. Rusho and C. Gregory Crampton, *Lees Ferry: Desert River Crossing*, 2d ed. (Salt Lake City: Cricket Productions, 1992), 12–15.

13. Fairley, 164–65, 175.

14. Woodbury, 166; Fairley, 166. Polygamy is plural marriage (one husband, multiple wives), introduced as a religious tenet by Joseph Smith before the westward migration. It was practiced mostly by Mormon leaders who could afford more than one family, and was outlawed by the church in 1890 under pressure from the United States Congress, although it persisted in the remote Arizona Strip well beyond the pioneer era. From 1850 to 1890, perhaps 5 percent of Mormon men had more than one wife (Brigham Young had more than fifty); 12 percent of women shared a husband; and 10 percent of Mormon children were born to polygamous families, per Arrington, 199, 204, 244. Polygamy kept its adherents on the move from federal marshals operating out of Utah, thus, they were often explorers, town founders, or leaders who frequented the faithful in isolated communities.

15. Woodbury, 167–78; Fairley, 167–69. A Mormon militia originated with militant bodies organized in the 1830s and 1840s back East to fight persecution. Young revived the idea in the 1850s when it appeared that the church would go to war with the United States over regional control. The militia was recalled as a mounted unit to fight Indians during the 1860s.

16. Woodbury, 179–80, 190; Rusho, 20–23; Brooks, *John D. Lee*, 289–92.

17. Rusho, 17–18, 23, 29–33, 35; Brooks, *John D. Lee*, 303–314; Fairley, 171. Lee also had three wives and children living at Skutumpah through the early 1870s and had little chance to rest taking care of business at the three family sites. Folklore holds that Emma Lee named the farm when, upon first viewing the locale, she exclaimed "Oh, what a lonely dell!" But the name was in use before she arrived.

18. Rusho, 31, 34, 44, 55–60; Fairley, 171–75. Since the boat was lost in the accident and the bridge promised to be open within several months, the county chose not to reopen the ferry.

19. Today's motorist can also glimpse segments of the original U.S. Highway 89. Vestiges remain from Flagstaff to Kanab, but segments between Cameron and the Gap are most easily seen from a moving auto as they are within two hundred yards (east) of the present highway. This first regional automotive road was built in the 1930s to replace the emigrant road and contains many fine masonry culverts and bridge abutments no longer used in modern road construction. In 1911, the segment of emigrant road leading toward Flagstaff—which had crossed the Little Colorado River at Tanner's Crossing since the 1870s—was realigned to pass over a new suspension bridge built by the Bureau of Indian Affairs. The bridge, seen today beside the present highway at Cameron, determined the location and subsequent growth of that town.

20. Cecil Cram, interview by Michael F. Anderson, tape recording, 10–11 February 1994, Fredonia, Arizona. Arizona Strip residents always referred to the road as the "emigrant (or immigrant) road." The name Honeymoon Trail is likely an apt creation of the Bureau of Land Management who in the 1970s marked the trail from Lees Ferry west to Kanab. Cram guided the BLM in this task and he and the author retraced about 80 percent of the trail's length in spring 1995.

21. Wallace Stegner, *Beyond the Hundredth Meridian: John Wesley Powell and the Second Opening of the West* (Boston: Houghton Mifflin Company, 1953), 123, 128.

22. Stegner, 128–33; Frederick S. Dellenbaugh, *A Canyon Voyage: The Narrative of the Second Powell Expedition* (New York: Putnam, 1908; repr., Tucson: University of Arizona Press, 1984), 170–71. Some believe that Powell's men may have been killed by Mormons. Since Powell knew little if any of the Paiute language in 1870, and Hamblin served as interpreter when the Indians supposedly admitted their guilt, it is possible that Hamblin rendered a "faulty" interpretation. Powell, too, may have been willing to accept a dubious explanation because the deceased had not been friends—he had serious disagreements with the elder Howland and Dunn while on the river—and in any event, could prove nothing and needed Mormon and Indian assistance for his upcoming survey. The principal problem with this theory is lack of an adequate motive.

23. Fairley, 178.

24. Powell apparently represented himself as an official government agent at the peace conference, though he had no authority to do so, and thus may have helped end the war.

25. Stegner, 137–39; Dellenbaugh, 4–8.

26. Dellenbaugh, 144–45, 151–64, 261–62; Stegner, 142, 144.

27. Dellenbaugh, 174, 185, 241–43; Stegner, 139; Rusho, 31. Prospectors found fine placer ("flour") gold all along the canyons of the Colorado, but it proved impossible to extract at a profit. Charles Spencer tried in 1910–11 at Lees Ferry, as did Robert Stanton within Glen Canyon using a mammoth river dredge, but both failed. Powell had other reasons for ending the second river trip at Kanab Creek, mainly, his belief that the second granite gorge downstream would be dangerous given the river's seasonal flow and his disinterest in further adventure promising no scientific rewards. He may also have wished to avoid painful memories at Separation Rapid.

28. Clarence Edward Dutton, *Tertiary History of the Grand Cañon District* (Washington: Government Printing Office, 1882), 159–61; USDI, NPS, "Thunder River Trail," by Michael F. Anderson, National Register Nomination, 30 June 1992, copy in Professional Services, GCNP.

29. Fairley, 182; Stegner, 273.

30. Francois E. Matthes, "Mapping the Grand Canyon," *The Technology Review* (January 1905): 1–25.

31. Matthes.

32. Fritiof Fryxell, "Memorial to Francois Emile Matthes (1874–1948)," *Proceedings of the Geological Society of America* (July 1955): 153–68.

Arizona Strip Settlement

33. USDI, NPS, HAER, "Zion National Park Roads and Bridges," by Michael F. Anderson, August 1993, traces this slow, regional road development from the 1850s through the early 1930s.

34. Poor transportation hampered north side mining enterprises even when Mormons had a mind to pursue them. Note that a few church members like Dee Woolley and Dan Seegmiller did stake and work some mining claims on the Arizona Strip. Others worked as mine laborers, and provided support services to gentile miners such as those at Silver Reef, Utah.

35. George H. Billingsley, "Geology of the Grand Canyon" (Museum of Northern Arizona and GCNHA, 1974): 170–78; Owen B. Wright, "Background and History of the Arizona Strip District," manuscript, 16 June 1972, *Reference File— Arizona Strip*, GCNPRL; Elizabeth Coker, "Historical Resources of the Kaibab National Forest," USFS report, 1978, copy in Cline Library, Northern Arizona University, 24; Anna Brown, interview by

Michael F. Anderson, tape recording, 9 February 1994, Kanab, Utah.

36. The author found no evidence of patented mining or homestead claims north of the river within Grand Canyon National Park other than Hance's asbestos claims.

37. The Kaibab Plateau lumber industry did not begin until after the late 1940s when postwar demand and improved roads made it economically feasible.

38. Coker, 25; USDA, USFS and USDI, BLM, *Man, Models and Management: An Overview of the Archeology of the Arizona Strip and the Management of Its Cultural Resources*, by Jeffrey Altschul and Helen C. Fairley, 1989, 203, hereafter noted as Fairley; Angus M. Woodbury, *A History of Southern Utah and Its National Parks* (Salt Lake City: Utah State Historical Society, 1950), 189–90; Sharlot Hall, *Sharlot Hall on the Arizona Strip: A Diary of a Journey Through Northern Arizona in 1911*, ed. C. Gregory Crampton (Flagstaff: Northland Press, 1975), 83–84.

39. Anna Brown interview. Mrs. Brown managed the youthful maids, waiters, and other Utah Parks employees at Grand Canyon Lodge through the 1930s.

40. This pattern is well illustrated along the Virgin River downstream of Zion National Park and the Little Colorado settlements downstream of Holbrook, Arizona. Annual flooding of the latter fickle stream caused abandonment of three of four towns established in 1876. By 1886, only Joseph City survived and its residents had to rebuild and relocate their dams and ditches almost annually until the early 1900s.

41. A "sink" is formed by collapse of a limestone cavern, after which debris fills the depression allowing water to collect and form a small lake. Jacob and Greenland Lakes on the Kaibab Plateau are examples. These sinks, along with small springs and cattle tanks formed by damming intermittent drainages, were the only surface water sources on the strip other than the Virgin River far to the west, central Kanab Creek, and the Paria River far to the east.

42. USDI, BLM, *Opportunity and Challenge: The Story of the BLM*, by James Muhn and Hanson R. Stuart, (Washington, D.C.: GPO, 1988), 34–35; Darrel Hevenor Smith, *The Forest Service: Its History, Activities and Organization* (Washington, D.C.: Brookings Institute, 1930), 158–59. The 1906 law permitted the Secretary of Agriculture to allow entry to agricultural lands within forest reserves; the 1909 law enlarged a homestead parcel to 320 acres; the 1912 law required only a three-year residence as opposed to the earlier five years.

43. A.M. McOmie, C.C. Jacobs, and O.C. Bartlett, *The Arizona Strip: Report of a Reconnaissance of the Country North of the Grand Canyon* (Phoenix: Arizona State Press, 1915), 18. McOmie travelled from Phoenix to the Arizona Strip via Lees Ferry in 1914 to assess water and agricultural resources. Governor Hunt sanctioned the trip to discover what lay north of Grand Canyon and

to encourage settlement, if favorable. The party arrived during a period of wet years and their report likely spurred immigration. Coincidentally, McOmie's party was almost certainly the first to drive an automobile nearly the full breadth of the strip along the emigrant road. See also Fairley, 200–203; "As Self-Sufficient as Possible," manuscript, [1960s], in *Reference File—Arizona Strip*, GCNPRL, which identifies through oral accounts small Arizona Strip communities; and Wright.

44. Nellie Iverson Cox and Helen Bundy Russell, *Footprints on the Arizona Strip* (Bountiful, UT: Horizon Publishers, 1973), 1–6; James E. Cook, "The Arizona Strip," in *The Arizona Republic*, 12 January 1969. The quote is from Mardean Church, interview by Michael F. Anderson, tape recording, 9 February 1994, Kanab, Utah. The same quote might be applied to Chamberlains, Hamblins, Judds, and a few other local families with equal accuracy.

45. Fairley, 199; Hall, 62; Dart Judd, interview by Michael F. Anderson, tape recording, 20 May 1992, Fredonia, Arizona. Mr. Judd, born at Kanab in 1896 and a Fredonia resident since 1901, recited the names of the twenty-seven families living here before 1910 along with the lots assigned to each and the homes in which they lived. Note that Kanab Creek in the Fredonia vicinity was considered too shallow and sandy for irrigation until a flood in 1886 scoured and deepened the creek bed. Note also that the lumber mill in Fredonia recently ceased operations.

46. Church members were required to give a percent of their income for communal activities and expansion. Since early pioneers had little cash, they could tithe labor or products of equivalent value. Livestock were a common tithing medium, thus the church had to maintain "church herds," which were used to feed laborers on projects, bartered, or sold for cash. For an excellent history of Pipe Spring and the immediate vicinity, see David Lavender, *Pipe Spring and the Arizona Strip* (Springdale, UT: Zion Natural History Association, 1984), who traces ownership and uses through modern times.

47. Fairley, 186–97, gives an excellent account of large-scale cattle operators on the Arizona Strip and is referenced liberally in the following paragraphs. Information of value is also found in Marlene Wright, "Conserving the Natural Resources of the Arizona Strip," [1955], *Reference File—Arizona Strip*, GCNPRL; Earl Cram, "A Brief Ranching History of the Jensen Tank, Tuckup, and Slide Mountain Areas," 14 August 1975, *Reference File—North Rim—History*, GCNPRL; and Wright. See also Lavender, 35–38, who gives slightly different dates and more information on the Pipe Spring property.

48. Most sources agree that VT stood for Valley Tan or Valley Tannery, a distinguishing trademark for skins prepared by the United Order of Orderville tannery in Long Valley, Utah, which implies OUO ownership or another church outfit.

49. Cecil Cram, interview by Michael F. Anderson, tape

recording, 10–11 February 1994, Fredonia, Arizona. Mr. Cram, born the same year his father homesteaded the Cram Ranch in 1916, grew up in Kanab and House Rock Valley.

50. Cecil Cram interview; Aldus "Blondie" Jensen and Bob Vaughn, interview, 6 September 1974; "Cowhide" Adams, interview, 3 and 6 September 1974; transcripts of the latter two interviews in *Reference File—North Rim—History*, GCNPRL.

51. Blondie Jensen and Bob Vaughn interview. These men ran cattle on the strip for many years after 1900, and recalled cattle grazing on the broad Powell Plateau as well, making their own way down to Muav Saddle and up the other side, and sometimes straying farther into the canyon.

52. USDI, NPS, "Thunder River Trail," by Michael F. Anderson, National Register Nomination, 30 June 1992; Ron Mace, interview by Michael F. Anderson, tape recording, 19 May 1992, Fredonia, Arizona. Mr. Mace has wrangled horses and run cattle on the strip since the 1910s and is intimately familiar with the Thunder River area. The Esplanade is also found south of the river, beginning roughly at the South Bass Trail and continuing west. Note that the Crazy Jug trailhead is likely the same as that used by 1870s prospectors and Clarence Dutton.

53. Dart Judd interview; Coker, 20–22. Residents also grazed horses, goats, and sheep, though most of the large sheep herds arrived seasonally from outside the region. Transience ended in 1935 with implementation of the Taylor Grazing Act which required land/water ownership to obtain permits. Sheep disappeared from the plateau by 1945.

54. Ron Mace interview; Paul McCormick, interview by Michael F. Anderson, tape recording, 20 May 1992, Fredonia, Arizona; Stanley White, telephone interview by Michael F. Anderson, 21 May 1992.

55. Cecil Cram interview.

56. Cecil Cram interview; Ben and Sarah Hamblin, interview by Michael F. Anderson, tape recording, 9 February 1994, Kanab, Utah.

57. Cecil Cram interview.

58. W.L. Rusho and C. Gregory Crampton, *Lee's Ferry: Desert River Crossing*, 2d ed. (Salt Lake City: Cricket Productions, 1992), 96, 105–106; Cecil Cram interview.

59. Snow closures today are by choice since the state highway department, USFS, and NPS could plow if they wanted to and had the funds, but none of these agencies, much less local residents, had the equipment to keep roads open during the earlier era.

60. Dan Seegmiller, Dave Rust, Jim Owens, as well as others identified later also guided hunting parties at the North Rim.

61. John Young was one of many sons of Brigham Young who made southern Utah and northern Arizona his

home. Just a few of his enterprises included contracts to supply ties to the Atlantic and Pacific which led to his establishment of Fort Moroni at Flagstaff; extensive cattle interests on the Kaibab Plateau; and the dude ranch idea, failure of which would lead to financial difficulties with his cattle company.

62. [John Rich Sr.], "Buckskin History: Kaibab Plateau and Grand Canyon," [ca. 1980], manuscript, copy in possession of Sarah Hamblin, Kanab, Utah; Woodbury, 190–91; *(Flagstaff) Coconino Sun*, 10 November 1892. Photographs in Cecil Cram's possession complement those in the Edward Lamb Collection at NAU, and depict the party at Flagstaff, Lees Ferry, Kane Ranch, and on the plateau.

63. Michael F. Anderson, "North and South Bass Trails Historical Research Study, Grand Canyon National Park, Arizona," 1 November 1990, 50, 53 (photo), 55, 64; *Williams News*, 14 September 1905; Joseph McAleenan, *Grand Canyon Trails* (New York: H.S. Nichols, 1924), 30–69 passim. McAleenan's is an account of a 1917 cougar hunt but is descriptive of hunting parties at the turn of the century. He used the Bass trails to reach the plateau and the central corridor to return to the South Rim.

64. USDI, NPS, "History of Legislation Relating to the National Park System Through the 82nd Congress," comp. Edmund B. Rogers, 1958, Part I, 3–6 and Part II, 1–3; John P. Russo, *The Kaibab North Deer Herd: Its History, Problems and Management* (Phoenix: Arizona Fish and Game Department, 1964), 125–26. Eagles and perhaps other raptors were also targets.

65. James T. Owens, as told to Annie Dyer Nunn, "Government Hunter No. 1," *Field & Stream* (May 1937); Annie Dyer Nunn, "He Returns as a Famous Man," in *Amarillo Sunday News and Globe*, [ca. 1928]; transcript copies of both in *Reference File—Owens, Uncle Jim*, GCNPRL. See also Robert Easton and MacKenzie Brown, *Lord of the Beasts: The Saga of Buffalo Jones* (Tucson: University of Arizona Press, 1961), 2, 15–17, 55–56, 120. Uncle Jim worked at several other ranches in Texas and Indian (Oklahoma) Territory between 1876 and 1905.

66. Lund, Utah, served as an important regional railhead until a short spur from Lund, prompted mostly by escalating tourism, reached Cedar City in 1923.

67. Easton, 120–25, 132–35; Carolyn Niethammer, "Sincerely Yours, C. J. Buffalo Jones," [September 1978], magazine article from unknown periodical, copy in *Reference File—Jones, C. J. "Buffalo,"* GCNPRL; Owens; Dart Judd and Cecil Cram interviews. Judd remembers the 1906 drive and buffalo being fed and kept overnight within Fredonia's town limits; Cram remembers the buffalo sharing grass and water with House Rock Valley cattle herds and the Woolley permit trade in the 1940s.

68. Niethammer; Easton, 135; Owens; "Uncle Ben" Swapp, interview, 1951, transcript in *Reference File—Owens, Uncle Jim*, GCNPRL. *Arizona Daily Sun*, 18 April

1950, in an article entitled "Game, Fish Commission Seeks End of Houserock Range Battle," reads that Owens sued for wages and the court awarded him title to the herd. Forest Supervisor Clark wrote that he had seen this title in Uncle Jim's possession. Hall, 82, notes that Owens and Woolley were the only two partners in 1911 and that only twenty-six head remained as Jones had taken his share to New Mexico, and outlaws after the valuable robes took their toll. Hall saw third generation offspring (one-quarter buffalo), indicating that the experiment went at least one step beyond initial cross-breeding.

69. John H. Clark to Lon Garrison, letter, 25 December 1951, *Reference File—Owens, Uncle Jim*, GCNPRL. Clark was USFS supervisor of the Kaibab Forest and Game Reserve, 1907–1912.

70. Owens.

71. Zane Grey, *Roping Lions in the Grand Canyon* (New York: Grosset and Dunlop, 1924), 1–2, 47. Clark, in his letter to Garrison, explains that the USFS rarely assigned Owens to guide someone, but he was allowed to choose from among the many who requested his services. Other sources indicate that Owens was very selective about whom he guided.

72. Grey's *Roping Lions* explains this type of hunting in detail. Hall, 80, reports Owens' tally in 1911 at 184 lions killed and 12 roped.

73. Thomas Heron McKee, "'Uncle Jim' Owens and His Dogs Have Killed 1500 Cougars," *The American Magazine* [1924], copy in *Reference File—Owens, Uncle Jim*, GCNPRL.

74. Owens. NPS permits and letters noted later indicate Owens' activities here in the early 1920s. He had cabins at Bright Angel Spring and White Sage Flat near Ryan, but also lived in a cabin at VT Park, the Woolley Cabin near the head of the Rust trail, and in any number of caves, one of which was along the mail trail from Kanab to Lees Ferry. He, like cattlemen, also stayed in the Muav Saddle Cabin beneath the Powell Plateau, the salt cabin at Greenland Lake, and the cabin at Jacobs Pools.

75. Various sources give the number of buffalo as eighty to a hundred at the time of sale, sale prices ranging from one hundred dollars per head to ten thousand dollars for the lot, and the year of sale as 1924, 1926, and 1927.

76. Annie Dyer Nunn to Lon Garrison, letter, 16 May 1952; Billy Tober, New Mexico State Registrar of Vital Statistics to Lon Garrison, letter, 17 April 1952; both in *Reference File—Owens, Uncle Jim*, GCNPRL.

77. Hall, 80; Cecil Cram, Anna Brown, Mardean Church, and Ron Mace interviews. These are just a few of the people who knew or met Owens and added to the composite portrait.

78. Most sources noted above tell these stories. His attributes are also recorded in interviews with Sarah Hamblin, Cowhide Adams, and others.

79. Russo, 36–37, 43–45, 154; Report of the Kaibab Investigative Committee, 8–15 June 1931, copy in *Reference File—U.S. Forest Service*, GCNPRL. Arizona Strip residents recognized the overgrazing problem earlier and numbers actually diminished from an estimated twenty thousand cattle and two hundred thousand sheep in 1890 to nine thousand cattle and twenty thousand sheep by 1906, but there were still too many animals for the range to recover.

80. Russo, 51–54; Mardean Church interview.

81. Russo, 38–39; Cowhide Adams interview. The quote is from Ben Swapp in Fairley, 214.

82. Russo, 48–49; Cowhide Adams interview. Adams contends that the controversy over federal hunts revolved around out-of-state hunters and that the USFS hired guides like Adams to lead hunters away from state game officials, which seems supported by Fairley, 214–15. What is certain is that organized sport hunts continued unabated in 1924–28 while the lawsuit lingered, and the state joined in the hunts in 1929.

83. Russo, 57–60, 94.

84. The old Ryan ranger station also served as a checking station.

85. Russo, 59. This was presumably in Slide Canyon, west of Mangum Spring. A map attached to the 1931 Kaibab Investigative Committee report does not show this camp.

86. Information on hunting camps is based mainly on interviews with Mardean Church. Other sources include the author's interviews with Cecil Cram, Ron Mace, Billy Swapp, Steve Church, Anna Brown, Paul McCormick, Ben Hamblin, Sarah Hamblin, Stanley White, and Johnny Nelson 19–22 May 1992 and 9–10 February 1994. Sources in Church's possession include 1960s letters, permits, and financial reports which illuminate later camp business matters.

87. The lodge building is now a residence in Fredonia.

88. Pine Flat also had a "cook shack." These camps used a smaller "fly camp" to the west near Kanab Creek Canyon. Coker, Appendix B III, notes that Moquitch burned in 1948; others indicate it was the least popular camp and any burning may have been to clean up the area.

89. Mardean Church recalled that the USFS imposed no controls on Paiute and Navajo hunters. They took whatever deer and nuts they needed and jerked the meat at their camps. The rim was the boundary between the national park and national forest and hunting was restricted to the forest. Guides had no desire to hunt below the rim, anyway, since the terrain was too hard on men and stock.

90. A partial list of the men and women who guided and worked at the hunting camps: Nate Adams, Ernie Appling, Dinkie Brinkerhoff, "all the Bundys," Jack and Mary Butler, Hayden, Sytha, Jack, Mardean, and Steve Church, Cecil Cram, Ben Hamblin, Spike

Heaton, Chucky Jake and other Paiutes who were considered excellent guides and packers, some of the many Judds, Ron and Evelyn Mace, Marley Meeks, Billy, Tuffy, and George Swapp, Johnny and Bill Nelson, Bob and Bill Vaughn, Slim Waring, Weaver and Stanley White.

91. Walapai Johnny Nelson, interview by Michael F. Anderson, tape recording, 9–10 February 1994, Fredonia, Arizona. "Walapai" is not a Hualapai Indian, but grew up near the reservation where his father served as a Mohave County deputy sheriff and likely was the same man who drove Farlee's stage. Considering the cowboy guides as extended family is not just figurative, since a great number of Arizona Strip residents are related going back five and six generations.

92. Sarah and Ben Hamblin interviews; Coker, Appendix B III, notes that the Saddle Mountain buildings were burned upon the camp's closure.

Tourism Arrives

93. Michael F. Anderson, "Human History of the Thunder River Trail in Grand Canyon," research paper, December 1991; USDI, NPS, "Thunder River Trail," by Michael F. Anderson, National Register Nomination, 30 June 1992; both in GCNPRL. Local residents kept a visitor register, pots and pans, and other small camp items at Camp Cove from the 1920s to the 1950s.

94. The Churches held grazing permits on the Esplanade above Thunder River for many years, as did local cattlemen Carlos Judd and Bob and John Vaughn. The Churches grazed sixty of their best saddle stock here, about half the number needed for their various enterprises.

95. J.W. Powell named Tapeats Creek in 1872 after a Southern Paiute man who claimed the water. Thunder Spring and River acquired their names from the incessant roar of continuous whitewater within the river's narrow gorge. The United States Board of Geographic Names confirms the names, thus a river indeed flows into a creek.

96. See Michael F. Anderson, "North and South Bass Trails Historical Research Study, Grand Canyon National Park, Arizona," 1 November 1990, GCNPRL, 49–72, 120 (photos), and Appendix C, for detailed trail history and a description of Muav Saddle Cabin.

97. Anderson, "North and South Bass Trails," 66–70. NPS development was in response to criticism that they wanted to add lands along the northwest rim to the national park, yet had done nothing to open that area to visitors. Once the desired lands were secured by proclamation of Grand Canyon National Monument in 1932 (added to the park in 1975), they discontinued development. USGS benchmarks placed along the North Bass Trail in 1906 still mark the original path.

98. Quentin Rust, interview by Michael F. Anderson, tape recording, 10 February 1994, Kanab, Utah. Mr. Rust,

grandson of Dee Woolley and fifth son of David Rust, today follows in his forefathers' footsteps as a guide to southern Utah and the Arizona Strip. See also Zeke Scher, "Riches of the North Rim," *Denver Post's Empire Magazine* (5 March 1978): 10–15.

99. *(Flagstaff) Coconino Sun*, 11 July 1903; Joseph C. Rust to Stanley T. Albright, letter, 24 August 1993, with attached copy of David Rust's diary (Rust Diary), 4 July 1906 through 22 September 1907, author's possession. Local resident Jesse Knight invested five thousand dollars in the company in 1908 while another, Israel Chamberlain, consistently helped with trail construction. See also [John Rich Sr.], "Buckskin History: Kaibab Plateau and Grand Canyon," [ca. 1980].

100. Quentin Rust interview. A few sources credit Woolley with starting the trail in 1901 or 1903. Rust's diary indicates some form of trail in place when he started work in 1906, but it was likely a remnant of Matthes's several-day effort in 1902. A review of Rust's diary of earlier years, in the possession of his descendants now living in Utah, might confirm or disprove any trail work prior to 1906.

101. Rust Diary, 4 July, 9 July, 24 July, 17 August 1906. The first party to use Rust's trail included a Mr. Mansfield, Miss Mansfield, Miss Hewitt, and Hetty White. The campground along today's trail known as Cottonwood Camp was used by Rust as a base camp that he called Cottonwood Grove.

102. Rust Diary, February through March and 21 September 1907.

103. Rust Diary, 11 December, 20 December 1906; 27–31 January, 13 February, 15 February, 28 February, 4 March, 7–8 March, 18 March, 10–14 April 1907. Rust is vague about the routes of his trails and the agreement, but clearly he had built a trail connecting to the Bright Angel and made an agreement with Cameron by September 1907. Rust gathered four hundred "shade tree" cuttings and planted an unknown number at his camp; some of these are presumably the mature cottonwoods seen at Phantom Ranch today.

104. Quentin Rust interview; Joseph Rust letter, 24 August 1993; Sharlot Hall, *Sharlot Hall On the Arizona Strip: A Diary of a Journey Through Northern Arizona in 1911*, ed. C. Gregory Crampton (Flagstaff: Northland Press, 1975), 65–66; Joseph McAleenan, *Grand Canyon Trails* (New York: H. S. Nichols, 1924), 117, 127–29, 131–32. Quentin Rust states that because Woolley and Rust had no patented claims, the NPS evicted them from the new national park in 1919 without compensation. This would be consistent with policy at Grand Canyon where the NPS sometimes compensated residents for improvements and always for private land, but never for "business value." With no private land and scant facilities at Rust Camp by 1919, Rust would be out of luck. The cable cage was probably never reattached after 1917, but the NPS used the cable strand to build a wobbly wooden suspension bridge in 1921.

105. Adonis Findlay Robinson, ed. and comp. *History of Kane County* (Salt Lake City: Utah Printing Company, 1970), 101–103; Frank L. Farnsworth to National Park Service, letter, 1 August 1964, *Reference File—North Rim—History*, GCNPRL; Hall, 62–63, 66–73. Robinson details the trip to Kanab and generally to VT Park; Farnsworth confirms a wagon road to Greenland Spring by 1896; Hall fills in the details of the Woolley route in relating her 1911 trip along the same road—she likely camped near the Woolley Cabin.

106. One might argue that Nathaniel Galloway, whom Julius Stone hired to guide him on a pleasure trip through Grand Canyon in 1909, pioneered "commercial" river rafting, but the Stone trip seems to have been Galloway's only paid venture.

107. Quentin Rust interview; Doc Marston to Ken Sleight, Wonderland Expeditions, 19 November 1968, *Reference File—Kolb Part 1—Emery amd Ellsworth*, GCNPRL. See USDI, NPS, HAER, "Zion National Park Roads and Bridges," by Michael F. Anderson, August 1993, 19, 22–23, for Rust's involvement in regional road boosterism.

108. "Map of the Grand Canyon, Kaibab National Forest, Grand Canyon National Monument, Grand Canyon Game Preserve," sixteen page brochure, [1913–17], *Reference File—U.S. Forest Service*, GCNPRL.

109. Blondie Jensen, Elizabeth Mather, and Edwin Rothfuss, interview, handwritten transcript, no date; William B. Waltman, "Greenland Lake Project," report, 1964; both in *Reference File—North Rim—History*, GCNPRL. See also [NPS], "Addition to the Historical section of the Operational Prospectus for Grand Canyon National Park," manuscript, no date, *Reference File—"Wylie Way" Camp*, GCNPRL. Melissa Jensen was the daughter of Frank Scott Brown, one of the first USFS rangers at VT Park, and grew up on the plateau. Aldus "Blondie" Jensen, a native of Fredonia, also served as fire warden at the old fire tower atop Bright Angel Point. Signal fires here had a different meaning than Bass's used the Bass family knew how many people Bill had led out and only needed to know *when* he would return. The Wylie's never secured a USFS lease, but the agreement is identified in Elizabeth Wylie McKee to NPS, letter, 6 December 1922, *Reference File—"Wylie Way" Camp*, GCNPRL.

110. Bill Bass likely borrowed the tent-cabin idea from Wylie soon after the Yellowstone operation opened, and the concept immediately gained popularity at Grand Canyon. Many Grand Canyon Village residents lived in tent-cabins until the NPS and Fred Harvey Company started building bungalow housing for employees in the middle 1920s (tent-cabins were also used in many other western parks).

111. Anderson, "Zion National Park Roads and Bridges," 26–31. The federal government was responding to the dawn of the automobile age with varied types of road legislation for park, forest, and interstate roads. The Federal Aid Road Act of 1916 allocated seventy-five million dollars for "postal"—just about any—roads. Similar legislation continued through the 1930s. The McKees' understanding of an eventual Union Pacific takeover is inferred from Stephen Mather to Mr. Wylie, letter, 10 March 1922; J.R. Eakin to Mather, letter, 22 July 1925; and Mather to Eakin, letter, 30 July 1925; all in *Reference File—"Wylie Way" Camp*, GCNPRL; and Wylie's understanding concerning Zion as noted in Anderson.

112. Waltman; Blondie Jensen et al interview; Elizabeth Wylie McKee letter, 6 December 1922; Superintendent's Annual Reports, 1919–20, 1923–24; "A Journey to North Rim of Grand Canyon," *Hotel Monthly* (October 1919): 46–62. Skidoo Point was named by a Cedar City travel group that, since about 1900, had made frequent trips to the North Rim and invariably stayed at "Skidoo Camp" atop Skidoo Point, also known locally as Harris Point, but later renamed Point Imperial. See Thomas McKee to Raymond Carlson, editor of *Arizona Highways*, letter, September 1951, *Reference File—Owens, Uncle Jim*, GCNPRL; and *Hotel Monthly* article.

113. *Hotel Monthly* article; James J. Durant to Mr. James T. Owens, letter, 7 June 1922; varied NPS camp, transportation, and grazing permits, 1921; James T. Owens to Thomas McKee, letter, 24 March 1921; Thomas McKee to Mr. Carlson, letter, 30 June 1951; James T. Owens to D.L. Reaburn, letter, 12 May 1921; Superintendent [D.L. Reaburn] to Mr. Owens, letter, 2 May 1921; Stephen T. Mather to James T. Owens, letter, 28 October 1921; D.L. Reaburn, "Authorized rates for trail trips," price list, 8 March 1921; all in *Reference File—Owens, Uncle Jim*, GCNPRL. No concessioner ever established a camp at Cape Royal, but the NPS built a campground there in 1931 and also maintained one near the Point Imperial turnoff at Neal Spring that had been started by late 1920s road crews.

114. Anderson, "Zion National Park Roads and Bridges," 30–32, 39–40. The Parrys were initially involved with the Union Pacific and W.W. Wylie in the 1917 Zion concession, and their tourism company had other names, including the Zion National Park Company. After the Union Pacific gained control of Zion's concessions in 1923–24, the Parrys continued their tour business, but reorganized.

115. Thomas D. Murphy, *Seven Wonderlands of the American West* (Boston: L.C. Page and Company, 1925), 231, 233–34; Arno B. Cammerer to Mrs. McKee, letter, 4 August 1922, *Reference File—"Wylie Way" Camp*, GCNPRL. Hades Church also offered tourist supplies and gasoline at the Will Rust facility when the road alignment ran through Will Rust's camp. USFS contractors realigned the road to its current location on the east side of VT Park in the 1930s.

116. Elizabeth McKee to NPS Director, letter, 8 January 1925, *Reference File—"Wylie Way" Camp*, GCNPRL. Will Rust made improvements in 1925 and later in the decade, then sold out to Ed Cox, a close friend of

Uncle Jim Owens. The Cox family owned Kaibab Lodge until the late 1980s.

117. The Parrys had a complex schedule of as many as a dozen package tours by 1924, and prices varied from trip to trip, year to year. Most trips originated at Cedar City after the Union Pacific reached there in 1923, but some ran from the older railhead at Marysvale and one connected with the Santa Fe system at the South Rim via a central-corridor saddle trip. Many of their price brochures are found in Zion National Park's library and archives.

118. Cammerer letter, 4 August 1922; Elizabeth McKee to Colonel W.W. Crosby, 2 letters, 11 August 1922 and undated; Elizabeth McKee to D.S. Spencer, Union Pacific System, 17 January 1923; Arno Cammerer to GCNP Acting Superintendent Bolton, letter, 10 May 1923; Acting Chief Ranger C.M. West to Bolton, letter, 21 May 1923; all in *Reference File—"Wylie Way" Camp*, GCNPRL.

119. Scher; Rich. By 1923, there were several gasoline stations at Fredonia, and one each at Jacob Lake, run by the Bowmans; VT Park, run by the Churches; and Bright Angel Point, run by the McKees. The Bowmans could remain open year round because the state kept, and still keeps, U.S. Highway 89A open during the winter.

120. Superintendent's Annual Reports, 1922–23, 1923–24, 1925–26. [GCNP Superintendent Crosby] to J. C. Roak, letter, 20 June 1922, *Reference File—U.S. Forest Service*, GCNPRL. Early North Rim park rangers included Cal Peck (1920), C.M. West (1921), Parvin E. Church (1923), and Assistant Chief Ranger Winess (1924). These men bunked just about anywhere they could find a roof, including Uncle Jim's cabin at Bright Angel Springs, the Woolley Cabin, and at any of the USFS cabins until they built quarters at Bright Angel Point in 1924. The NPS and USFS cooperated to extend phone lines from the ranger station at VT Park to the Wylie Camp in 1923. NPS rangers also stayed in the McKee's tent-cabins at a reduced rate.

121. Superintendent's Annual Report, 1923–24. Evidence of NPS/USFS cooperation is found in a dozen or more letters found in *Reference File—U.S. Forest Service*, GCNPRL. The USFS station at Quaking Aspen may have been informal, based in or near the cabin built here by Mitzie Watts Vaughn of Kanab. The USFS closed its Bright Angel Ranger Station when Harvey Meadow was placed within Grand Canyon National Park, but kept rangers at Big Springs, Dry Park, VT Park, and Jacob Lake at least until 1930.

122. Elizabeth McKee to NPS, letter, 6 December 1922; Elizabeth McKee to NPS Director, letter, 20 February 1924; Elizabeth McKee to J. R. Eakin, letter, 17 August 1924; Elizabeth McKee to NPS Director, letter, 8 January 1925; Stephen Mather to Mrs. McKee, letter, 17 January 1925; [Elizabeth McKee] to the Director, letter, 20 November 1926; all in *Reference File—"Wylie Way" Camp*, GCNPRL. The NPS

reduced the permissible side trip fee to six dollars per person, and later to five dollars as roads improved.

123. J.R. Eakin to the Director, letter, 22 July 1925; Stephen Mather to Mr. Eakin, letter, 30 July 1925; J.R. Eakin to Stephen Mather, letter, 15 June 1926; Thomas McKee to Mr. Eakin, letter, 19 June 1926; all in *Reference File—"Wylie Way" Camp*, GCNPRL.

124. [Elizabeth McKee] letter, 20 November 1926; Thomas McKee to J. R. Eakin, letter, 23 November 1926; Thomas McKee to J.R. Eakin, letter, 15 December 1926; J. R. Eakin to Thomas McKee, letter, 20 December 1926; Thomas McKee to J.R. Eakin, letter, 25 February 1927; J.R. Eakin to Thomas McKee, letter, 28 February 1927; [NPS], "Addition to the Historical Section…"; all in *Reference File—"Wylie Way" Camp*, GCNPRL. The Church family took over the Jensen and Vaughn saddle trip concession in 1927–28 and ran it for many years, but were Utah Parks Company subcontractors.

125. The USFS extended its Grand Canyon Highway to Bright Angel Point by 1919 in conjunction with the Wylie Camp. This difficult 2.2-mile segment does not appear on maps in 1917 when tourist activities still centered at Harvey Meadow and the Woolley cabin, but does appear on a 1919 map two years after the McKees established their camp.

The NPS also built two roads to Point Sublime in these years, the first originating near the checking station at Little Park and the second along today's alignment beyond the Widforss trailhead. The NPS in the 1930s dropped Point Sublime as an encouraged tourist destination and has maintained the road only to fire road standards since that time.

126. Detailed sources for the 1920s central corridor are Debra Sutphen's and Michael F. Anderson's national register nominations for the South and North Kaibab Trails, copies in GCNPRL; and Teri Cleeland's "The Cross-Canyon Corridor Historic District in Grand Canyon National Park: A Model for Historical Preservation," (M.A. Thesis, Northern Arizona University, 1986). Today's rigid steel suspension bridge replaced the fearsome 1921 wood-and-cable bridge, which tended to whip sideways in the breeze.

127. Superintendent's Annual Reports, 1927–28, 1932–33, 1936–37; "Grand Canyon Lodge," manuscript press release, no date, *Reference File—G.C. Lodge*, GCNPRL; USDI, NPS, *Architecture in the Parks: National Historic Landmark Theme Study*, by Laura Souilliere Harrison (Washington, D.C., GPO, November 1986), 285–99.

128. M.R. Tillotson to R.E. Taylor, County Supervisor, letter, 25 August 1928; Charles H. Burke to the State Highway Commission, letter, 5 June 1928; both in *Reference File—G.C. Lodge*, GCNPRL. Superintendent's Annual Report, 1927–28.

PHOTO CONTRIBUTORS

Throughout this manuscript, due to space limitations, the publisher has often abbreviated the names of organizations, institutions (and/or their respective collections), and individuals who have granted permissions for art reproduction in this publication. The publisher wishes to gratefully acknowledge these contributors and give full credit as follows:

Michael F. Anderson

Arizona Historical Society, Pioneer Museum, Tucson, AZ
W.W. Bass Collection

Boston Public Library, Print Dept., Boston, MA
Alexander Gardener Collection

Michael A. Buchheit

Teri A. Cleeland

Cecil Cram

GRCA Grand Canyon National Park Museum Collection, Grand Canyon, AZ
Grand Canyon Archives
Fred Harvey Collection

Hayden Library
Arizona Collection

Henry E. Huntington Library
Pierce Collection

Kansas State Historical Society, Topeka, KS
ATSF Collection
Santa Fe Railroad Collection

Mrs. Martha Krueger

Mohave County Historical Society, Kingman, AZ

Museum of New Mexico, History Library, Santa Fe, NM
School of American Research

Museum of Northern Arizona, Flagstaff, AZ
Charles H. Vary Collection

The National Archives

NAPHS Northern Arizona Pioneers Historical Society
(see *Arizona Historical Society*)

NAU Northern Arizona University, Cline Library, Special Collections & Archive Dept., Flagstaff, AZ
Cataract Canyon Collection
Kolb Collection
Louis Grundel Collection
Edward T. Lamb Collection
Morley Fox Collection
J.W. Powell Display Collection
Russel Wahmann Collection
Williams Scrapbook Collection (assembled by Hugh and Hazel Clark; photos courtesy of N.S. McDougall, L. Polson, I. Smith, and H. Lockwood)

Mr. David Scott

Seaver Center for Western History Research, Los Angeles, CA

Sharlot Hall Museum Library/Archives, Prescott, AZ

Mrs. Mary Larkin Smith

University of Arizona, Special Collections, Tucson, AZ

INDEX

Index compiled by Earle E. Spamer